UNDER THE EDITORSHIP OF

LEONARD CARMICHAEL

SECRETARY, SMITHSONIAN INSTITUTION; FORMERLY PRESIDENT, TUFTS COLLEGE, AND DIRECTOR, TUFTS RESEARCH LABORATORY OF SENSORY PSYCHOLOGY AND PHYSIOLOGY

AN INTRODUCTION TO

Therapeutic Counseling

E. H. PORTER, Jr., Ph.D.
SYSTEM DEVELOPMENT CORPORATION,
SANTA MONICA

HOUGHTON MIFFLIN COMPANY
BOSTON · The Riverside Press Cambridge

BF
637
P833ι

CONTENTS

FOREWORD

THIS IS NOT an easy book to classify. It does not fall within the category of persuasive expositions of a single orientation in psychotherapy, though the author makes no attempt to conceal his own convictions. It is not a comparison of psychotherapies, though the reader must necessarily emerge with a better conceptual framework with which to make comparisons. It is not a book to be read straight through, though it will yield much to the person who pauses frequently to think. It is not a text in the traditional sense, though it should be of great value to classroom groups.

What is it? How are we to understand these paradoxes? As I see it, it is a book which above all helps the counselor or therapist to *consider*. It helps him to consider, thoughtfully and with a richness of detail, the issues which arise in counseling and psychotherapy. It assists each counselor to recognize his own goals, and to weigh and think about them. It helps him to perceive his own attitudes, toward himself and his client and to consider their appropriateness. It aids him in formulating and evaluating the hypotheses he holds in therapy. Above all it stimulates him to think deeply about the way he is implementing his purposes, his attitudes, and his hypotheses in the therapeutic relationship. The book cuts through the descriptions of therapy and the theories of therapy to the operational and functional level. It is safe to say that the therapist whose thinking has been invigorated by this book will be far more keenly aware of what he is doing, and why. In this process of becoming aware of one's own aims, feelings, and hypotheses, one cannot help but become more sharply aware of other possible formulations, and thus the breadth of thinking about therapy and the likelihood of improvement in one's therapeutic functioning are greatly enhanced.

In all the questions, devices, examples, and recorded interview excerpts in which the book abounds, there is astonishingly little pressure on the reader to agree with any particular point of view. The author seems to be saying — "Here is an issue. Here are a variety of ways of thinking about it. Have you considered all of these possibilities? Have you found a way of behaving which is meaningful for you, and in line with the basic organization of your own attitude?" To study and ponder these issues, and to formulate one's own point of view and way of behaving, is rewarding indeed.

This is an exceedingly practical book. In it Dr. Porter has distilled the experience and the wisdom which have come from a number of years of effective therapeutic work. He has used this background as a basis for selecting the issues which are pertinent for every therapist. What do you feel, and think, and do, in such and such a situation? This is the pattern of the whole volume, and one would be hard put to it to find problems occurring in counseling which are not dealt with in this book. Whether it is a highly specific question such as how to deal with the client's relative who wants to know about his progress, or a very general question such as how to create the most favorable psychological climate for therapy to take place, the issue is considered in these chapters. Note that I say *considered*, not *answered*. The reader will instead find a number of answers, and may proceed to choose his own on the basis of having recognized more deeply what is involved in each problem.

If I may inject a personal word, I was among the doubters when the author conceived this book. I felt that problems considered on paper could do little to help counselors to recognize and deal with their basic attitudes, and might do real harm by causing them to believe that psychotherapy is a bundle of tricks, a golf bag full of techniques carefully chosen for every purpose, including a niblick to get the unwary counselor out of any sand traps. Consequently the ingenuity which Dr. Porter has shown in developing devices which compel self-examination and facilitate attitudinal reorganization, incites my admiration. He has succeeded where to me failure seemed almost certain. The fact that he has enlivened such thought-provoking material with occasional touches of dry humor not only reveals something of his personality, but adds zest to the meaty material.

All in all, I cannot imagine a program of training for counselors or therapists which would not be enriched by this book. No matter what the orientation, whether client-centered, psychoanalytic, or eclectic; no matter what the specific purpose, whether to train psychological therapists, medical psychotherapists, educational counselors, vocational or guidance workers, psychiatric social workers, religious counselors, or marital and family counselors, the materials of this volume are germane and pertinent. It is to be hoped that it will have wide influence in stimulating constructive thinking about significant issues and problems in the growing field of psychotherapy.

CARL R. ROGERS

PREFACE

My CENTRAL PURPOSE has been to provide the reader with a series of experiences involving questions or issues basic to the field of therapeutic counseling. Regardless of theoretical leanings or loyalties, sooner or later the student must come to deal with these issues. It is not of great importance whether the student favors certain "answers" at a given moment; however, it is crucial that he be aware of the questions he is answering and that his answers are hypotheses.

Conceivably the issues presented should have been handled in a neutral fashion. I have tried to handle them openly, but not neutrally. To pretend I am neutral would be to act falsely. My concern with the non-directive or client-centered hypothesis in psychotherapy is plainly apparent, but the book is organized in such a way that readers who wish to increase their acquaintance with a client-centered orientation can do so while others may readily disregard this aspect of the material.

This book, in dealing extensively with techniques, stands in apparent contradiction to the major characteristic of non-directive therapy, for non-directive therapy is not a technique nor a body of prescribed techniques. It is best described in terms of the central hypothesis that each person has within himself the capacities to order and reorder his behavior without external manipulation by another. To the extent that a counselor endeavors to implement this hypothesis in his interviewing, he may be called non-directively oriented. To the extent that the procedures he uses are consistent with the central hypothesis, he may be said to be using client-centered or non-directive techniques. A given technique is not directive or non-directive inherently but only in relation to the non-directive hypothesis. The reader will find that techniques considered non-directive a decade ago are no longer used: as inconsistent procedures have been uncovered they have been discarded.

It has not always been easy to discard techniques even when their interventionist nature has been clearly evident. Therapists are not cold-blooded experimentalists. They seldom, if ever, experiment with clients to see what happens just as they seldom, if ever, experiment with their children. When a technique has been utilized in apparently successful cases the counselor is prone to continue its use. This is both understandable and commendable. Even so, it is not the path we must travel to determine the validity of central hypotheses in psychotherapy.

Not all of my co-workers are in agreement with an emphasis upon technique-training for beginners. One of the reasons has been alluded to above: the significance of a technique is relative to the hypothesis it implements. This would imply that consideration of the hypothesis and its implications should be primary. A second disagreement arises out of the expectation that an emphasis upon technique will lead the student to conceive of therapy solely as an intellectual, technical skill and not as involving the personality, values, philosophy and feelings of the counselor. My answer is two-fold. First, the beginning counselor must do *something* when he enters the interview. If he enters the interview with a hodge-podge of ideas and notions and skips from one procedure to another, he is quite unlikely to learn much about the effectiveness of any of his procedures. It seems quite certain that he must deal with a procedure in a consistent manner if he wishes to determine for himself its suitability. I have designed this book, in part, to give the beginner enough vicarious experience so that he can approach his interviews with at least a minimum of consistency and with a background for observing the significance of what happens. In the second place I would answer that I know of no faster way of learning how deeply involved the counselor's personality, values, philosophy and feelings are than for the beginner to get into the interviewing situation with a set of techniques or skills sufficiently developed to permit the operation of the therapeutic process.

In brief, despite the disagreements of my co-workers and despite the apparent contradiction of a book on technique when technique is considered incidental to the non-directive hypothesis, it is my conviction that dealing with techniques as tools can materially help the counselor to deal with his interviewing procedures more intelligently. I believe that I am at one with therapists in all frames of reference in my conviction that reading any book, doing any and all kinds of exercises and mastering all written material completely will not make a person a psychotherapist. And yet, in another sense, every person is already a therapist. My goal is to assist the interested person in becoming better through intensive consideration of issues on which decisions must be reached. It is incidental to my goal whether the decisions reached agree with mine.

As the reader comes to grips with the basic issues he will wish to know what evidence is available for the various sides. I only wish it were possible to list sources which presented the evidence for each point, but much of this is not yet available. In most instances we have only conjecture. Since I do not wish to recommend one set of conjectures over another, I have not prepared the usual bibliography which carries the implication that *these* are the sources the student *should* read. What I have done is to present in Appendix C a number of books which can serve as starting points, and a list of periodicals which most often carry articles of interest. Starting from these sources the student can follow his nose and sooner or later be led to every area of importance.

My indebtedness is as great as it is widespread. Were I to list those who have materially assisted in the shaping of my thinking, the list would contain a number of my former instructors, a host of my colleagues, all of my clients, a great number of students, and a number of my friends who have patiently listened while I tried out my ideas on them. I am specifically indebted to the University of Minnesota for permission to reproduce material from *Trends in Student Personnel Work*, to William U. Snyder and to Houghton Mifflin Company for permission to reproduce material from *Casebook of Non-Directive Counseling*, and to McGraw-Hill Book Company for permission to reproduce material from *Counseling With Returned Servicemen*. I should like to express my gratitude to Earl Zinn, Carl R. Rogers, John M. Butler and a number of unidentified therapists from whose cases I have drawn excerpts. Special thanks are due John M. Butler for his continued help throughout the time I struggled with the manuscript, and to Virginia M. Axline and Douglas D. Blocksma who worked with me closely in the original planning. J. V. Cunningham of the English Department at the University of Chicago has convinced me that there really is some use to beginning courses in English. He worked with me on the galley proof and has made communicable many ideas I had deftly concealed by my untutored style. My appreciation is sincere. The greatest debt is to the unnamed clients who have made this venture possible by their willingness to be phonographically recorded.

E. H. P., Jr.

Chapter I

INTRODUCTION

The Importance of the Counselor's Attitudes

Training in adjustment counseling seems clearly to consist in two highly related aspects. One is the matter of the counselor's attitudes. A second is the matter of his skills. While they may be separated for some purposes of discussion they remain in fact interdependent. Neither can be fully appreciated apart from the other. The techniques or skills which the counselor employs are expressions and implementations of his attitudes just as surely as the responses of the client constitute expressions and implementations of the latter's values and perceptions of reality.

A very great deal has been said in the past several years about the importance of the counselor's attitudes. Far and above the greatest bulk of these comments have, however, been very limited in scope and meant to provide a warning to the unwary. The gist of the warning is to prevent one's own attitudes from interfering with the interviewing process. The student is advised of the ever present danger of projecting his own difficulties, values and attitudes onto the client. It is quite apparent to the student that the warning should be followed: the dangers are obvious even at first glance. It is not so obvious, however, as to just how one is supposed to avoid these pitfalls. The student who looks twice at such a warning sees with an uneasy eye that knowing what not to do and then not doing it can be a real problem. A warning is not enough. Psychoanalysts have for years attempted to guard against the projection of their own attitudes into the therapeutic situation by undergoing an analysis themselves in order that they might know themselves deeply and control their actions. Clinical psychologists and vocational guidance people have often sought their salvation in an increasing dependency upon standardized tests administered and interpreted in standardized ways.

There exists, however, a rather specific avenue for the control of one's attitudes which has as yet not been nearly adequately exploited. This path lies in the counselor's continuing concern with: (1) knowing precisely the nature of the techniques he uses and the attitudes which they express or implement; and, (2) understanding his techniques in terms of the psychological climate which they create.

In a sense this avenue is broader in scope and more basic in the demands it makes upon the counselor than the avenue of knowing or solving one's own problems first or using techniques which avoid the counselor's being involved by keeping the counselor out. To illustrate this let us consider first some typical situations in which self-knowledge or self-avoidance is deemed important. The client expresses to the counselor some part of his problem. The counselor asks him to elucidate some phase or aspect of the expression. Or the counselor may choose to interpret the meaning of the material presented. The counselor may choose to respond in a reassuring manner or he may elect to inform the client or suggest to the client something calculated to be of assistance to him. Always, however, the counselor is faced with certain inescapable questions. "Why did you select that particular aspect to probe?" "Why did you not probe here?" "Why do you think that that particular interpretation was the best one or the correct one?" "Why did you choose to reassure the client at that particular point?" "Why did you think that this was the point to show the way?" Or phrased even more pointedly the questions stand: "When you chose to probe here and not there are you completely certain that those were not points where your own difficulties made you see the topics as important?" "When you interpreted to the client as you did are you completely certain that you weren't interpreting the meaning which similar events had for you?" "When you reassured the client there are you completely certain that you were not alleviating your own anxieties?" "Are you completely certain that you weren't suggesting a way out of your own difficulties when you made this suggestion to the client?"

In the face of such ever present questions it is most understandable that the counselor-in-training is met on every side with warnings. It is clear that it would be the counselor's responsibility to turn in at least a pretty fair proportion of creditable answers. Yet even more basic questions may be put to the counselor. "Why probe at all?" "Why interpret at all?" "Why support at all?" "Why suggest and persuade at all?" Such questions as these strike at the very foundations of our most accepted concepts of how to deal with people. They strike at our whole system of ideas about the nature of personality.

These questions are being asked and they are questions for which the counselor must seek answers. It is quite apparent to anyone who cares to read the literature that the questions are not just intellectual in nature. They seem to generate considerable heat. They are questions which can be put to almost any human being capable of communication with the result that the answers are immediate and delivered with all the depth of conviction that the person's life span can put behind them. But the answers that are forthcoming from different people are diverse. They seem clearly to represent expressions of attitudes rather than descriptions of basic data of observation.

Counselors do not respond to the client strictly on the basis of chance. The counselor has aims which he endeavors to reach through his use of techniques. These aims are based upon certain values which the counselor holds. These values vary from one counselor to the next. It cannot help but be confusing to the beginner to read in diverse fields, find such apparently solid agreements to what proponents of different viewpoints want, and yet see such exceptionally strong disagreements as to the ways the values are to be achieved. Further, it cannot help but be confusing to the beginner (as well as to the old-timer) to understand how the other person apparently gets results when it seems so obvious that he is operating on a completely incorrect theory of personality and using techniques which cannot be anything but harmful or ineffective.

It is not the intent of this volume to attempt an answer as to what values should be accepted. But it is the intent of this volume to expose the student to experiences which are designed to assist him in studying what his own attitudes are. Any student of Psychology knows that what a person says he believes may be markedly different from what he actually believes. It is a basic assumption of this book that if the counselor can be trained to see the attitudes which are implemented by the responses he makes and the psychological climates they may likely create, the counselor is in a better position to change in the direction of the values toward which he aims.

Common Immediate Interviewing Aim

Quite aside from general aims or goals of therapy and quite aside from the criteria by which the depth or effectiveness or completeness of therapy may be judged there is an immediate counseling aim to which nearly all, if not all, counselors will agree openly or by implication. This aim is so simple and so obvious as to be quite easily overlooked and yet it is so central as to occupy a very great deal of the counselor's energies. The aim referred to is to keep the client expressing and exploring his attitudes as freely as possible. The agreement seems general that unless the client can bring himself both to express and explore the problems which are of concern to him there is little probability that he will achieve the help which he seeks, no matter how clear the problems may be to the counselor.

Different devices or techniques are used to create psychological climates intended to safeguard the willingness the client brings to the interview for free expression, intended to persuade the client into expression and exploration, intended to support him through the difficulty of expression and exploration, and intended to facilitate the client's tendencies toward freedom in expression and exploration. The counselor may simply reassure the client that to talk of his difficulties is the thing to do, that it is safe to do so, and that he will be thought none the less of for going ahead. The counselor may attempt to persuade the client into expression and exploration by indicating that it is the only way the client can be helped, by pointing out to him that his defensiveness is only serving to thwart his desires for help, by pointing out to the client that it is not the counselor's problem to be solved but the client's, by holding up before the client the possible consequences of not going into his problems and achieving a solution. The counselor may seek to reassure the client by pointing out that others have had similar difficulties and worked them through, by pointing out that the feared consequences of free expression and exploration are not based in fact, by pointing out that some difficulty is to be expected and is all a part of the game. The counselor may seek to facilitate the client's expression and exploration by actively endeavoring to demonstrate his understanding of the client's way of viewing the things of which he speaks.

Not all counselors are in agreement as to the effectiveness of these several devices nor do all counselors find themselves in practice using one device to the exclusion of others no matter how doubtful they may feel others to be. In any event, and unfortunate though it may be, the counselor is constantly finding himself using techniques which are based upon sweeping generalizations as to the nature of personality not yet verified by experimental evidence. Some of these generalizations are openly recognized. Others remain unrecognized. On many such generalizations we operate daily but feel doubtful of depending upon them completely, feeling that too much remains unknown to give us reasonable certainty of their validity.

When the counselor utilizes some sort of reassurance, persuasion, moralization, instruction or coercion he is making an assumption as to limiting factors in the capacity of the client to continue on his own. When the counselor utilizes an attempt to understand the client as the client perceives the situation he is operating on an assumption that the client does not need energizing from an external source but has the capacity to continue on his own. Eventually we may learn what the truth really is. In the meantime we must view such assumptions as hypotheses subject to evaluation.

Assumptions regarding the capacity of the client to express and explore problem areas take different forms. Some counselors feel that basically the client is possessed of sufficient capacity that without external assistance the client can go ahead. Others feel that the client may be in reality a victim of his defenses, defenses which block him beyond his capacities to continue without external assistance. Still others may fall between these extremes with the feeling that the client may work through many of his defenses on his own but be blocked by some of them. Quite aside from stated positions it is interesting to note that apparently no counselors propose the meeting of every resistance or difficulty of expression with the most forceful methods available. No counselor proposes that the client be continually presented with reassurances, persuasions and moralizations to go ahead when he is going about as fast as he can anyway. Upon the contrary, when the client is proceeding satisfactorily counselors seem to feel no need to introduce motivating devices. Further, there seems to be a generally accepted rule that the strength of the motivating devices to be used by the counselor should be appropriate to the strength of the blocking. The techniques vary from bluntness to subtlety according to the apparent strength of the defenses. The interesting aspect of this variability lies in the fact that it expresses an observation about the effects of the use of external motivation which is not usually openly recognized, or, when it is considered, is so puzzling as to be often disregarded. The observation is simply that the use of external motivating devices may produce effects just the opposite of what is intended. In short, to persuade, reassure, instruct, or moralize may result in an increase, not a decrease, of resistance, a refusal to continue the expression and exploration of attitudes.

In suggesting that this undesired effect of external motivation is not openly recognized the writer means to imply that counselors usually restrict their questioning of such undesirable phenomena to the concepts they already hold. In other words, the counselor meets what he perceives as a resistance, the resistance must be overcome, the client can't do it so the counselor must, and accordingly the counselor employs some form of external motivation. If the technique employed doesn't work the only explanation must be in terms of the strength of the resistance, the inappropriateness of the particular technique chosen, or the counselor's ineptness in the use of that technique. This type of reasoning when carried to its ultimate conclusion leads to the client. If it were not for the way in which the client operates, if it were not for the experiences of the client which have so shaped his emotional life as to cause him to be blocked at some points, if it were not for deep forces within him that produce blocking beyond his control there would be no need for the application of external motivation. When we reason in this way we in effect deny the problem of undesirable effects of external motivation. We say, in effect, that such results are unfortunate but accountable for on the basis of the resistance phenomena and the skill of the counselor in dealing with them. Reasoning in this way does not lead us to consider an explanation of the negative results as possible direct and lawful outcomes of the use of external motivation itself.

Suppose we were to go outside of our customary framework of thinking and ask what is involved if we assume negative results of external motivation are direct outcomes of the presence of external motivation regardless of the existence of an initial resistance. As was suggested in an earlier paragraph it is when such a recognition is given the problem that the puzzlement becomes so great as to throw us back upon our earlier ways of thinking and lead us to disregard the problem. As we construct our thinking on this new assumption we reach an immediate implication that the counselor should avoid the use of external motivation. We ask, "Is it possible for the results which the counselor wishes to achieve, an initiation and facilitation of the client's expression and exploration of attitudes, to be achieved *without* the use of external motivation?" It is small wonder that we should be puzzled. To ask the question is only to raise two more. "Is the client possessed of enough internal motivation to overcome his own blocks and, if so, how can it be mobilized and made to operate effectively?" For many people the questioning will have gone far enough at this point. Many people feel the evidence is overwhelmingly in favor of the notion that, for the most part, the client will not have sufficient inner capacity to overcome his own resistances by himself. For others the answer is not so obvious as to the limitations of the client. A whole new line of thinking is developing upon the basis of the observed effects produced when the counselor seeks only to understand the client as the client sees himself and his own environment. The reported effects of such a way of responding to the client suggest that initiation and facilitation of expression and exploration is possible without the use of external motivation. It further suggests that a greater capacity for going ahead does exist within the client than is apparent in the face of other techniques.

It is entirely too early to say that the evidence which may be cited in behalf of the necessity for external motivation is in conflict with the evidence bearing against it. In science we have faith that some day unifying concepts will help us to understand such apparent conflicts in the same way that the concept of attraction between masses and the concepts of density and displacement helped us to understand why apples should fall on heads and helium-filled balloons rise into the air. It is, however, not at all too early to say that the apparent conflicts can be deeply puzzling and lead us into many a cul-de-sac. The student may well be bewildered when confronted with obvious examples where the institution of external motivations is followed by significant movements in the therapeutic process, with obvious examples where the therapeutic process does not move forward but apparently reverses, and with obvious examples where external motivations are called for by all the usual criteria and yet significant movement takes place in their absence. We cannot argue about what takes place but we can argue extensively, to say the least, as to what the events mean. To repeat once more, it is not the purpose of this volume to propose that the student follow any one set of meanings but rather to provide him experiences which will help him to see more clearly the events which do transpire. This is done in the hope that it will broaden the bases on which he arrives at the meanings which satisfy him. Or even greater is the hope that the student can reach such a point of security in his thinking that he will not need to have "answers" but only hypotheses which he constantly seeks to improve.

Why Therapy Needs the Client

No matter to what viewpoint we turn for ideas on the therapeutic process it is immediately obvious in each instance that the techniques proposed are aimed at bringing about changes within the client. There can be no question that where individuals are thinking of therapy they are thinking of how these changes can be brought about. The therapeutic process, the process of change, does not take place in the counselor or therapist. Therapy presupposes the client. Further, it is only in terms of changes within the client that we can judge whether or not an experience meant to be helpful has been helpful. Stated in another way we might say that no technique can be evaluated on the basis of its place within a logical structure but must be evaluated on the basis of the consistency with which it is related to the initiation and facilitation of a therapeutic process within the client.

We can say that a therapeutic process has taken place when a client with an attitudinal-behavioral organization which causes him and others discomfiture and which restricts the capacities of the client to live a free and constructive life comes to a different attitudinal-behavioral organization which is accompanied by an increase in feelings of well being and by a release from elements restricting the degree of self-realization or self-actualization. These changes are what may be described as outcomes of therapy. We may step up closer by regarding the process of therapy. Therapy seems to be constituted in the process of the client's reorganizing of the meaning of events in his life and in the process of the client's learning new attitudes, new ways of feeling, toward himself and his environment. In the following chapters exercises will be provided to help the student increase his facility in recognizing these processes as they appear in interview material taken from phonographic recordings or reconstructed from notes in verbatim style.

COUNSELING PROCEDURES

PRE-TEST

Before starting out on the various exercises meant to help the learner develop insight into his attitudes and skills, he may wish to get a picture of his starting point. There is no real answer as to just what his score will mean. Rightness and wrongness in counseling procedures, as may well be seen from the opening chapter, are concepts strictly relative to the counselor's whole set of values. The scoring will not be on a right or wrong basis but will provide a profile picture of counseling procedures favored. It will be to the reader's advantage in obtaining a truer picture of his procedures to let further concern about scoring or the meaning of the scoring wait until after the test has been taken and to answer each item according to his real convictions.

Part I. Aptness of Response [1]

Instructions. In this part of the test a series of excerpts from interviews are presented. Each excerpt is an expression by a client con-

---

[1] The test as given is a modification of a test developed by Virginia M. Axline and E. H. Porter, Jr., for use in a short-term training program. For a description of this program see Blocksma, D. D., and Porter, E. H., Jr., "A Short-Term Training Program in Client-Centered Counseling," *Journal of Consulting Psychology*, v. XI, no. 2 (Mar.–April) 1947, pp. 55–60.

cerning an aspect of the situation he faces. Little or no information is given you about the nature of the person speaking. No further information on the case is available. You will not even know where in the course of the interview series the expression takes place. In brief, you are presented with isolated client expressions.

Following each such client statement is a series of five possible counselor responses. You are to select the one response which seems to you to be the most apt response you could make in reply to the client. Where no response seems best, select the response which best approximates the response you would like to see.

1 Woman — age 47 — Quite tense

"I really don't know what to do. Ah —, I really don't know whether to go back to teaching school. It gets on my nerves so — I can't hardly stand it — but I've got tenure and a good salary. Or else make a clean break and really do the thing I am interested in. (*Slight pause.*) But that would mean starting in at the bottom with a very small salary and I wouldn't know whether I could do that or not."

1. Could you tell me a little more about your new field of interest? It is quite important that we think about this clearly.
2. Well, before you jump into something new you should be very sure that it is really more worth-while and will provide at least the security and feeling of contribution that teaching brings you.
3. Well, now, possibly we can help you with that decision. Probably we can give you some tests which will furnish you with some idea as to whether you might expect to be successful in the line of your new interests. And maybe we could explore some of the things which give you dissatisfaction in your teaching work.
4. This indecision of yours is an understandable thing and stems from the conflict between your uncertainty over the new line of interest and your mixed feelings of dissatisfaction with the teaching job yet hesitance to leave the security which it affords.
5. It's really a tough decision, isn't it? Whether to take the risks of starting out in the new field or whether to stick by the security of the irritating teaching job.

2   Girl — age 19

"I tell you I hate my father. I hate him! I hate him! I hate him! And there's no reason for it. He is a minister — a good and righteous man — . He has never laid a hand on me — but I have this terrific feeling against him — and it makes me feel so terrible because — there is no reason for it. It's a sin to hate your father — especially if you don't have any real reason for it. I — it worries me."

1. Of course you feel guilty about hating him so, especially since you can't put your finger on what he has done to make you hate him. And then, too, even though you see only your hatred of him you'll find that underneath it all you have some love for him and this plays a part in your feelings of guilt.
2. I guess everyone at some time or another goes through a period when they hate one or both of their parents. It's really not at all uncommon. Most people find that they can work out some way of getting along until things settle down.
3. This is certainly something which you will want to get cleared up. Happy relationships with parents are too constructive a thing to a person, not only now at your age, but in the future as well, you won't want to jeopardize what it can mean to you.
4. It worries you that you should hate your father without reason and yet feel sinful for hating him.
5. I think we ought to get to the root of that worry. Tell me about your father: all about him. You say he's never laid a hand on you, but maybe he has *not* let you do a number of things *you* wanted to do. Can you think of anything along this line?

3   Man — age 30

"I have the queerest feeling. Whenever anything good happens to me — I just can't believe it. I act as though it never happened. And it worries me. I wanted a date with Myrtle — and I stood around for weeks before I got up enough courage to ask her for a date and she said 'yes' — and I couldn't believe it. I couldn't believe it so much that I didn't keep the date!"

1. You've got to grow up, fellow, and get a little more realistic idea about women. They're human, too, you know, and want dates just as much as you do.
2. It just doesn't seem real when something good happens.

3. You have probably denied to yourself so strongly that anything good could happen to you that when it does it seems unreal.
4. I am wondering whether or not these feelings of unreality are associated with any particular area of your life. Would you like to tell me more about what you mean when you said, "Whenever *anything good* happens to me"?
5. Well, I'm not too sure that you should be so worried about it. It doesn't mean anything in itself, really. I think we'll be able to get to the bottom of it all right.

4 Man — age 59

"I couldn't let my son help me now that I'm down and out. I've got that shred of pride left — because you see I remember when he was a kid I didn't turn my hand to help him. I traipsed around the country — his mother died when the kid was born — and I let the relatives push him around and stuck him in foster homes — and now — It certainly was like a knife stuck in me when we met the other day and he said, 'We can make a go of it together, Dad — I've got a little money saved up.' No — No — I won't let him do it. I will clear out of here. It'll be hard — but — I haven't done *one* thing for him — or anyone else — for that matter."

1. Have you investigated the possibility of an old age pension? Possibly something could be worked out there that wouldn't make it necessary for you to impose on your son or accept help from him.
2. What was your married life like? Had you and your wife planned for a child?
3. Your behavior in the past makes you unworthy of the help your son wants to give you now, is that what you mean?
4. Have you thought about what it will mean to your son if you don't let him do this thing which he wants to do for you?
5. I see what you mean. You feel that you don't deserve the help he wants to give because in the past you did nothing to earn it. And your statement that you never have done anything for anyone else makes it look as if it might be a real problem to you to accept responsibility *for* helping others, and to accept help *from* others.

5 Man — age 35

"I'm determined to get ahead. I am not afraid of hard work. I am not afraid to take a few hard knocks — if I can see my goal out there in front. And I'm not averse to climbing over a few people – who get in my way – because this means a lot to me. I can't be satisfied with just a mediocre job. No, I want to *be* somebody."

1. You see yourself as a deeply ambitious person, is that it?
2. You feel that you just have to be out on top no matter what you may do to others.
3. What do you suppose is behind this strong determination of yours to get ahead?
4. Would you be interested in taking some tests to determine in what areas you might expect to be most successful? It might be of real help to you, although it is possible with your drive that you could be successful in a number of fields.
5. Strong ambition can be a real asset to any man. Are you really sure, though, that you mean it when you say you're not averse to climbing over those who get in your way? Couldn't that turn out to do you more harm than good?

6   Man – age 21

"Shall I marry her? Or shall I think of *my* future? If a fellow is going to think of his future – if he's got ambition and drive to get ahead – he's got to be hard – and forget all about sentiment – But I do love Marie – I really do – And she's been my inspiration – if we broke off, I don't know what I'd do. I don't know whether I should be able to do a thing – I don't know. On the other hand, I can't afford advanced study and marriage too. And Marie says, if we can't get married now, she isn't willing to wait – I don't know what to do. I love her, but if she loved me, would she say, 'Now or never?' That's the thing I can't answer."

1. That is, you can't decide whether to marry and risk your future or whether to plan for your future and risk losing out on the marriage. They seem so dependent on each other.
2. It is not really so much a problem of indecision between marriage and vocational plans as it is the deeper problem of whether you should be dependent upon your own self-approval or dependent upon her approval of what you do.
3. I am wondering, there, if you can't have both the career and marriage. Have you two discussed ways and means of increasing your income by extra work or by her working? Most universities or schools would cooperate with you. And besides there just isn't time

for expensive entertainment among married students working their own way. There would not be the demand for social activities that you might expect to find out in a community.

4. I think you have got to take into account how Marie will feel if you go ahead and decide to follow your studies and not get married now. What will it do to her? The decision you make ought to take into account what is best for both of you.

5. I think you may have hit on something significant there; how much she loves you. Could you tell me a little more about that? How she acts toward you and your ideas?

7 Girl — age 29

"I'm afraid to be alone. I really am. I'm afraid I'll kill myself and I don't want to — but I get so depressed. I get caught in a terrific clutch of fear — It's unreal, but it's there. And I get so worked up I could scream. I want to get outside and I'm afraid to go out in case I run in front of a car — and I'm afraid to stay in — I'm afraid of myself — I'm afraid to go to the doctor and get an examination. I'm afraid he'll tell me it's cancer. My mother had it. My grandmother, my aunt. I've lived with it all my life — and it's hell — and when this first came up — See — I break out in a sweat just talking about it. Christ, is there any help!"

1. Aside from your fear have you experienced any symptoms which lead you to think you really might have cancer?
2. This terrific fear just never lets you alone.
3. If you have any reason at all to think that you might have cancer, you really should try to control your fear enough to have a medical examination.
4. Would you like to try this: Whenever you experience one of these fears call me on the telephone, either here at the office or at home, and talk it over with me. Talking it over oftentimes helps a person to get a grip on himself.
5. My guess is that if we trace these fears a bit we'll find that they are not as real as you feel them to be. I think you are punishing yourself for something about which you feel pretty guilty.

8 Woman — age 30

"I've lived in this town for ten years now — and in the same apartment for seven years — but I don't know anybody. At the office I just can't seem to make friends. I just freeze up — I try to be nice to the other workers, but I feel all stiff and uncomfortable inside. And then I tell myself that I don't care. People aren't dependable — Everyone is out for himself. I don't want any friends — and sometimes I think I really mean that."

1. Well, I'll tell you what I can do. I can arrange for you to join a small social group at the "Y". I send quite a few people there who have difficulty in making friends. Most want to start out by taking ceramics, leather tooling or some other handicraft. This gives them something to do as a basis and permits them to make friends slowly and at their own pace. How does that sound to you?
2. Possibly if you could tell me a little more about how you go about trying to make friends we could get a clearer idea of what is involved.
3. It's gone on so long it almost has you convinced — is that what you mean?
4. Maybe your not wanting friends is just to protect you from something else.
5. That's a pretty unhappy situation, to be without friends, and one that I would really work on. There are a number of things that you might do to learn how to make friends and the sooner you start the better.

9   Man — age 42

"But can't you tell me what to do? Can't you make a few suggestions? I'm willing to do *anything* but I just don't know which way to turn. I'll work *hard* to help myself — if you'll just tell me whether you think it will help me or not — and whether you think I can get over this personality problem. If you'll just tell me what to do, I'll be so grateful to you."

1. Maybe one of the important parts of your situation is that you don't have real confidence in yourself. Do you see?
2. Really, it's not so important what you do so long as what you do is a product of your own self-dependence. You've got to learn to do the things which are good and right because *you* feel they are — not me.
3. I gather you just don't feel capable of working this out yourself?
4. Before it would be possible to answer any of your questions satisfactorily I'd have to have quite a bit of information about you, about

your family, your childhood, your work, your relationship with your wife and so forth.

5. Well, you've really asked for a lot there, all right. I think I can best answer you in this way: We'll work together talking over these things that bother you. You'll think of some things and I'll think of some things that maybe you've missed. And maybe between the two of us, we'll get to the bottom of all this and figure out a path for you to follow that will solve most if not all the problem. I wouldn't worry too much about it. I think we can be fairly sure of making headway.

10   Man — age 35

"I expect, that if I took this job — with the understanding that I'd be given the opportunity to prove my value to the firm — and had a chance for promotions — yes, I believe that's the soundest way to go about it. It's not as spectacular as I would like to have it — No, I don't really want a spectacular job any more — just a good solid job with a future. Yes. I'll take this job and discuss my plans with the boss quite frankly and honestly. Then my wife and I can get some feeling of permanence and we can buy a home and really think about the future here in this city. The kids need an anchor, too. They haven't had that — but from now on we are all going to have our feet down on solid earth."

1. That's fine. The long way around can be the short way home. I think you've really got your feet on the ground now for sure. The kind of thinking you're doing is certainly the most constructive.
2. That sounds good to me. And if you run across any difficulty in thinking through how you're going to present your problem to the boss, or if you want any help in planning how to make yourself more promotable — just remember that I'm always here to help you.
3. I'm wondering if you've investigated the promotional policy of the company to see if the path you want to follow is the one most likely to lead to promotion?
4. Of course! The spectacular may be appealing but the more mature way pays off.
5. It may not be spectacular but I gather the soundness of it is what really appeals to you.

11   Man — veteran — age 30

"What's the use of anything? No one plays fair and square with a guy. The fellows who stayed at home got all the plums. They all took advantage of us while we sweat it out at the front. I hate their guts — every one of them. They are all double-crossers. And my wife —" *(long pause.)*

1. You started to say something about your wife?
2. You feel they took advantage of you and it really makes you boil.
3. You've been taken advantage of and it makes you pretty angry. Well, that's natural.
4. I understand how you feel about that but it's going to block you from getting ahead if you don't try to get away from it.
5. You've got lots of company with your anger. It's justifiable in so many cases. But you'll forget it as time goes on and you get established again.

12   Man — age 33

"I tell you I am in one hell of a fix! I'm in love with the swellest girl on the face of the earth — and she loves me. I'm sure of that. But I'm not worthy of her. I can't ask her to marry. I've got a criminal record. She doesn't know about it — But I know it'll come out some day — No. I couldn't marry and have children. I've got a record that proves to the world that I'm a first class son-of-a-bitch."

1. Well, it would certainly be unfair to her to marry and to discover about your past later. Don't you almost have to tell her about it now?
2. You feel afraid to face her with your record because she might turn you down and you just couldn't stand that.
3. Could you tell me a little as to why you're so sure that she wouldn't be able to accept you if she knew about your past?
4. Possibly if you were to have her come in to see me I could talk with her and lead her to see that your past is your past and does not necessarily mean that you couldn't have a happy future together.
5. You see yourself as unworthy of her beyond all shadow of a doubt.

13   Man — age 27

"I've come to the conclusion that if I'm not happy in the work I'm doing, then I'll get another job. And that's what it adds up to. I've hung on because I spent four years in college getting ready to do it. *Now* I think I'd be a lot happier if I chucked the whole thing and entered this other field — even if it does mean starting at the bottom and working my way up — ."

1. You feel that you'd be a lot happier if you could just escape your work and start out in a field where you are more adequate, is that it?
2. Whether this is the field in which you'll end up no one can say, but it seems to me quite sound that you are counting more on yourself.
3. Have you thought of the possibility of working out a combination line? It seems a shame to just toss out all you've lined up so far.
4. You've decided that you'd do better to change.
5. How much study have you given this new field?

14 Girl — age 23 (physical handicap)

"I can't do any of the things my sister does. I can't dance or go riding or date the boys. I'm a — I look at Charlene — and I wish I was her. You can't know the feeling I get deep inside me — I want to be able to have pretty clothes like hers — and to go out and have a good time. It makes me sick inside me — But she can't help it — She was born that way. And I can't help it because I was born this way — and I get this feeling. I *love* my sister. Really I do — but I just cried and cried — until I was sick. I want the things other girls have. I can't help it — I'm only human. I know it's a sin to feel as I do — but she has *every-thing* and I have nothing."

1. I'm wondering — since you aren't going to be able to engage in physical activities as your sister does — I'm wondering if there aren't some other sources of activities which might be satisfying.
2. I can appreciate why you'd envy her so but since you can't compete with her it's not much use in using up your energies with envy. You've got to buckle down and build a world that satisfies you.
3. In other words, you feel envious of your sister because you can't compete with her and you feel guilty about your envy because you love your sister too.
4. I'd like to get a better idea of just how you react to her directly and how she reacts to you in some of these situations.
5. You say in one breath that you envy your sister. You say next that you love her. Now couldn't your feelings of guilt be due to these conflicting feelings?

15 Man — age 27

"I got out of the Navy last month and I thought, 'Now what?' I looked
for a job — and right there I ran into a snag — I couldn't make up
my mind what to do — I thought I ought to go back to school and finish
up and I thought I'd be happier if I signed up for more Navy — and
then I looked for a job — and nothing stood out as a clear choice. Everything looked good and everything looked bad — and I felt — well, what
the hell? Am I going nuts? Am I always going to be so messed up inside
of me that I won't be able to move in *any* direction?"

1. You're wondering just what's at the bottom of it all.
2. Let's go ahead and discuss some of the things — why don't you
   want them and why do you want them — maybe we can find a clue
   that will point out the answer.
3. This is a thing which so many G.I.'s have faced. It'll disappear
   largely in time. Why not just take something until you get your feet
   back on the ground?
4. No, I don't think you need to remain messed up or really that you're
   messed up now. You're confused, yes, but if you set your mind to
   it, you'll overcome your confusion and move ahead in a more natural
   manner.
5. You're confused — and alarmed with your confusion. This is to be
   expected when you suddenly find yourself facing the necessity for
   making decisions after a long period of having even minor decisions
   made for you.

16 Man — age 35

"I know I could make a success of that business. All a person needs
is a little over-all vision, some common sense, and the courage to try it.
I've got that — So — If I could just get ahold of the cash — I'd sure take
the plunge."

1. If you'd think it wise I could give you the name of an Investment
   Counselor who'd be glad to go over the proposition with you and
   possibly give you some good leads on how to seek financial support.
2. That's fine! One must feel sure of himself if he expects to make a
   go of something. To go into something hesitantly can really make
   it get all mixed up. You're on the right track and I wish you success.
3. If you could get the cash to start, you feel sure you could make a go
   of it.

4. You feel sure you could be successful because you now see what is involved in making the thing go. When you see things clearly assurance follows.
5. Have you figured out what the risks are as yet?

17 Girl — age 18

"Oh, I couldn't work through my problem without help. You ask me questions and tell me — Because I wouldn't be able to — Honestly — I haven't got any idea how to go about it. I don't want to — It's like down at the office — I can't go ahead on my own — I just can't — I want to be told — then it's not my fault if things go wrong — And they would go wrong — because I don't know how things should be done, I feel sɢ helpless."

1. You say it's not your fault if things go wrong even after you've been told what to do. Can you tell me what you mean there?
2. You feel that you just aren't capable of doing things unaided.
3. It's not really that you can't go ahead on your own — it's just that you think you can't. That's one of the problems we can work on — to build up your confidence in yourself.
4. Well, I could suggest some of the things you might talk about here in our interview and some of the things you might think about between interviews. I might also suggest some things for you to do about your office work that ought to make it a little easier for you.
5. You feel dependent upon someone else for nearly everything you do, don't you? And it probably makes you panicky when people throw you on your own, too. But when people tell you what to do you don't have to assume the real responsibility and hence it's not your fault if things go wrong — they just didn't tell you enough.

18 Man — age 46

"Well, this new man came into the company. He's a big shot — Has all the answers. Thinks he's going places. But, by God, he doesn't know George P. Quipenque! I'll get ahead of him if I have a stroke trying!"

1. You feel that you must be out in front. That it is really important to you to be the better man.
2. It's a fine thing to try to get ahead but do you think that by starting out with such an attitude toward him you're going at it right?

3. And that will probably take a lot of careful planning and thinking. You'll want to go carefully.
4. He really makes you want to beat him out.
5. Let's wait a minute there. Why is it so important to you to want to get ahead of this man?

19

"It's not that I don't want to do something about it — I just — well — I know what I *ought* to do — but for some reason or other I just can't — do a thing."

1. Maybe if we talked over what you've thought of doing, we could figure out what is best to do. It's possible that the answer is something new.
2. Let's try to get at what's behind this blocking. Tell me more about it.
3. Behind this blocked feeling you're experiencing is a conflict in your desires: you want to and you don't want to.
4. You're blocked by something and you don't know what it is, is that what you're saying?
5. Are you sure you know what you ought to do? It seems to me that if you really had a clear idea of what you ought to do you'd be able to go ahead.

20   Man — age 60

"I've got it all figured out. There's nothing for me to live for any more. My wife's dead. My kids don't need me. I'm too old to get a job. Just the fifth wheel on a wagon. And I'm tired of it all. I'm going to end it all — Put a bullet through my brain. And rest in peace."

1. You feel there's nothing left in life for you.
2. When things add up for a person like they've added up for you it really does make it tough to face. And sometimes there doesn't seem to be a way out. Yet — I think that if you'll stick with me on these interviews we may be able to find a way out.
3. How long have you felt this way, may I ask?
4. Escaping is one way, all right, but have you thought of what it would mean to your children to have you commit suicide?
5. It seems to me that you are looking for a way to escape an otherwise intolerable situation.

21 Woman — age 43

"I've decided that this is not going to help me. All it does is make me realize what *I* have to do and I'm sick of taking responsibility — I don't think I'll come back any more."

1. Of course it has to be your decision — I can't force you to come — but you certainly aren't going to settle anything by backing away from it.
2. This has been too painful to you and now you want to escape the situation which produces the pain.
3. It just doesn't seem to fill the bill for you.
4. I'd like to know what your thinking has been in coming to this decision.
5. Sometimes taking responsibility can be a pretty demanding thing. Possibly if you decided to continue coming we could reach a point where you enjoyed responsibilities.

22 Man — age 41

"I've been married four times and each time I've thought, 'Boy, this is the real thing!' But none of them has ever been like this girl. She's the most beautiful girl you ever saw — And dance! And she dresses like a million dollars. She's out of this world!"

1. You're *really* enthusiastic about *her.*
2. How does she compare with your other wives? How did you feel about them before you married?
3. If she's anything like you seem to feel she is, she must be quite a catch. Maybe this time you'll stick.
4. Doesn't it strike you as odd that every time you've felt the same way?
5. Just stop and analyze what you've said. The points which you mention as her good points are rather superficial. You are still a bit immature, I'm afraid.

23 Man — age 29

"I keep remembering how I walked out on Mary and the two kids. Five years ago — The law never caught up with me — I thought I was pretty smart — But now — God, but I was a heel. I don't see how I could do it. And I'm so ashamed I can't look people in the eye. Now

I can't find her — Not a trace. Her relatives won't tell me where she is. I don't blame them — But how could I have done it? Just because it was tough going. I tell you, I'll *never* have any self-respect. Never! And I — I don't know what to do — or how I can even *try* to rectify my big mistake. I don't know — !"

1. There are a number of things you might do to try to find her. You could list her as a missing person and get police help. You could get a private detective agency to handle it for you. You might even be able to get a court order that would force the relatives to give her address.
2. When did you decide that you wanted her back? Tell me about the circumstances.
3. The hopelessness there seems pretty clearly connected with the feelings of guilt.
4. Are you at all sure that you should try to go back to her? If you left her once maybe you'd do it again. Possibly you just didn't get along at all well and you were forced to leave her.
5. As you see it then, your behavior is just plain unforgivable.

24 Man — age 39

"There is no other way to handle this than to destroy them completely. Remember this man was supposed to be my best friend — and he took my wife away from me — and after the divorce he married her — and then he pushed me out of the business. But I've got the evidence to ruin him. I could clean him out — and put him behind bars for the rest of his life. (*Laughs bitterly.*) Wouldn't that be something? My ex-wife married to something kept behind bars and not a dime left to live on?"

1. Your desire to destroy them seems to me to be largely a desire for revenge. It may have grown out of the rejection and denial you experienced from both of them.
2. Wanting to get even is understandable but don't you think that is going pretty far? I certainly wouldn't do anything I'd regret later.
3. You want them to suffer at your hand just as they made you suffer at theirs.
4. After all that I can see where it would be really satisfying to see them suffer. Do you suppose, though, that you could get at them in some less drastic way?
5. Has anyone else ever crossed you like that: in business, among your friends, when you were a kid in school?

25 Girl — age 28

"I just looked at her — She isn't so attractive as I am — She isn't smart — and she has no style — and I asked myself — 'How does she fool so many people?' Why can't they see through that sticky-sweetness? She can always do up a job in a hurry. Everyone is always admiring the way she does things — and I can't stand it. It just makes me sick. She has everything I want. She got my job — She got Bill — took him right away from me — and then denied it — when I put it to her. I just told her what I thought and she said 'I'm sorry.' But — well, I'll show her."

1. Is she pretty much like the other girls with whom you've been thrown in contact?
2. You feel that she always gets what you really should have.
3. It sounds to me as if you're taking a pretty strong attitude against her. We all have prejudices against people but they seldom, if ever, do us any good.
4. You've got a case of plain, old-fashioned jealousy brought on by being thrown into contact with someone possibly a little more capable and slicker than yourself.
5. Why don't you try to watch the things she does and beat her at her own game? If she's a four-flusher, you ought to be able to get the best of her.

Part II. Aptness of Response in Different Situations [1]

Instructions. In this part of the test are ten examples of possible exchanges between counselors and students. The counselor starts each exchange. The student replies. The counselor's response to the student is presented as a multiple choice problem. You are to choose the counselor response which you feel is the *type* of response you would be more apt to favor, if you were in the situation. The wording used may not strike you as being the best, but disregard this factor as long as the response is the same *type* as you would favor.

---

[1] This part of the test is based on a series of such items presented in "A simple measure of counselor attitudes," *Trends in Student Personnel Work*, E. G. Williamson, editor (Minneapolis: University of Minnesota Press, 1949), pp. 129–135.

26

Financial Counselor: How do you do? I'm Mr. Smith. Now what is it that I can do for you?

Student: Well, sir, I'm not just too sure. I have a situation that I'm not too clear about and I don't know whether I need to get a loan, or whether I'm not planning well enough on what I have, or whether I'm a victim of the inflation, or just what. And I thought — well, I mentioned it to one of my profs and he suggested I ought to see you, so here I am.

Financial Counselor:

1. A little too confusing to dope out yourself, is that it?
2. Well, I hope that I can help. It's the kind of thing we want to do here: help you get lined up.
3. Let me get a piece of paper here. Okay: shoot! What's the story?
4. Chances are that it is a combination of factors; it usually is for most students.
5. Well, it strikes me that you're doing the right thing here. Sound financial planning can be a real help.

27

Marriage Counselor: All right, Miss Ex, what is it that you wanted to see me about?

Miss Ex: I wanted to talk with you about my fiance and what you think about whether or not I should marry him. My whole relationship with him is such a changeable thing. One day we are all set to get married and the next day we want to call it all off. We've set a time now, two weeks from tomorrow, when we are either going to get married or quit seeing each other. Now *I* think we can make a go of it, if he will just be a bit more considerate of my feelings. I know I'm what you call a neurotic but why can't he help me overcome it?

Marriage Counselor:

1. Well, now I certainly can't give an answer to your situation just like that, but I do think it is clear that whatever decision you reach should be one which is the most constructive for the both of you.
2. I'd like to hear a little more about what you feel he could help you overcome.

3. I'm wondering here how much of your relationship might be a way of looking for help for something inside that troubles you: the same thing that brings you to me.
4. While you paint a picture of incompatibility at times, I'm thinking that it may be possible to reach some resolution of this conflict. It may be more apparent than real.
5. I gather the whole situation is a somewhat confusing one to you and one for which you want to work out an answer right away.

28

Fraternity Counselor: Hi, Ed. How'd the game with the upper classmen go?

Fraternity student: Aw to hell with 'em! Good Lord, I tried to do my best, but when Joe got so darned mad at me when I miscounted trumps it just made me — well, I try — I do try — but when they as much as tell me that my best isn't enough, it just points out to me more and more clearly that I'm just a sad sack.

Fraternity Counselor:

1. Look, Ed, have you ever just stopped to consider the source? Like the guy that got kicked in the face by the mule?
2. In other words, when someone attacks you, you tend to feel guilty about it.
3. In other words, when you did your best and he found fault, it tended to make you feel rather worthless.
4. Now look, my friend, if you're going to let something like that throw you, you are a sad sack, for sure.
5. Tell me, Ed, is it only in bridge games that you feel that way?

29

Student Activities Counselor: I wanted to talk with you, Tom, about the difficulties which seem to exist between your staff and the newspaper staff.

Student: Well, if you ask me, it's high time that pack of mutts got straightened out. Every time they print that sheet all they do is criticize. They run down every last thing we do. I've done everything I can do to work with them. They're so infernally superior. They ought to try to put a good foot forward for a change. But, I'll help in any way I can.

Student Activities Counselor:

1. I'd like to hear your side of the story completely. Want to tell me more about it?
2. What you say about them may be true, Tom, but let's remember that we've just got to work together in order to exist.
3. From the way you see it, I can understand how it would be very provoking.
4. From the way you see it, then, you're pretty well justified in feeling angry, but you're willing to help.
5. I gather you resent being made to feel inferior.

30

Religious Counselor: All right, Marian, we have half an hour now. Would you like to go ahead in your own way?

Student: I don't know just how to begin. It just seems that everything here is so negative. In all the classes they just tear things apart — and put nothing in their place. Now it really doesn't bother me but I like to see the good side of things. To me religion has always meant a lot, but with all this analysis and taking things apart and explaining things mechanically, it just makes me wonder if there really is a God. And I want to see things constructively.

Religious Counselor:

1. You feel disturbed by these destructive activities.
2. Sometimes it takes a lot of thinking to absorb conflicting ideas.
3. You want to be constructive but these destructive activities stand in the way, is that it?
4. I'd like to get a little clearer idea of how this conflict works out. Could you give me an idea, say, by a more specific example?
5. Have you thought of the possibility of asking your instructors just how they relate the two sides? Maybe you could get some help by a more complete discussion.

31

Faculty Counselor: Come in. What can I do for you?

Student: Dr. Allen, I'd like to get some help from you on my schedule for next winter quarter. I've talked with several people about what J ought to take but they all tell me different things and it's so hard for me to know what to choose. Gee whiz, I'm only a Freshman and I just don't know what is best, so I decided finally that I ought to come to someone who could give me some expert advice.

Faculty Counselor:

1. If I follow you correctly there, you feel pretty sure that this is something that requires outside help, it's something you can't decide for yourself.
2. Are you speaking now of what major field you want to get into, or what you are going to take for electives?
3. Well, now maybe if you depended a little more on yourself, on what you can do and what you want to do instead of what others say, you'd get along a little better.
4. I'm wondering there if your difficulty isn't more a matter of developing self-reliance than a matter of selecting courses.
5. Sure. I'd be glad to help. Sometimes it's a bit brutal getting adjusted to the college set-up.

32

Student Discipline Counselor: I expect, Al, that you know why you've been sent for. Bringing liquor into the dorm was a violation of the University rules. Were you aware of that?

Student: Yes, I am aware of that and I appreciate the fact that it was a foolish thing to do. I do not intend to try to justify myself in any way. It was childish. I can understand that such things cannot be tolerated by the university. I had an impulse to try it and I got caught. I am ready to accept the consequences.

Student Discipline Counselor:

1. All right, Al. I'd suggest you keep up the same attitude. I don't like to jump you any more than you like to be jumped. I'll let you know what the Dean decides.
2. All right, Al. I gather you wish to stand squarely on your own two feet in this matter. I'll let you know what the Dean decides.
3. You feel, then, that the treatment is just. You'll be hearing from the Dean as soon as he has reached his decision.
4. I hope you'll recognize this is something the Dean's office must do

and that we don't like it any more than you do. You'll be hearing from the Dean soon now.
5. What's the score on this now? What the devil was it that prompted you to take a try at this?

33

Counselor at Student Union: How do you feel about coming here, Joan? Do you feel it has been of any help to you?

Student: I think it's wonderful! I've never had a chance like this before in all my life. People are so friendly here. Oh, of course, I realize that there are others here who are just learning, too, but I just don't feel afraid any more. I think the university is to be most wholeheartedly congratulated for providing the chance for students who might otherwise go through school as wall flowers.

Counselor at Student Union:

1. That's just grand, Joan. I'm glad you're getting so much out of it.
2. You'll probably simmer down a bit as it becomes old stuff to you, but it's sure fun now, isn't it?
3. Keep at it, Joan, you're on the right track.
4. I'm rather wondering whether this same feeling is carrying over into other areas of your life.
5. Feeling pretty pleased and grateful, is that it?

34

Dormitory Counselor: How are things coming along, Joe?

Dormitory Student: Okay, I guess, except for that new roomie I got stuck with. He's a heel! He thinks he knows everything — a big shot. But I'll figure out some way to handle him, all right. And he'll know he's been handled, too. I'm not taking any guff off a peanut like that.

Dormitory Counselor:

1. You feel you must be out in front of him, that it's really important to you to be the better man, isn't that it?
2. Do you think that's a very constructive attitude to take toward him?
3. Why should this thing be so important to you?

4. You feel pretty angry with him and want to put him in his place, is that it?
5. I see what you mean. A guy like that is a real pain in the neck.

35

Guidance Counselor: All right, Ralph, what was it you wanted to talk about?

Student: What I want to do is to narrow my interests down to one or two areas or objectives which can give me a source of economic support, of financial security, and yet give me a feeling of intellectual achievement. It seems to me that the time has come when this immature lack of direction has got to be straightened out.

Guidance Counselor:

1. Just how far has your thinking gone in this problem?
2. You know where you want to go and it's high time you got there, is that it?
3. That's a fine goal, Ralph. Let's see what we can do about it.
4. I expect that first we'll have to get a measure of your strengths and weakness and interests and then see how things seem to stack up.
5. Um hm, I see. You're beginning to become concerned about growing up.

Part III. Immediate Counselor Aims

Instructions. In this part of the test you will be presented with the first ten consecutive responses in an interview with a veteran. Following each response are five alternative formulations of aims or purposes which the counselor might wish to follow. You are to choose the alternative which you feel indicates the best aim or purpose which the counselor might try to effect at this particular point in the interview.

36

"Say, what's the matter with this town? You go down the street and don't see anyone you know! You can walk into restaurants and they give you the cold shoulder! You look for a job and they have to see your discharge papers and ask a lot of nosey questions!" [1]

The counselor should reply in such a way as to try to:

1. Indicate he understands the veteran's disappointment and bitterness.
2. Convey to the veteran the idea that attitudes so often taken toward service men could easily cause them to feel bitter and rejected.
3. Get the veteran to continue talking so the counselor can get a little better idea of what he has to deal with in this case.
4. Lead the veteran to consider that his reactions may be in part due to his own attitudes.
5. Indicate to the veteran that in all likelihood he has an incorrect slant: that the town is probably not as unfriendly as he presumes.

37

"It wasn't this way overseas. It was tough there, but you had your job and you did it. I was tail gunner in a Fortress. I could have let the armorers look after my guns, but I never let it go at that. I always checked 'em over myself to make sure they were right. The whole ship was no better than any man in it, and if one gun went out, you were likely to be done for."

The counselor should reply in such a way as to try to:

1. Lead the veteran to explain more fully just what all this means to him.
2. Point out to the veteran that the present situation calls for different behavior than did the service situation.
3. Convey to the veteran the feeling that you can sympathize with how difficult the civilian situation can be.
4. Let the veteran know that you recognize his feelings that in the service his life had a real purpose and he counted.
5. Help the veteran to recognize that his feelings of bitterness might be due to his not being in a position where he can feel he belongs and others count on him.

38

"You see these guys going around here with good jobs who have had

[1] The responses of the client-serviceman in items 36 through 45 are from *Counseling with Returned Servicemen* by Rogers and Wallen. 1946. Courtesy of McGraw-Hill Book Company.

it nice and easy all the time we've been gone, and it just makes you sore. Don't you think yourself that there are a lot of fellows who got their draft boards to defer 'em on pretty weak excuses, and then just stayed home to make lots of money and have it soft? It makes me boil, just like it used to when my older brother would sneak out on a Saturday afternoon, leaving me with all the work!"

The counselor should reply in such a way as to try to:

1. Get the veteran to recognize that criticism of others is not the "solution" to his situation.
2. Convey an appreciation of how the veteran sees the situation as one in which he feels taken advantage of.
3. Draw the veteran's attention to the two topics he has brought up: feelings of being taken advantage of now and an earlier life experience with his brother.
4. Provoke the veteran into a further explanation regarding the childhood situations with his brother.
5. Indicate your own feelings that his feelings of being taken advantage of are at least in part justified however unfortunate they may be.

39

"You know, it's a funny thing, but when I go in to ask for a job, I just feel shaky all over. It's the silliest damn thing! Why should I do that?"

The counselor should reply in such a way as to try to:

1. Help the veteran to minimize his concern over this symptom.
2. Connect for the veteran the facts of his feelings of rejection which are being experienced and his anxiety symptoms.
3. Express in simple terms that you can see how his reactions must puzzle him and cause him concern.
4. Lead the veteran to consider what he might do about this condition.
5. Lead the veteran into a more complete exposition about the condition he reports.

40

"I think it would be a screwy thing to do, really, but I think sometimes that I will sign up again with the Army. It would be easier than all this red tape of getting a job, and you would always be sure of where your next meal is coming from. And they are a good gang of fellows there, too. But I think that would be a foolish thing to do."

The counselor should reply in such a way as to try to:

1. Draw to the attention of the veteran that he feels two ways about his situation, that he is ambivalent.
2. Get the veteran to furnish further details about either or both sides of his ambivalence.
3. Bring the veteran to drop his escapist attitudes.
4. Bring the veteran to the realization that the readjustment situation probably does not call for such stringent action.
5. Check on your own understanding that the veteran sees the situation as so difficult to beat that even something foolish might be the best way out.

41

"My mother doesn't have much, and she pretty much lived on the allotment I sent home. I never know just what to do about that. It seemed to me that I had a right to keep enough to enjoy myself on — oh, I didn't do any high living — of course some of the fellows sent home more, but it seemed to me that I was doing pretty good if I sent home —— dollars out of the —— dollars I was getting paid. What do you think? Doesn't that seem fair to you?"

The counselor should reply in such a way as to try to:

1. Help the veteran to see that his question about his rightness or wrongness is a side issue, he should think more along lines of what he is going to do now.
2. Bring the client to see more clearly that he is saying at one moment he was right and at the next moment is saying that he doesn't know.
3. Direct the veteran to talking about his relationship with his mother.
4. Reduce the veteran's anxiety and uncertainty by indicating that you are sure he did what seemed best even though he may have doubts about it now.
5. Indicate that, as you see it, he feels he did do right by his mother, but at the same time he is not really certain that he did.

42

"When I was young, my mother used to always watch over everything I did. You see, I was the youngest, and she was always worrying about me. She was the kind that worried about whether I had my rubbers on when I went out. I didn't mind it so much then, but after

I got away from home — Of course she was really a good mother. Just about everything she did was for us kids."

The counselor should reply in such a way as to try to:

1. Draw to the attention of the veteran that there might be some connections between his prior question of doing right by his mother and the way she handled him as a child.
2. Determine whether or not he means that even though she may have handled him in a way of which he disapproved nevertheless he feels she was essentially a sacrificing person.
3. Convey your understanding of his feelings of gratitude and love for his mother.
4. Induce the veteran to accept that he probably should consider his relations with his mother more fully.
5. Provoke the veteran to talk further about his mother and their relationship.

43

"Sometimes I think, 'Gosh, you can't go drifting around here always. You have to pick out a job and stick to it.' But you know that isn't so easy. It's been nearly three years I've been in the Army, and I don't know what I want to do now."

The counselor should reply in such a way as to try to:

1. Lead the veteran to feel that the counselor has faith in the veteran's ability to overcome the problem.
2. Lead the veteran to disclose what plans he has considered regarding the future.
3. Suggest to the veteran that his apparent inability to pick a job may possibly be because he doesn't want a job just yet.
4. Imply that the counselor understands the veteran to be saying that he feels torn between knowing what he ought to do and the handicaps he faces in doing it.
5. Indicate to the veteran the values which he might derive from vocational testing and information.

44

"When I'm feeling discouraged, I wonder if there will ever be anything that will appeal to me again. Maybe I've lived my life. Maybe that time over there was the best we will ever see, and from here on in it will just be pretty second-rate in comparison."

The counselor should reply in such a way as to try to:

1. Convey to the veteran that he, the counselor, sees that such an attitude, if continued, would be quite likely to make the whole thing come true and that the veteran might well divert his thinking to constructive issues.
2. Evoke from the veteran a more concise formulation of what is meant by "second-rate."
3. Indicate he understands the veteran's feelings of disillusionment.
4. Point out to the veteran the fact that in service where he had no adjustment problems he was happy but now when he is faced with problems of adjusting to a new life he is meeting with discouragement and unhappiness.
5. Get over to the veteran that his concern with the future is a natural by-product of his discouragement and is not something which is of real importance and about which he should worry or be concerned.

45

"I don't know whether I have any abilities that are good for anything. I've forgotten all I knew about the shoe industry, and I don't think I want to go back there anyway. And what else do I know? What I know about handling a machine gun won't be much use unless I go in with racketeers, and I certainly don't know any other lines of work."

The counselor should reply in such a way as to try to:

1. Get over to the veteran that the counselor appreciates that the veteran feels the work situation looks pretty hopeless.
2. Get over to the veteran that regardless of his lack of immediate work skills he must nevertheless be aware that he still has his capacity to learn.
3. Bring the veteran to consider the possibility of going back into the shoe industry until he gets his feet on the ground and decides where he wants to go.
4. Bring the veteran to discuss why he does not want to return to the shoe industry.
5. Bring the veteran to recognize the contradiction between his present low assessment of his abilities and the fact that he has demonstrated real ability in the past.

Part IV.   Accuracy of Perception of Client Attitudes

Instructions.   In this part of the test are ten consecutive statements made by a thirty-five-year-old man who has sought help because of inability to hold a job for any length of time. Each statement is followed by four possible counselor responses. You are to select that alternative which you feel most accurately reflects the client's attitude, the situation as it appears to the client; the alternative which if spoken to the client you feel would be most likely to evoke an immediate reply of, "That's right!"

In considering each alternative counselor response, read it as a tentative statement, a questioning statement which asks of the client, "Do I understand you correctly? Is this what you mean?"

46

"So I've come to see if *you* can help me to find work. (*Pause*) I suppose if I did get work, I'd just bungle things — something would go wrong — at least I'd probably be pounding the streets again in a few weeks."

1. You want work and yet you feel that if you do get it, something would go wrong anyway.
2. You feel that your lack of self-confidence makes you incapable of holding a job even if you could get one.
3. This inability to hold a job has been troubling you and you're turning to someone for help.
4. You feel that it's pretty futile to try again.

47

"Oh, well, I guess it's all — sort of — hopeless. The days go on, everybody's busy excepting me. (*Pause*) My wife says the papers are full of stories about there being a shortage in manpower. (*Pause*) Maybe that's what's wrong with me — (*bitter laugh*) a shortage of man power in myself."

1. You feel that you're not quite up to it, is that it?
2. You feel that you're not busy because of your own shortage, is that it?

3. That's what you feel, is it, that this hopelessness may be something within you.
4. In other words, you just feel pretty inadequate.

48

"I wonder if you know what it feels like to have a family depending on you, and never knowing from one week to the next where their food will come from? Have you ever spent Christmas in line at a firehouse waiting for a charity basket?"

1. It's the blows to your pride that make you feel bitter, is that it?
2. You're wondering if I can appreciate what a humiliating experience it can be.
3. You're wondering if I have ever been in such a spot.
4. It's a pretty desperate spot when you have to go to such length to provide.

49

"What do you think I ought to do — jump off a bridge, or look for another job to lose?"

1. There just doesn't seem to be any way out.
2. You've just given up, is that it?
3. You're feeling discouraged now, is that it?
4. You'd like to know if I can't suggest a possible solution.

50

"You know, last year I really thought I was going places. I worked at the Stoneworks for four months before I had a bad break; I stood up for — oh, well, you're probably not interested." (*Pause*)

1. You feel, do you, that to explain it to me would only bore me?
2. Things looked pretty hopeful for a while but then the bottom just dropped out, is that it?
3. You'd really like to tell me about this but you feel uncertain about going ahead, is that it?
4. I take it you felt pretty deeply disappointed.

51

"Well, it was just that I stood up for a non-union man who had been fired unfairly by a union foreman. And when I spoke up in union meeting I got booed down. Soon after that I was walking the streets again. (*Pause*) Oh, there may have been other reasons for my getting out, but that's the one that sticks in my mind."

1. In other words, while there may have been other factors involved, you feel fairly sure the most important thing was connected with your defense of this man.
2. In other words you feel there was a connection between your defense of this man and being let go.
3. You feel you were also treated unfairly and you just can't get it out of your craw.
4. That's the reason that sticks in your mind but you feel there may have been other reasons.

52

"Well, maybe it's just that I'm no good. I get good jobs — but after a while I get that old fear of losing my job."

1. You feel this fear of losing the job somehow operates to make you lose the job, is that it?
2. As I get it, this fear of losing out makes you wonder if it's not that you just don't have what it takes to be a success.
3. You get good jobs but you worry about losing them, is that it?
4. Just wondering if there isn't something that might be wrong.

53

(*Angrily*) "Did you ever have anything grab onto you so you couldn't shake it loose? Well, mister, I have! I've got a habit that if I don't cut it out, I'm going to ruin myself and my home — and everything!"

1. In other words, this thing is just driving you over the precipice unless you can bring it under control.
2. It's a habit you can't shake and will be ruinous.
3. This thing bothers you quite a bit.
4. In other words, you feel you just don't have enough will power to meet this thing.

54

"You see, it all started back when I was a kid. We had a club in high school — all fellas — and we used to go out and drink beer. We did that every week — even after we were out of school. (*Pause*) Well, beer got to be quite a habit with me. My folks were German and we always had it around the house, so they didn't care. Well, that was okay, but when I got married and found out I couldn't hold my jobs, than I began to drink more and more. Even my old cronies thought I was going to the dogs nights and told me to lay off. (*Pause*) If you could just get me to quit drinking, I'd be okay."

1. You began to lose jobs and then started drinking too much.
2. This drinking is something you want to conquer.
3. You feel that you used drink to drown your disappointment in yourself.
4. It may have started out innocently enough, but now it's become something that is a real problem to you.

55

"My wife says I can't be depended on — and I guess maybe she's right. She's a good woman — always is very saving, and doesn't ride me any more than I deserve, I guess, because I've been a poor bread-winner. But, my gosh, she's complained ever since we were married that I wasn't always honest with her." (*Pause*.)

1. And it makes you angry, is that it?
2. You feel your anger is because of the way she'd "ride" you, is that it?
3. She may have been justified in a lot of criticisms but in this she's gone just too far, is that it?
4. She criticized you a lot but probably no more than you deserved but her complaint about your honesty with her you feel you don't deserve, is that it?

Part V. Free Response to Attitudes [1]

Instructions. In this part of the test you are presented with twenty consecutive responses made by a twenty-one year old veteran who

[1] The test as given is a slight modification of a test developed by Douglas D. Blocksma for use in a short-term training program described in Blocksma, D. D., and Porter, E. H., Jr., "A Short-Term Training Program in Client-Centered Counseling," Journal of Consulting Psychology, v. XI, no. 2, 1947, pp. 55–60.

has presented himself to the counselor after being referred by an academic adviser. You are to write on a separate sheet the response which you feel you would most likely make or which would be most helpful to the client. Do not read ahead in making your reply but reply only on the basis of each response in turn just as you would expect to do in an interview.

56

"My name is Robert Doakes. My adviser said that you are a personal counselor, and before I can take a music aptitude test that I had to come and see you."

57

"He said that it's just because I've had no experience and was too nervous that he wouldn't recommend me for music courses. Now, what do you think about this?"

58

"Do you think that talking about it is going to do any good?"

59

"How much time can you give me?"

60

"Well, sir, here's the problem that I was mulling over in my mind all the time I was overseas. I'm interested in music theory and composition. I'm twenty-one years old. Now, do you think I'm too old to be great?"

61

"Well, I know that I'm too old to be a pianist."

62

"You see, I've never had any lessons on any instrument, and I don't know how to play. I'm just interested in music of all kinds. What I want to know is, do you think I'm too old to start?"

63

"Yes . . . You see, one thing you ought to know is that my father is a lawyer, and he wants me to be a lawyer, too. He thinks that music is a pansy profession. He says that music is fine for homosexuals."

64

"But I like music so darn much that I don't want anything to stand in my way of some sort of musical career."

65

"You know, a thought just occurred to me that maybe I want to be a big shot artist just to show my father how wrong he has been."

66

"Sure. You see, when I was in high school, when I should have been seriously studying and working, I was only interested in sports, and was a poor student in school. But since I've gotten out of the service, I feel more and more that I've got to get going, that I've got to begin to *get* somewhere. I can't go on forever, just living off the folks."

67

"Well, I know this for sure. I want to get started on something. I want to do real well in whatever I do. I want to make good. In my work, I don't want to just work for money, like most people do. I want above all to like the job I choose. I want to be completely absorbed and totally interested, in fact I want to love my work. Money alone won't satisfy me, although I want to make a comfortable living."

68

"And I might as well tell you this. I feel embarrassed discussing it, but for a long time I've been bothered with obsessions. I constantly try to keep clean. I feel the need to be perfect in everything that I do; even on little routine jobs, I worry for fear it isn't done exactly right. And that perfection spreads to so many things. I brood about trivialities. I lie awake worrying whether I've put things back in place. Or, I brood as to whether things will be changed at home when I go away."

69

"I so often wonder what caused me to be that way. Can you tell me?"

70

"Yeah — you see, I've thought a lot about this. But you understand that I'm not ready to blame my parents for all this. They've always been immaculate with themselves, and with the house and with me, and since childhood I've always had to be neat and clean. Once I went to see our physician to talk over my obsessions, and he told me that my parents were the cause of my trouble. Now that may be, but I can't say that for a fact."

71

"Well, sir, this discussion doesn't seem to be getting me anywhere."

72

"Well, I honestly believe that in spite of everything that I can handle this problem without further help."

73

"In fact, I actually seem to see things more clearly after talking with you. But it's just too embarrassing to tell you the whole story."

74

"Well, one of the reasons I really need help, you see, is that the police have threatened to lock me up if I molest the little girls any further, in our neighborhood."

75

"You know, I really don't feel worthy of taking up the time of a busy person like you."

This completes the pre-test. The directions for scoring your responses and the significance of the scores are given in Appendix A. It is recommended that the student not consult the scoring discussion until after taking the pre-test as it will undoubtedly change his set toward the test and make the results less meaningful for him as a learner.

Chapter **III**

SELF-EVALUATIVE ATTITUDES

AND PSYCHOLOGICAL CLIMATE

A great deal of current thinking is devoted to the notion that the attitudes which an individual holds toward himself, his self-evaluative attitudes, are merely by-products of deeper personality factors and that these self-evaluative attitudes hold significance only as indicators of the deeper personality factors. Much of what is to appear in this and in following chapters can be better understood in terms of a converse notion, namely that the deeper personality factors may in many cases be by-products of or constructs inferred from the operation of self-evaluative attitudes. From such a point of view the self-evaluative attitudes lose their significance as indicators or symptoms of something else and take a place as central determinants of behavior.

Self-evaluative attitudes are defined here as attitudes regarding the worth, competence, capability, guilt, adequacy or other such evaluation of one's self as a person. Such attitudes may be consciously held or denied to consciousness. Against the recognition of unconsciously held negative self-evaluations the individual may defend himself and he may strive for the enhancement of positive self-evaluations.

These self-evaluations do not come with the physiology of the newborn child: they seem quite clearly to be learned. Nor are these self-evaluative attitudes learned in a formal learning situation, by having a smiling teacher face a class of eager pupils to say, "Now today, children, we will have our beginning lesson in how to feel worthless. Please do not become confused and learn to feel guilty as that comes in the higher grades. Just stick with the lesson in worthlessness." No, self-evaluative attitudes are learned, but not in such a way. It seems much more likely that the learning is indirect and as a coincidental part of everyday situations. The term psychological climate is used here to designate that aspect of a situation with which an individual, child or adult, is faced and which holds implications for him as to his value as a person.

The remaining part of this chapter will be devoted to an illustration of a typical attitudinal learning situation and to exercises through which the student can come to develop a greater appreciation of the notion that the attitudes he holds toward others may play a highly significant part in how the others come to evaluate themselves. The illustration and first two exercises relate to childhood situations. The later exercises relate to interview situations with adults. The illustration follows.

A SAMPLE EXERCISE

Johnny and his Mother

1. *Mother:* "Johnny, go to the bathroom. You're squirming around like a Whirling Dervish."
2. *Johnny:* "No."
3. *Mother:* "Go on! You have to go, don't you?"
4. *Johnny:* "No."
5. *Mother:* "Well, go anyway."
6. *Johnny:* "I don't want to!"
7. *Mother:* "Now go on before you have an accident."
8. *Johnny:* "I'll get a hatchet and chop you all up!"
9. *Mother:* "Why, Johnny! That's a terrible thing to say. You wouldn't really want to hurt me, would you?"
10. *Johnny:* "Yes."
11. *Mother:* "Now this is silly. You just march yourself on into the bathroom this instant."

Here we have an apparently very simple training situation. Its simplicity is, however, much more apparent than real. Let us analyze the situation for the psychological climate each participant sets for the other and the self-evaluative attitudes which might be learned by each.

The mother starts things off (1) with the implication to Johnny that he is not capable of taking responsibility for his own bladder tensions, that the responsibility for initiating action with regard to his own needs lies outside of himself. From such a psychological climate Johnny may be receiving lessons in such attitudes as "I am incapable of accepting responsibility," "I am irresponsible," "What others tell me to do is the right thing to do."

Johnny resists (2). While it is more conjectural to propose what climate this creates for the mother it is possible to say at least that it is denying and rejecting. Such a climate may bear the implication for the mother, "I am a failure," "I am inadequate as a mother."

The mother continues to set the same essential climate for Johnny in her reply (3). She has also added a new element by her disregarding and denial of Johnny's attitude. The implications still remain that Johnny is incapable of being responsible for himself and not responsible for initiating his own actions. Further, there is the implication that Johnny's wishes don't count. Such a climate may constitute a further lesson for Johnny that "I am incapable and irresponsible" and may also constitute a lesson in the attitude "I am unworthy; my ideas and wishes don't count."

Johnny's further resistance (4) would seem to set again a denying, rejecting climate which would hold the same implications of inferiority and inadequacy for the mother.

The mother's next response (5) seems to emphasize the attitudes already discussed. The climate which her attitudes create would appear to involve more heavily at this point the implication for Johnny of "I am worthless; my wishes just don't count at all." It is also possible that Johnny may be learning "To try to be yourself is futile."

At this point (6) Johnny makes a more clear-cut expression of his feelings. Quite aside from the motives which may be prompting his not wanting to comply, the expression of his "not wanting to" is clear. It seems reasonable that the denying, rejecting attitude may hold a further lesson of inadequacy and incompetency for the mother. It might be true that this situation holds for the mother an implication of her unreasonableness and authoritativeness. Such an implication might tend toward the establishment of the feelings, "I'm too bossy" and "Sometimes I'm just unreasonable."

The mother's exasperated order (7) seems to reinforce the previous implications for Johnny with a possible greater emphasis upon lack of responsibility for self and upon his lack of worth as a person with rights to his own desires and wishes.

Johnny's retort (8) is a clear-cut expression of hostility. In addition to the denial and rejection of the mother which is involved, his reply constitutes an implication to his mother that she has gone too far, that she is wrong in such utter disregard of him. From this it might be that the mother receives a lesson in the attitude toward herself of "I am guilty."

The mother's moralizing and cajoling response (9) sets up two clear-cut lessons for Johnny. First is that he is guilty for expressing his hostility and second is that he is guilty for possessing feelings of hostility. It seems quite probable that even though no one told him directly that he was guilty and bad for possessing and expressing hostility the lesson is clearly there for him to learn to feel, "I am guilty when I feel angry and I'm guilty if I express anger."

Johnny's terse affirmation (10) of his attitudes only serves to reaffirm the implications of inadequacy, incompetency and guilt of the mother.

The mother's closing statement (11) would appear to be a crowning re-emphasis and reinforcement of all the attitudinal lessons she has unwittingly set for Johnny to learn. One can easily imagine in fifteen or twenty years from now Johnny's working through his attitudes of worthlessness, irresponsibility, guilt, inadequacy and incompetency. These attitudes may be faced as he speaks of his mother or it may be that they will be faced as he speaks of his boss or of his instructors. Such attitudes as these, attitudes toward himself, are not likely to be left at home with mother. It is also likely that he will have a whole series of defenses, ways of perceiving events, which will enable him to sufficiently twist the external reality so as to avoid his having to face his own feelings toward his own self. One can just hear him saying, "I used to have a wild temper but I don't any more. I've grown up."

And one can see him sending out barbed and caustic comments to a weaker opponent — but in a laughing manner and all as a joke. One can hear him saying "That's pretty simple stuff to do," but neatly avoiding any contact with the task which might face him with a proof of his fancied inferiority.

By self-evaluative attitudes are meant such feelings about self as Johnny might have learned. By psychological climate is meant such actions and attitudes as the mother displayed and which held for Johnny implications as to his value as a person.

At this point the issue becomes more complicated. There can be no doubt as to the validity of a psychological climate as it has been defined here. The actions and attitudes of others do hold implications for another as to his value as a person. Very often these implications are conflicting in their positive and negative tones. They may be very subtle and hard to recognize but they are there for us to seek out.

It is not so certain, however, that just because various lessons by implication are inherent in a situation they will be learned by the person toward whom they are directed. Several factors are apparently involved. One factor is the body of lessons which a person has already learned, how he already feels about himself. We are all familiar with the person who feels himself inferior no matter how much we try to reassure him and try to point out his strengths. We are also familiar with the person who seems to go right on feeling confident despite experiences which would seem nearly catastrophic failures to most of us.

A second factor involved would seem to be the matter of the material on which an individual's attention is focused. In the example given, Johnny is rather obviously attending to the issue of whether or not he should go to the bathroom. In such a case the attitudes of the mother form the ground of the figure-ground relationship and are not responded to in a clear, conscious manner. However, it may be that the matter of becoming enmeshed in the attitudinal lessons is less likely to occur when the individual perceives the attitudes directed his way in a more clear-cut manner. This is certainly true in psychotherapy where at times the counselor will be attacked directly or indirectly. Were he to become involved in the rightness or wrongness of the issue he would be lost. His job of responding to the fact that the client feels strongly this way or that may be his salvation.

A third factor is what is termed here a "proving experience." By a proving experience is meant an experience which tends to confirm the implications set in the psychological atmosphere. To illustrate the concept we might think of a five-year-old boy who says to his mother, "I'll help you clear the table, Mother. I'll carry out the dishes." Should the mother doubt his adequacy and competency and express her feelings, we might expect her to reply, "No! Well, OK. But do be careful and don't drop them." If at this point Johnny stumbles on that skate he left by the stove and the dishes do fall and break, it is much harder to deny that his mother wasn't right in her feelings. Such an experience tends to prove the implications of her attitudes as to his inadequacy and incompetency.

In Exercise I which follows another relatively simple situation is presented. Again the setting will be a childhood situation. This time it involves a Mr. W who has been observing children at play in a community play yard. He has noticed that the children apparently delight in climbing on objects about a foot off the ground and then jumping off. Mr. W decides to make a "jumping-board," a plank a foot wide and three feet long with a supporting block at one end about a foot high, so that the children can run up the plank and jump off. The scene described in this exercise takes place in front of Mr. W's home near the play yard as he begins to make the "jumping-board." Four children are standing off at a distance of six to ten feet watching silently as Mr. W begins to saw off the plank. Gradually the children close in to a "no working" distance. No explanation was offered by Mr. W as to what was being prepared. The conversation started as given below.

Read through the exercise once bearing in mind that you are looking for the psychological climate which Mr. W sets for the children and the children for Mr. W. Bear in mind, too, that you will wish to make inferences as to the self-evaluative attitudinal lessons they are setting for each other to learn. When you have finished your reading go back and make a careful analysis, much as was presented for "Johnny and his Mother," jotting down your reactions on a sheet of paper. You may be interested in comparing your analysis to the analyses made by members of a class in counseling who were presented this exercise. Their responses follow the exercise.

EXERCISE 1

Mr. W and the Jumping-Board

1. *Mr. W:* "Where do you think we ought to saw it? About here?"
2. *Children:* "Yeah. About there."
3. *Mr. W:* "Am I sawing it straight?"
4. *Children:* "Yeah, you're going straight."
5. *Mr. W:* (*Continues sawing, and then*) "Am I going straight?"
6. *Children:* "Yeah, you're going straight."
7. *Mr. W:* (*After more sawing*) "Am I still going straight?"
8. *John:* "No, you're going crooked now."
9. *Mr. W:* "Okay, which way shall we go now? This way?"
10. *Children:* "Yeah, that way."

(The sawing was completed and the nailing started.)

11. *Mr. W:* "Now, let's see. Where should we put this first nail? About here?"
12. *Jim:* "No, put it here!" (*Indicates spot about half an inch away.*)
13. *Mr. W:* "Here?" (*Puts nail on indicated spot.*)
14. *Children:* "Yeah, that's right."

(Nailing continues in the same manner until completed. Children then play by running up and jumping off the board. This continues for several minutes.)

15. *Mr. W:* "I wonder if this hadn't better be washed off, if we are going to paint it this afternoon? Will you kids be here?"
16. *Children:* "Sure, we'll be here."
17. *Mr. W.:* (*Picking up one end of the board*) "Who wants to help carry it over to the hose so we can wash it?"
18. *Chuck:* "I do." He picks up the other end of the board.
19. *Children:* (*In chorus*) "We want to help, too."
20. *Mr. W:* "Okay, you help on the sides."

(The procession goes its way to the hose. Under some direct instruction the children all have a turn at washing the board. Immediately thereafter the children are again playing on the board with the result that the board was rapidly getting dirtier than before.)

21. *Mr. W:* "Gosh, it looks like the board got dirty again. We can't paint it when it is dirty like that."

22. *Ellen:* "We'd better wash it off again."
   (The group then proceeds to rewash the board with the hose.)
23. *Mr. W:* "Now I wonder how we can keep it clean until this afternoon so we can paint it?"
24. *Ellen:* "Don't anyone put his feet on it again. You'll get it dirty again."

Here are the responses to this exercise made by members of a class in counseling procedures as the responses were reconstructed from notes taken during the discussion period. The responses are presented in the order made.

A. "This is a situation in which Mr. W deals with some kids by leaving responsibility with the kids, but with some structuring."
B. "Yeah, he structured for sure. A question can lead or direct. Note the 'Yes' responses at the outset."
C. "By including the kids he got the children to participate and to accept responsibility."
D. "He certainly recognized the integrity of the children as persons."
E. *(Instructor)* "What do you think the children might learn to feel about themselves in this situation?"
F. "That they can decide things for themselves: that they are capable of making decisions."
G. "Well, they could be learning that children can be helpful. Most of the time it seems to me that they learn how unhelpful they are."
H. "They are learning confidence in themselves."
I. "It seems to me they could be learning that real acceptance of responsibility involves self-denial. They could be learning such a real acceptance of responsibility."
J. "They're learning that at least one adult considers them worthwhile. They could be learning to feel worthwhile; a feeling of worthiness."
K. "Sure. Self-respect."
L. "How about this? Couldn't they be learning that adults are trustworthy?"
M. *(Instructor)* "How about Mr. W? What might he be learning?"
N. "Oh brother! I can just see him. He must have gotten a lot of self-satisfaction with what he was able to do."
O. "Yeah, I can just see him saying to himself, 'It works: anarchy doesn't necessarily follow!' "
P. "He could be learning that a rejection of a paternalistic role leads to satisfaction."

Q. "He's certainly developing a better understanding of personal integrity in others."

If we go back and view the responses made to the exercise by the counseling class members, we will see quite readily that they did not approach the material in the same manner as was exemplified in the analysis of the "Johnny and his Mother" example. In that analysis each response was inspected for the psychological climate it created and the potential self-evaluative attitudinal lesson it set to be learned. The class members did not bring themselves to such a close inspection. It may pay to consider more closely what they did do since they fell into a thinking trap which the reader may wish to avoid in working out these exercises.

Notice particularly the first four responses: A, B, C and D. In each case the respondent describes an activity in which Mr. W engaged or an outcome of his activity. No reference appears to the attitudes upon which Mr. W acted nor to the lessons which these attitudes set for self-evaluative learning on the part of the children. One would not want to deny the correctness of these first responses the class members made but one could say that they missed the point.

For the most part responses F through K represent fairly reasonable inferences of the possible self-evaluative lessons the children may have learned. Others could be added. Notice, however, that there is still no reference to Mr. W's attitudes, to the psychological climate.

Response L is particularly interesting because it draws attention to the possibility of the development of generalized evaluative attitudes toward others as well as toward self.

Notice further that following the instructor's query about Mr. W's possible learnings, Response M, only the first response following, Response N, even remotely relates to Mr. W's possible feelings about himself as a person. No direct references are made to the possible lessons in worthiness, adequacy and competence. Responses O, P and Q are clearly descriptive statements as to what Mr. W may have learned about his actions, or as to how Mr. W may have perceived the results of his actions.

In the following exercise, Exercise 2, try to stay as closely as possible to an analysis of the psychological climates provided and to the implications for the participants as to how they should feel about themselves.

EXERCISE 2

Jim Gets A Lickin'

Jim's parents are sitting in the living room of their small house enjoying a chat with one of the father's business friends. Outside one can hear the voices of several children at play. As happens frequently, the sound of crying becomes audible.

1. (*Jim, a 5 year old, bursts in the front door, quickly looks from one adult to the next with a half-smile on his face. With one hand still on the open door, Jim speaks.*) "She pushed me first!"

2. (*The visitor rises, looks out the front window and sees a little girl sprawled and sobbing on the grass beside an overturned tricycle.*) "Well, you shouldn't have had much trouble pushing that kid around, she's only about half your size."

3. (*The mother rises and strides to the window.*) "What did you do, hit a little girl?" (*She looks out and sees the child, then turns toward Jim and scowls.*)

4. *Jim:* "No, no, Mother. She pushed me first!"

5. *Mother:* "I've told you a thousand times, Jim, not to hit little kids — kids smaller than you are. We just don't do it."

6. *Jim:* "No, no, no, no, no, no. She pushed me first."

7. *Mother:* "That's not the point, Jim. She's smaller than you are. You'll have to go to your room for ten minutes."

8. *Jim:* "No, no, no, no, no. Please don't, Mother."

9. *Father:* "You know what the rule is, Jim, you know what happens when you do things like this. What happened?"

10. *Jim:* "She pushed me, then I pushed her."

11. *Mother:* "And knocked her off her tricycle. She's smaller than you are, too. Into your room, now."

12. *Jim:* "No, Mother, Mother, Mother. I don't want to. I don't have to."

13. *Father:* "I'll count to three." (*An invariable rule used by parents. When violated, a moderate spanking always follows.*)

14. *Jim:* "No, seven."

15. *Father:* "All right, seven then. One — two — three —"

16. *Jim:* "No, no, no, no, no."

17. *Father:* " — four — five — six —"

18. *Jim:* "No, no, no. I'll hit you." (*Runs to bedroom door but does not enter.*)
19. *Father:* "Seeeeeeevvvvvvvv — better hurry!"
20. *Jim:* (*Near tears.*) "No, no, no, no, no. I don't have to."
21. *Father:* " — ven!" (*Picks Jim up, carries him to bedroom, and administers spanking.*)

The following material is a suggested analysis of this situation with which the reader may wish to compare his own efforts. As there are four people involved in the situation the problem of analysis is increasingly complex and, in spots, obscure. It does seem possible, however, that at least the inferences given below are reasonable.

1. Jim's behavior strongly suggests that he feels both guilty and justified and that he anticipates being punished or at least meeting disapproval. Such attitudes may well imply to the parents that they have failed in their efforts to keep Jim in line.

2. The visitor's caustic comment directed at Jim certainly implies that Jim is guilty of the act, guilty of being a bully, worthless. Such attitudes directed toward their son might well imply to the parents that they are failures — incompetent and inadequate.

3. The mother's behavior confirms the attitude of the visitor toward Jim, and may constitute a further lesson in guilt and worthlessness.

4. Jim's rejection and denial imply that the visitor and the mother are wrong and unfair: that they are incompetent and guilty.

5. In this response the mother reaffirms her attitudes toward Jim, especially by the moralizing attitude of "It is bad to do what you did. We don't do those bad things." The lesson in guilt is evident. The lesson in incompetence is also there, that is, "You can't do it yourself, I have to teach you and take responsibility for you."

6. Jim again denies the mother and reaffirms his attitude of her incompetence and guilty inconsiderateness.

7. The mother reaffirms her attitudes and puts a crowning denial on Jim's efforts by passing sentence. The implications of guilt and worthlessness are only exaggerated.

8. Jim again denies the mother, thus implying her guilt of one-sidedness, and enters a plea for mercy. Such a plea sets up a con-

tradictory implication of the mother as an understanding person. It seems likely that many of life's situations are comparably contradictory in their implications for people.

9. Another contradictory implication appears to exist in the behavior of the father toward Jim. First the father implies that Jim is somewhat worthless in not accepting the punishment for guilt and next the father implies that Jim is of worth and has a right to be heard.

10. Jim's reaction is not at all clear in its implications for the father. We might interpret Jim's response as a straightforward presentation of the situation to the father in a trusting manner. This would hold implication for the father as a trustworthy, just person. Or we might interpret Jim's response as a defensive (in this case a justification or rationalization) response to the father, in which event it would imply the father is unjust and untrustworthy.

11. The mother's instant insistence on her viewpoint, a rejection of Jim's rights as an equal person, might well imply to Jim that he is inferior, that he is unworthy of justice, as well as implying that the previous implications from the mother are truer than ever.

12. Jim's next reply, ending in an overt resistance constitutes a rather complete denial of the mother as a worthwhile person and as a capable person.

13-21. The father's invocation of the punishment routine is not too clear cut in its implications for Jim. The reaffirmation of the negative implications seems primary, yet there is some implication that Jim has some worth. Jim's responses seem also somewhat mixed in their implications. When he asks for a "seven-count" in place of the "three-count" it is possible that the implications for the father are of worth and compassion. Jim's continued and persistent resistance, however, would seem to be essentially negative in its implications for the father.

The exercises which have been presented were chosen deliberately to serve certain purposes. The first purpose was the demonstration of the concepts of psychological climate and of self-evaluative attitudes. The second purpose was to provide a context for the demonstration of the two concepts which could be easily "broken through," that is, a context in which the content (the words spoken) could be easily put aside to permit the observation of the climate and attitude possibilities. In the exercises to follow, the material is taken from treatment contacts with adults and the job of putting aside the content will be much more difficult. The student will have to be on guard, if he wishes to observe solely the psychological climate and its implications for self-evaluative attitudes.

The next exercise, Exercise 3, is taken from the opening of a phonographically recorded interview with a student enrolled in a remedial study course.

EXERCISE 3

Linda and Dr. A.

1. *Dr. A.:* "I was looking over your data sheet and information and all — (*Linda:* I know.) — and I see you are from Chicago."
2. *Linda:* "Mm hm."
3. *Dr. A.:* "Did you attend Roosevelt High?"
4. *Linda:* "Yes, I did, mm hm."

(*They talk for a moment or two about Linda's name and middle initial.*)

5. *Dr. A.:* "The — I noticed that you checked your new enrollment (*enrollment for the remedial course*) because you didn't know how to study well enough — ah — and then I checked on the 'problem-sheet' lists and I saw that you went rather heavy on — you worried about low grades and poor memory and so on. How well did you do in high school?"
6. *Linda:* "Well, I was just an average student."

(*Dr. A. continues to ask questions relating to her academic record for a few responses to which Linda supplies answers.*)

7. *Dr. A.:* "Well, now as you see it, what are, so far that you've been in college, what do you see your problems to be?"
8. *Linda:* "I haven't had any trouble at all only with my history but I believe I'm getting it better than I did but I just can't seem to concentrate. I don't know whether there's so much to it or what, but I just can't seem to pull it all together."

(*Dr. A. continues to call for academic facts for several more responses.*)

9. *Dr. A.:* "Well now — ah — again, I mean if you can't make a diagnosis of yourself but still you can't remember [what you study] — ah — well, what I mean, how do you see some of the problems to be? Are you, do you have any trouble studying at home?"

The student may find it difficult to analyze this excerpt, especially since the interchange does not appear to have the emotionally charged elements which were encountered in the earlier exercises and example. Nevertheless, basic attitudes are being implemented and expressed here just as surely as in the earlier material. The student will be left to deal with the possible significance of at least the following factors which may be observed.

1. Dr. A. clearly has accepted responsibility for the initiation and continued conduct of the interview period.

2. Dr. A. fails to respond to Linda's expression of improvement or to her expression of confusion.

3. Dr. A. rather directly states that Linda can't solve her own problem without outside help.

4. Linda readily supplied answers to Dr. A.'s questions.

Here are some leads to what may be involved. In connection with (1) above, remember that Johnny's mother took over the responsibility for telling Johnny when to respond to bladder tensions. In connection with (2) above, remember that Mr. W paid a great deal of attention to how the children felt about the jumpboard. In connection with (3) above, remember that Jim's mother also felt that Jim had to be taught about himself. And in connection with (4) above, remember that Jim did not comply as did Linda, he reacted in an opposite manner.

The next exercise is based upon an excerpt from a fourth psychoanalytically-oriented therapy session with a young man who was hospitalized for schizophrenia. The patient had just expressed feelings of guilt with respect to having gone into the cafeteria. The analyst, in reply, had just finished an explanation to the effect that it could not have been only the going into the cafeteria to eat, "but you felt guilty because of something else." The client reiterates his feelings and further mentions that he has given up going to the candy counter later in the day as being foolish.

EXERCISE 4

Jake and the Analyst

1. *Analyst:* "What was foolish about going up to the candy counter and eating some candy?"

2. *Jake:* "Well, it wasn't foolish, I thought if I didn't eat any second

course, I'd go up there, that's all. I had the plan mapped out. I'm glad I didn't take it. I don't know — I suppose I ought — I got that idea there."

3. *Analyst:* "And that leads us to believe that there is some reason why you feel guilty about eating candy, too. What does eating candy make you think of?"

4. *Jake:* "Home, right away now. That's what it means."

5. *Analyst:* "And what does home make you think of?"

6. *Jake:* "My mother."

7. *Analyst:* "And what does your mother make you think of?"

8. *Jake:* "Oh, children, babies. Those ideas are put in my head. I don't know, I've got those thoughts again in my head. That's what is put up there to me."

9. *Analyst:* "Yes, and as you think of babies, what comes to your mind?"

10. *Jake:* "Girls, I guess. B—— R—— " (*Girl's name.*)

11. *Analyst:* "B—— R—— " (*Repeats name.*)

12. *Jake:* "Yes." (*Very long pause.*)

13. *Analyst:* "You see, you have guilt about B—— R—— . You undoubtedly have sex feelings about her and something within yourself has been trying to convince you that is wrong. That same part of your personality is making you feel guilty about eating candy. You see, it connects right up with the thoughts that come, that somehow you — one part of you is trying to make you believe that all of that is wrong. Well, we know it isn't."

For many students it may again be difficult to avoid entanglement with the content of the excerpt. It would be quite easy to quarrel with, for example, the reasonableness of the analyst's interpretations, with the suitability of the introduction of interpretations in the fourth interview, or with other aspects of his procedures. To the writer it appears significant for the psychological climate involved that: (1) the analyst is clearly leading the interview; (2) the analyst clearly provides the meanings of the patient's thoughts during his free association; (3) the analyst clearly is not concerned with the significance which the patient might attach to his ideas, but is concerned with the significance which the patient ought to attach to his ideas. To the student is left the possible implications of these events for the client's attitudes toward himself.

In the closing exercise an excerpt is taken from a college counseling case in which a student has been referred to the counselor by a dean.

EXERCISE 5

Frank and the Counselor

1. *Counselor:* "I don't believe I know much about why you are here. The Dean mentioned you sometime ago, but I know very little about it."

2. *Frank:* "Well, the Dean and Professor R. wanted me to see you. They said you were a good psychologist, and that if you studied me you might be able to diagnose my adjustment. They think I'm not getting along very well, and if you diagnosed what was the matter, you would be able to help me."

3. *Counselor:* "They think you need some help, and you're trying to do what they wish?"

4. *Frank:* "Well, they say I'm not doing as well as I should, and if you studied me, you could say why."

5. *Counselor:* "Well, now I'll tell you, Frank, I really haven't had much luck helping students with problems that the Deans think they have. I don't know whether I can be of help to you along that line or not. When a student is concerned about some problem that *he* thinks he has, then frequently we can work out something together, but otherwise, I don't believe I get very far. I wonder, quite aside from what the Dean thinks about you, whether you feel there is anything about your situation that is causing you concern?"

6. *Frank:* "Well, I don't know — I suppose I don't live up to my ability."

7. *Counselor:* "That is something you feel a little concerned about?"

8. *Frank:* "Yes. I don't know, I guess I procrastinate; I just don't get things done on time. I don't see why. I've thought about that a lot and tried to analyze it but I don't seem to have helped it."

9. *Counselor:* "So you feel you really do procrastinate, and that you've been unable to do anything about it."

These factors are observable which may be important for the psychological climate in which Frank is to work. (1) The counselor conducts himself in such a way as to leave with Frank the responsibility for what he wishes to do about dealing with his own situation. (2) The counselor leaves it to Frank to deal with his situation in the way he sees fit. (3) The counselor tries to understand Frank's situation as Frank sees it.

Chapter IV

RESPONDING TO THE INTERNAL

FRAME OF REFERENCE

In the previous chapter an effort was made to help the student become more sensitive to what events might mean to the individual who is the target of those events. It constituted a first step toward trying to get inside the client's skin, to appreciate what he may think and feel. In this chapter we shall try to go a step farther in this direction; we shall also try to develop elements of skill in responding to the client's internal frame of reference.

There are important reasons why we must become adept at distinguishing between an internal frame of reference (how the *client* sees himself, how *he* feels about the situation) and an external frame of reference (how the *counselor* sees the client, how the *counselor* feels about the client's situation).

Foremost among the reasons for distinguishing between these two reference frames is that psychotherapy is a process which occurs within the client — not the counselor. We are forced to deal with the reality the client holds no matter how much insight as counselors we may have into the errors of perception the client makes. It is the meanings which the client has come to learn from the experiences his life has held for him that constitute the reality to which he responds. It is toward a re-evaluation of these meanings which is more complete, more nearly correct, and less denying that therapy attempts to help the client.

Clinical observation has led us to the conviction that an individual by himself does not often get far in an attempt to re-evaluate his experiences, that he is too prone to get caught up in his own biases with little or no re-evaluation forthcoming. But clinical experiences with helping the person past such blocking points have not led us to consistent convictions. One line of observation has led to the hypothesis that the individual must be led or taught in some way to see his own biases, to see how he defends himself from dealing with meanings whose existence he has denied. Another line of observation has led to the hypothesis that the individual can come to see through his defenses when his perceptions (which function as defenses) are accepted by the counselor as the individual's best explanation of events as he looks at things *now*, and when these perceptions are not challenged by the counselor through different ways of looking at the events such as might occur should the counselor choose to interpret, probe, moralize or support.

A second reason why it is important for us to be able to distinguish between the internal and external reference frames arises out of the fact that the two hypotheses discussed in the preceding paragraph do exist and their implications for counselor conduct are markedly different. To the extent that the hypothesis of the essential impotence of the client in the face of his defenses is valid the emphasis upon an external reference frame, upon *not* accepting at face value the client's view, upon "seeing through" the client becomes of importance. To the extent that the hypothesis of the essential ability of the client to reduce his own defenses and to achieve new and more complete meanings is valid the emphasis upon an internal reference frame, what the client sees the situation to be, becomes of importance.

To illustrate the sense in which the terms internal and external frames of reference are used here Figure 1 is presented on the opposite page. To read this diagram start at the top center and read, "As the client talks to Counselor I (or Counselor II) he talks of: XYZ and/or $\Phi\Sigma\beta$ and/or $\Delta 0+$, and the client also demonstrates or reveals much of his personality by the way he acts in the interview." Then follow the arrows for each of the Counselors. The essential distinction is evident in Counselor I's responses based upon what *Counselor I* sees as significant in the client's situation

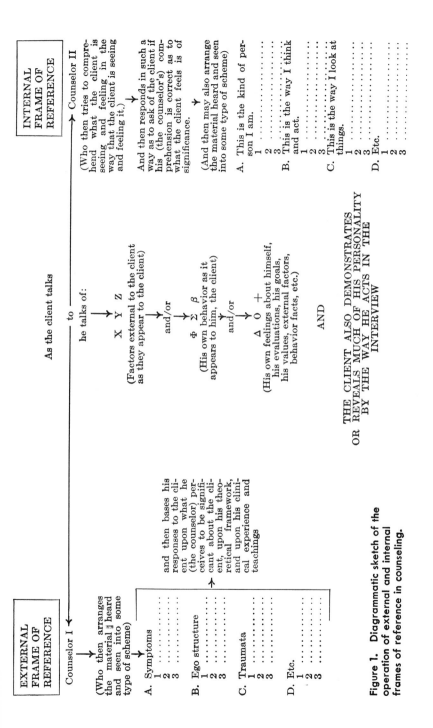

Figure 1. Diagrammatic sketch of the operation of external and internal frames of reference in counseling.

and in Counselor II's responses based upon what Counselor II is able to comprehend as to what the *client* sees as significant in his situation.

It should be closely noted that both Counselor I and Counselor II attend to the client's perceptions and behavior. This fact often leads to confusion in trying to understand the difference between the terms internal and external frames of reference. Counselor I obviously takes into account the $\Delta O+$ perceptions, the internal feelings of the client. He also recognizes that XYZ and $\Phi\Sigma\beta$ are in final analysis only the client's perceptions of external events and are therefore internal to the client. But Counselor I uses his comprehensions differently: he comprehends the client's perceptions and behavior in terms of the significance which he, the counselor, can attach to them. Thus Counselor I, by responding to what he feels is of significance in the client's situation, is responding to something external to the client even though his, the counselor's, perceptions are based upon the client's perceptions. Counselor II strives to eliminate his own judgments of significance and to comprehend the perceptions and behavior of the client solely as it appears to the client, except for entirely secondary purposes such as later research or later diagnosis and may be said to be responding to the internal frame of reference.

In Exercise 6 below are a series of statements from a case record of a first interview. Following the client statements are a number of different "thoughts" a counselor might have in reaction. Some of these thoughts represent thinking based upon an external frame of reference: some upon an internal frame of reference. You are to identify upon which frame of reference each thought is based by noting the appropriate abbreviation on a separate sheet of paper. Upon completing the exercise, the reader may wish to compare his answers with those suggested for this exercise at the end of the chapter.

EXERCISE 6

Identifying the Base Frame of Reference

S. is introduced to counselor and they go together to the interviewing room. S. is an attractive, well-dressed girl, whose smiling appearance and friendly manner give no indication of emotional disturbance.

Throughout the interview she smiles frequently, even when speaking of matters about which she is disturbed.

1–C. Will it trouble you if I take some notes while we talk? It's helpful to me in going back over what we've said.

1–S. No, I don't mind at all.

2–C. Perhaps you'd just like to go ahead and tell me what's troubling you.

2–S. Well, it's hard to say just what it is. It's just that I've never been happy. My parents have been wonderful to me, they've given me everything, but it just doesn't do any good. I feel that I'll never be happy until I have some affection, someone to love me and care for me.

2–C. IN EX 1. This is a case of all care and no affection.

IN EX 2. It appears to her that her folks have given her most everything but affection.

IN EX 3. She's speaking nicely of her parents now but the hostility will be more overt later.

IN EX 4. I wonder what the real reason is for denying her parents this way.

3–S. Mother's very nervous. She's the kind that wants to do everything for her children. She tries to choose our friends and everything we do. Even girl friends — at first she likes them and then she begins to talk about them. I had one friend — she was really a fine girl — we talked about music and art and things like that, but mother didn't like her.

3–C. IN EX 1. It sounds more like the mother needs help.

IN EX 2. I notice that she defends her mother a bit. She may be afraid to express hostility openly.

IN EX 3. She seems to feel the mother tries to do too much for her.

IN EX 4. I wonder how the girl reacts to such treatment.

4–S. I was so furious once that I just wanted to have it all over. I took a lot of pills just to end it. And another time I ran away from home. I like it up here at College, but I just am not really happy, I don't seem to be happy doing the things the others do, I don't have the same interests. They go out and rave about their dates and I have dates too, but I don't see what's so wonderful.

4–C. IN EX 1. Oh, oh! Suicidal tendencies. Perhaps she had better be referred to a psychiatrist.

IN EX 2. She seems to turn her hostilities inward upon herself.

IN EX   3. She resented her mother's treatment completely but doesn't seem to be getting any satisfaction even now.

IN EX   4. She seems to deny almost any source of possible satisfaction.

5–S.   I feel very disgusted, very unhappy up here. But when I'm at home mother worries about me and tries to do everything for me and she won't go out and do anything for herself, but when I'm away she does.

5–C. IN EX   1. She feels it's better for the mother when she's away but that she, herself, can't feel happy either place.

IN EX   2. She must be pretty dependent on the mother to tie her up at home like that.

IN EX   3. She is trying to talk herself right back into going home.

IN EX   4. This sounds like a projected dependency.

6–S.   I've kept at her to join the Red Cross or go out and play cards and do things the other women do, but she won't.

6–C. IN EX   1. Who is overprotecting whom?

IN EX   2. She feels the mother needs something like that.

IN EX   3. Now here is the other side of her feelings toward her mother.

IN EX   4. The mother is apparently a source of frustration in more ways than one.

7–S.   My older sister wanted me to go away from home. She did everything to help me get here to college.

7–C. IN EX   1. It sounds as though the sister wants to help her.

IN EX   2. She seems to think well of her sister.

IN EX   3. She seems to think her sister felt she should leave home.

IN EX   4. I wonder what the sister's motivation was.

8–S.   Yes, it was the one thing I wanted, but now I still don't feel happy. I feel so useless. I'm interested in art and literature and all that but I can't do anything special. I hear the others talking, some of them play the piano and do things, but I just have nothing.

8–C. IN EX   1. She apparently had hoped college would do something for her — but it hasn't.

IN EX   2. I wonder just how she reacts in these situations that produce the feelings of uselessness.

IN EX   3. Now, what is the significance of the shift of topic from sister to uselessness?

IN EX   4. She apparently feels pretty much out of touch.

9-S. My sister is a beautiful artist — she's married and very happy. Her husband has a good job. They seem to be getting along fine. (*Long pause.*)

9-C. IN EX 1. This seems to be a painful and significant area for her.

    IN EX 2. She seems to feel jealous of her sister.

    IN EX 3. I just don't understand what she feels at all.

    IN EX 4. There must be something significant here.

10-S. Well, I graduated in February, and I was very unhappy at home. When I'd be going out my mother would always tell me my hair didn't look right, always looked mussy. I've always felt badly about anything people say about me. Once she threw out something of mine and I was so furious, I just took those pills . . . Then the time I ran away was when she didn't like my friends.

10-C. IN EX 1. She hates her mother pretty deeply.

    IN EX 2. She feels she is criticized unfairly: a bit paranoid.

    IN EX 3. She feels angry even with the little things.

    IN EX 4. She feels herself to be a very sensitive person.

11-S. I went to New York, but she came after me. I told her I wanted to stay on and be on my own, but well, I don't know, she just talked to me and cried and cried and some way got me to come home.

11-C. IN EX 1. She is a deeply dependent person.

    IN EX 2. She feels incapable of expressing hostility openly.

    IN EX 3. She doesn't know why she returned but she feels it to have been against her will.

    IN EX 4. She feels a deep affection for her mother that is covered up here.

So much for our attempts to discriminate between the internal and external frames of reference per se. Let us now proceed to consider more directly the matter of responding to the internal frame of reference alone.

It must be recognized at the outset that responding to the internal frame of reference in the sense of trying to understand how the client sees and feels is, by its very nature, a tentative process. Much of the time the client himself is mixed and uncertain as to just what he does feel. It is impossible to be always certain that our perception of the client's perception is correct. To the beginner it may often seem that he is reduced to the wildest guessing.

There are, however, certain criteria from which the counselor may infer that he has achieved reasonable accuracy. Clinical experience has strongly suggested that when an individual expresses an attitude and that attitude is rephrased in fresh words with no change in its essential meaning to the client (when the understanding of the client is communicated to the client) the client will typically respond in one or more of the following ways: he will confirm the counselor's response, expand upon or further explore the attitude, achieve a recognition of previously denied meanings or feelings, move on to explore a new attitudinal area. Clinical experience has further suggested that when the counselor has understood faultily and communicates a faulty understanding the client will typically respond in one or more of the following ways: he will correct the counselor with a re-explanation, reply with a "Yes, but —" answer, pause, change the subject abruptly, attack the counselor openly, simply continue with the expression of the same attitude from a new angle, resort to an analysis of the interview process and the counselor's techniques, resort to social conversation, terminate the contact, evidence distraction from his line of thinking and take his lead from the counselor's remarks, show some other evidence of being threatened by the counselor's response. These criteria are the sign posts which the counselor can use to guide him in the interview and to assist him in improving his response skill.

To illustrate quite briefly some typical response movements a few excerpts from a phonographically recorded interview are reproduced and discussed below.

A twenty-seven-year-old veteran referred for counseling has opened the interview by stating that twice he has failed to succeed on training programs and that he cannot decide what he wants to do next or how to go about finding out what he wants to do. The next response, the client's second response, is as follows:

Mr. Duke: "I can't go any further. I just don't know how I'm set up or how to go at anything."

Counselor: "Just kind of a feeling of helplessness as it were (*Duke:* That's right!) as to how to tackle it."

Mr. Duke: "That's right. (*Pause of 3 seconds.*) Sort of dissatisfied at home and a — well, I want to do something, but I don't know just exactly what I want to do. I've taken some accountancy and that didn't work. That's what my records showed I was most suited for, that sort of work, clerical work, but I just can't seem to knuckle down to do it and do anything with it."

In this excerpt we see the confirmation of the counselor's response — twice. We also see a step toward the exploration of a new attitudinal area, the home situation, which is abandoned for the moment to come up at a later point in the interview. We see a further expression of the client's attitudes toward his work possibilities. Note that this further expression is not just a formal report on historical events or his present status but clearly demonstrates his feelings of confusion, frustration, concern and futility with the situation.

Notice how the client's reply to the next counselor response appears to evidence a return to a less expressive level of activity.

Counselor: "That is, the tests and one thing and another seem to add up to that, but when you actually tried it, you found it just didn't pan out; in that sense?"

Mr. Duke: "That's right. —— So that's about all I know. (*Pause*) I know there's a few things I'd like to try, but I don't know how to get into it." (*Pause* — 15 to 20 seconds.)

In addition to Mr. Duke's drop in expressiveness we have the additional criterion of a poor counselor response in the pauses which occur. Pauses will certainly not always be a criterion of poor understanding as they appear at times when an individual is thinking or experiencing an emotion at fairly intensive levels. Notice, too, that Mr. Duke confirmed the counselor's response. While this criterion has been listed as one indicative of good communication, it will not function so always. In this case the recording suggests that his confirmation is more perfunctory than exclamatory. The counselor's response was not a complete miss: what the counselor replied to was the content or subject matter of Mr. Duke's response, not the feeling, and the counselor was apparently sufficiently correct to elicit a confirmation but no further elaboration of Mr. Duke's feelings.

Despite all the temptations the counselor might have experienced to learn *about* the client, the counselor in his next response continued to strive for an understanding of Mr. Duke's feelings. Again, the counselor seemed more successful in the accuracy of his response as we shall judge from Mr. Duke's reply.

Counselor: "Well, as I gather it, you are just pretty much at your wits' end as to where to go."

Mr. Duke: (*Very strongly*) "That's right. I know what I'd like, but every time I go down there (*to see the adviser*) I seem to run into a lot of red tape. (*Continues to give details of being sent from one adviser to another.*) So — I'm pretty well dissatisfied so far as that goes."

While in this reply the content does not seem to be of much significance we cannot fail to notice the return to a more explosive mode of confirmation of the counselor's response and expression of further feelings.

In responding to a client's feelings there are two basic aspects which apparently govern the effectiveness of the response in producing forward movement: the attitude which the counselor holds as he delivers his response and the actual formulation or wording of the response itself.

Let us discuss the attitudinal aspect first because it is felt to be clearly the most important single factor both in its influence on the client and in its elusiveness for the beginner. As was discussed earlier, there appear to be five basic attitudinal positions which the counselor may take: (1) a probing, questioning, leading, discussion-provoking intent or attitude; (2) a teaching, interpretive, "pointing-out" attitude or intent; (3) an evaluative, corrective, suggestive, moralizing attitude or intent; (4) a supportive, sympathetic, reassuring, tempering, easing attitude or intent; and (5) an understanding, comprehending, appreciating attitude or intent.

The operation of these attitudes in most therapeutic or counseling approaches is frank and open. It is the intentional response on one or more of these bases at points judged appropriate by the counselor that constitute the counselor's technique armamentarium. When the counselor is, however, trying desperately to struggle for understanding solely, the operation of these attitudes becomes much more subtle. It is not uncommon for student counselors to say something to the effect, "I can't understand why he didn't move ahead; I reflected every feeling that I could see was of importance." What the student counselor also failed to see was his operation from the external frame of reference, from what he (the counselor) thought of importance and the interpretive, teaching attitude which prompted him to "reflect" what the client *ought* to see. The writer recalls quite vividly a discussion with an advanced student counselor who for the first time in over a year of counseling experience recognized that when a client expressed ambivalent feelings the student's response was one of "pointing out" that the client actually *did* feel two ways in the matter. Another student counselor came to the recognition only after a year of experience that when a client expressed a strong negative self-reference that he, the counselor, always "toned down" his response in order to try to reassure the client. Still another common attitudinal mix-up comes from many students who ask, "Shouldn't you always or nearly always try to reflect the brighter, more constructive side of the client's remarks?" It is, of course, a moot question as to whether or not one should: but there can be no question that the attitude of trying to manipulate the client lies at the basis of such a query. It is not toward what the counselor should or should not do that this book is primarily directed but toward the provision of material to which the student counselor can react and then examine his own reactions for the attitudes which lie behind them. It is the contention of the writer that unless the counselor can and does ferret out his own attitudes the counselor operates more blindly than he needs.

No exercise in the identification of attitudes is provided. There are two reasons why not. The first reason is that the pre-test which makes up the body of Chapter II is, for the most part, ideally suited for such an exercise. The student who wishes to sharpen his ability to make basic distinctions in attitudes is referred to Parts I, II, and III particularly. The second reason is the difficulty in constructing an exercise which illustrates subtle attitudinal differences without giving a great deal of the counselor's own feelings at the same time. At the present writing it seems wiser to hope that these subtleties will become more apparent to the student as he engages in discussions with others and as he tries to bring forth his own reasons for wanting to respond to a client in a certain way.

Let us next discuss the second major aspect governing the effectiveness of the response to feeling: the formulation or wording of the response itself. A response may apparently vary in at least the several ways described and illustrated in the following paragraphs.

Content. The first major variable seems to be that of the content of the counselor's response. By content is meant largely the same words as used by the client. Oddly enough, experience has seemed to indicate rather overwhelmingly that responses which are essentially repetitions of the client's response do not convey an understanding of the client to the client. Oftentimes a repetition of the client's identical words will be met with a denial, a reply to the effect, "No, that isn't what I mean." Why this should be is not at all clear but the fact remains that it does happen. In the illustration below a recorded client response and counselor reply will be presented, analyzed, and a modification of the response suggested so as to point up the presence of content.

Client: "I always thought I was just like other people — and yet there was a little wonder — "
Counselor: "Just a little wonder on your part — "
Here the counselor has essentially repeated the words of the client. The reply was as follows:
Client: "At times. Not all the time but just sometimes. I just rack my brains why do I do such things — why in the hell do I do things like I do."
Notice that the client's response starts with a hedging and modifying of his former response.

The feeling the client first expresses can be perceived by attending to the key ideas and their relationship: "I *thought* I was — but — I *wondered.*" This is a typical expression of uncertainty and puzzlement. A response not using his words might well be something such as, "There's always been doubt," or "There's been this element of uncertainty," or "You're not really certain," or "It's been a puzzle to you."

A second illustration of a response loaded with content is the following recorded excerpt.

Client: "Well, the tests are all over and finished and I still haven't come to any conclusions. I don't know any more than I knew before."

Counselor: "Um hm. You feel that in spite of testing, in spite of the thinking which you did with your counselor, you haven't come to any definite suggestion, any definite solution yet."

While the counselor's reply in this instance is not a mere repetition of the client's words it is a repetition of the exact thought sequence phrased in slightly different terms. This is just as much a content response as the other illustration. Had the counselor asked himself, "How must the client be feeling in order to express himself as he has?" the counselor might well have replied in terms of the client's discouragement, such as, "You just didn't get the help you wanted," or "The testing just let you down," or "You're right back where you started."

In general, the counselor in responding to the client will facilitate expression and exploration of attitudes more readily if the counselor's response is devoid of the words used by the client and avoids a simple repetition of the client's thought sequence and is directed at how the client must feel in order to express himself as he does.

Depth. A second variable is the degree to which the counselor's response has depth rather than shallowness in responses to deep feelings and the degree to which it has shallowness rather than depth in response to shallow feelings. Stated in other words, the second variable is one of accuracy of matching the depth of the client's response.

This concept of depth is easily illustrated. Suppose a client responds in a deeply disturbed manner:

Client: "I just can't see any way out. I've thought of every possible angle. It's just terrifying to be possessed like this day after day, hour after hour, minute after minute, second after second: just a continuous paroxysm of fear."

The counselor would be responding in the shallowest possible manner were he to reply, "Sort of disturbed about this, is that it?" or "This is something that troubles you." To match the depth of feeling the counselor's reply might be more nearly, "It's just about as bad as it could possibly be," or "It's almost more than you can bear," or "It just couldn't be any more overwhelming."

On the other hand, should a client express such an attitude as:

Client: "In some ways my folks are nice people – but in other ways I just don't care for some of the things they do."

the counselor would be going far beyond the depth of the client's expression if he were to reply, "You feel pretty bitter toward your parents, is that it?" or "At times they make you really angry." It may very well be that the client will reach such deep and strong feelings, but it is certain that feelings of such strength are not apparent in his immediate expression. A more appropriate response would be, "That is, in part you're satisfied with them and in part dissatisfied," or "Your feelings toward them go in both ways, is that it?"

Meaning. A third factor of equal importance is the factor of the meaning conveyed to the client by the counselor's response. In the counselor's efforts to match the perceptions of the client he may find himself either adding meaning or omitting meaning. Some of the obvious ways in which meaning can be added or omitted are the (1) completion of the sentence or thought for the client, (2) responding to material which the client has only used for illustrative purposes, (3) out and out interpretation of significance, (4) responding to the last thing the client said.

This illustration is taken from a recorded case.

1. *Client:* "Seems as if anybody should know why they do things it would be the person who does them. I don't know why I can't. I can't understand myself. When I'm acting normal there's nothing to understand. Those times that you do things that are different from the ways you act other times, those are the things you don't understand. You don't understand why. Every once in a while I get an impulse I've gotta get up and go – "

2. *Counselor:* "That old wanderlust."

3. *Client:* "I don't think it's the wanderlust because after I get where I'm going I don't feel any better."

4. *Counselor:* "Uh huh. Feel like being on the move all the time."

5. *Client:* "Not all the time, just once in a while. About four times a year."

6. *Counselor:* "Settle down for a while and then you got to get up and move and then when you get to where you're going you're not satisfied any more than you were before. Stay another four months

somewhere and then get up and move again. Something pushing and driving."

In this series of exchanges the counselor has managed to both add and omit meaning from his efforts to understand the client. In (2), the counselor has made the error of (a) responding to the last thing the client said, (b) completing a unit of thought for the client, and (c) responding to material which the client has used as illustrative of the point he was trying to make. Let us repeat the client's first response and insert paraphrasing at the appropriate points to clarify the meaning or feeling he is trying to convey.

1. *Client:* "Seems as if anybody should know why they do things it would be the person who does them. (*I should be able to understand* . . .) I don't know why I can't. I can't understand myself. (. . . *but I can't.*) When I'm acting normal there's nothing to understand. (*Part of the time there's no problem but* . . .) Those times that you do things that are different from the ways you act other times, those are the things you don't understand. (. . . *it's when I act differently that has me really puzzled.*) You don't understand why. (*For example* . . .) Every once in a while I get an impulse I've gotta get up and go. . . . (. . . *this impulse to go, I can't understand.*)"

The counselor's naming of the client's impulse, "That old wanderlust," while it may be a perfectly correct and appropriate term for the impulse, nevertheless omitted the client's emphasis upon his inability to understand his own behavior. A more appropriate response might well have been, "That is, you feel you should be able to understand yourself but there are some parts of your behavior which are really puzzling to you," or "Some of your behavior, at least, just seems to defy your understanding."

In response (4) the counselor has clearly added meaning. The client has not implied in his response (3) that he is troubled with the impulse to go all of the time. The counselor in (4) has also omitted meaning since he has failed to catch what the client has expressed, namely, that the term "wanderlust" is inappropriate as no satisfaction follows giving in to the impulse. (Apparently in the client's thinking, wanderlust is associated with satisfaction which accrues to a person on arrival at a new place.) A more appropriate response might have been, "That is, you feel it's not a satisfaction with getting to someplace new that is behind your impulse to get up and go."

In response (6) the counselor, quite aside from his extensive content repetition from the client's earlier remarks, has ended his response with a definitely interpretive remark, "Something pushing and driving." The client has not made any such bold statement relative to the nature of the impelling forces behind his behavior. The counselor has added together the material given him by the client and the knowledge he already has of abnormal psychology to reach a conclusion about the situation. His observation may be in every way correct except one: it doesn't square with the client's perception as expressed so far. In response (5) the client is conveying the notion, "No, no. You've got the wrong idea here. I'm bothered only once in a while — not all the time." A more appropriate response might well have been as simple as, "Oh, I see," or "Just at times," or anything else which would have communicated to the client that he was understood in his corrective meaning.

Language. A fourth variable and one which is not likely to be as important as the foregoing three is that of the language the counselor uses in his reply.

While student counselors are often abjured to fit their language usage to the language usage of the client, it may very well be that this works in one direction only, namely, the language should not be more complicated nor technical than the client is accustomed to using. A great deal of clinical experience would suggest that the counselor's language should always be the simplest of which he is capable regardless of the client's complexities of terms. One possible and very plausible reason for this is that, if the counselor uses the simplest of language, it is most likely that he will be understood.

To illustrate the complexity of language in the counselor's response we might consider for the moment the graduate student in psychology who as a client stated in a late interview:

Client: "Boy, oh boy! The old psychological elevator has been working again. A lot of stuff has been coming up during the past week that I'd pretty effectively put down and out. Stuff from my childhood that I just don't want to remember at all."

A counselor could easily have responded:

Counselor: "A lot of repressed stuff, is that it, from which the defenses have been torn away?"

The client might have accepted this quite readily but might just as easily have been led off into an intellectual discussion of the phenomenon. It would have been just as communicative had the counselor replied:

Counselor: "Troublesome stuff that just won't be held down any longer, is that it?"

EXERCISE 7

Identifying Common Errors of Response

In this exercise a series of client statements are given. After each statement there follows a group of five possible counselor responses. One response will be more acceptable than the remaining four. Each of the remaining four violates at least one of the four criteria just discussed: content, depth, meaning, and language. Identify each alternative as being primarily:

> A — Acceptable
> C — Too loaded with content
> D — Inappropriate in depth
> M — Inaccurate in meaning
> L — Inappropriate in language

The writer's identifications appear at the end of the chapter.

A–*Counselor:* "Well, what is it that you wanted to discuss?"

A–*Client:* "Don't you think that corporations are pretty soul-less things? That is, they hire a person for their own purposes, they don't give a damn about you. Don't you think so?"

B–*Counselor:*

1. "I gather you feel rather strongly that corporations are all for themselves and the individual who works for them just doesn't count."
2. "I gather you want to know what *I* feel about such things."
3. "In other words, you feel that corporations rather consistently violate the integrity of the individuals whom they employ."
4. "In other words you feel that corporations are not strictly ethical in their relations with employees."
5. "You feel that corporations have no soul and they hire people only for their own purposes without caring about the people themselves."

B–*Client:* "Yeah, that's right. I've never worked in a place yet where they gave a damn about you. Right now I'm working for a furniture outfit and of course there's been a hell of a rush — and we've been working overtime a lot. Why, I could work 70 hours a week if I wanted to but life is too short for that sort of thing. I come home all tired out — Even so, I've been working at least 54 hours a week. But that only amounts to $70 a week. And do you get any appreciation from the company? Hell, no! They'd work you to death, if they had half a chance and no thanks either. They wanted me to work overtime today but I just told them that I was through working overtime. It just took too much out of me and I was through."

C–*Counselor:*

1. "I gather you feel that they don't really have your best interests at heart?"
2. "You're working for this furniture company but they want you to put in more overtime than you want and it isn't worth it to you so you told them you didn't want any more of it."
3. "You feel that there's more to living than having to work without recognition or appreciation but only for the impersonal dollar."
4. "That is, monetary remuneration is not enough to fill the need for acceptance and need for appreciation that exists within you."
5. "In other words, you feel that this just isn't the job for *you.*"

C–*Client:* "That's right. Why, you don't have any time to do anything except work. What good is money when you don't have the time or energy to do anything with it? Now I've been palling around with a salesman — we have been together and run around a bit. He makes just as much as I do and puts in about 30 hours a week. Now I don't see any sense to working harder — and twice as long, for that matter, as — than he does. So I figured that I might like to go into selling myself. I don't know just what kind to go into and I've never done any selling, myself, but I figure I can do it. After all, all you have to do is get along with people and I've always been able to do that. What do you think of the idea?"

D–*Counselor:*

1. "That is, it is not so much your *aptitude* which you hold in question here so much as the *suitability* of engaging in selling."
2. "I gather that this is a decision which has given you a great deal of concern: you just can't make up your mind."
3. "In other words you want to get an easier job so you'll have more leisure time."

4. "That is, money is no good if you don't have the time to enjoy it so you want to get into something like selling that won't take as much time and you feel confident that you could do it but you're uncertain about whether or not you should try it."
5. "You find selling pretty attractive in view of all its advantages — yet you're wondering whether it's really the thing to do."
D–*Client:* "Yeah — you see there are some complications — you see — well — I might as well tell you. You see, I'm on parole from Joliet. The parole board wouldn't mind if I changed jobs but I'm wondering if I could get a job with that hanging over my head. Do you think it would be all right if I didn't tell 'em I'd been in Joliet? It wasn't too serious, you know — car stealing — I got drunk one night and just took off with it. Other men get probation or 90 days but they really stuck me for it. There's another thing, too, I've been wondering about. You see, I think there's something wrong with me psychologically — I don't know what it is and I don't know these technical terms very well. Those whaddyya callems — those psychiatrists, I guess they are, said I had a psychopathic personality — whatever that is."
E–*Counselor:*

1. "That is, you're wondering whether or not it would be all right to get a job without telling that you are a parolee and you're also wondering whether or not there isn't something wrong with you psychologically, too."
2. "You've been wondering about both things, is that it: wondering just how much you should let out and wondering about your own make-up, too?"
3. "I gather both of these things have you very deeply puzzled: what you should do and whether or not something might be wrong with you."
4. "That's what puzzles you, is it, just what they meant when they called you a 'psychopathic personality'?"
5. "Both things are disturbing you, is that it: the ethics of the situation and possible personality pathology?"
E–*Client:* "You know, I wouldn't tell this to anybody else, but I've been committed six times. There's something wrong with me all right. You know, I've been wondering about that a lot lately. My sex life, for example. Here I am 37 years old and I just realize that — well — whenever I wanted it, I always go to a prostitute. A sort of an animal proposition."
F–*Counselor:*

1. "You feel that your sex life shouldn't be like that."
2. "All of these things summate to convince you that there must be an aberration in your personality."
3. "You've been committed six times and your sex life doesn't seem right to you and those things make you feel there must be something wrong with you."
4. "That is, as you begin to look at some of these things you are pretty sure they add up to something being wrong somewhere."
5. "As you think about these things it tends to make you a little curious about whether or not all is well."

F–*Client:* "Funny thing — I've been around a lot — had all kinds of jobs — rode the rods — I've had over 160 jobs in the last 15 years — and I don't know why. Maybe it has something to do with when I was a kid. I was big and strong just like I am now. But my eyes are very bad. You can see how bad they are from these glasses. I had to be very careful because I was always in danger of going blind and when some kid made a pass at me I had to take it even though I knew I was tougher. That sort of thing was hard to swallow."

G–*Counselor:*

1. "You've been around a lot, had all kinds of jobs but you don't know why. And you're wondering if it could be connected with your eyes and the way you had to act when you were a kid."
2. "I gather you feel that life as a child was made just unbearable for you and possibly that that had something to do with what you are today."
3. "In other words you feel that part of your present difficulty may be attributable to your myopia and the unfortunate psychological climate which resulted from it."
4. "I gather it made you feel pretty angry and frustrated to have to 'take it' like that."
5. "In other words, you're wondering if there couldn't be some connection with the rough time you had as a kid and the way you act now."

G–*Client:* "That's right — you'll never know just how bad it really was. And as I grew up — it got worse. Here I was bigger, stronger, and tougher than the rest and it didn't mean a thing. I grew up pretty headstrong. Didn't give a damn and had to have my own way. And when I couldn't get it or didn't like things as they were, why, I just took off. And most of the time I didn't like things as they were. Why, once I worked at the University —— and held 3 jobs in one week as a janitor, as an engineer, and as a —— in the hospital.

When I took off they went crazy trying to check up on just what I
did do. And another time I was working for —— Bank as a janitor.
I had stuck six months this time and I had my permanent job and
everything. I was really sitting pretty — all I had to do was stick it
out 'til retirement. And it was easy. Why, this fellow and me used
to go over to the bar across the street and drink and chew the fat
for an hour, sometimes even two. And they never caught us. Well,
one day I was really working — stacking bales. And the super came
around to check up on me. Well, that was all right — but he kept
following me around all day. That really got me. He had no business following me around. He was a busy man, he had other things
to do. Well, he stayed with me until the middle of the afternoon.
When he went I stopped right in the middle of everything and just
walked out, had a drink and went home — well, no — I went to a
burlesque show first. And I never even thought about the perma-
nency of the job. Well, mother argued with me — she's had a lot of
that to do — and she finally got me to call the super and tell him that
I was leaving — I never would have done it otherwise. Most jobs I've
just walked out of — no warning — no nothing — and there's been an
awful lot of that."

H–*Counselor:*

1. "You feel that your mother played a part in all this, too."
2. "In other words you've tended to persevere in the old habit patterns."
3. "Things grew from bad to worse and always in the same way: if
   you didn't like it you just left."
4. "That is, you feel you just grew up pretty headstrong and had to
   have your own way and if you couldn't you just took off and you
   feel that there's been an awful lot of it."
5. "You feel that maybe you have tended to overdo the headstrongness,
   is that it?"

H–*Client:* "Yeah. I don't know, life gets pretty complicated sometimes —
and when it gets too complicated I just pull up stakes. I never look
at myself — I've tried it a few times and there's just too much turmoil
and confusion — I take off instead."

I–*Counselor:*

1. "You feel it's easier to strike out again than to turn your gaze inward
   and really face yourself."
2. "You feel life gets too complicated and that you would rather take
   off instead of looking at yourself with all the turmoil and confusion."
3. "You feel you just don't have what it takes to really face up to
   yourself."

4. "That is, you notice that you tend to avoid facing things and tend to leave them."

5. "That is, you would sooner withdraw than undergo the anxiety of meeting your symptoms."

I–*Client:* "And how! Well, as I said, life is pretty complicated. Why is it that people get things into such a mess? I'm Jewish but nobody ever guesses it because I don't look that way and when these guys come over and start talking to me about these 'sheenies,' these 'Christ-killers' — well, I know that's ignorance — they just don't know — but why can't people be taken for themselves? I never ask anything about a guy. I take him as he looks to me."

J–*Counselor:*

1. "That is, you have some intellectual appreciation of prejudice but you feel it to be markedly unjust to the recipients of prejudicial behavior."

2. "I gather you are wondering just what kinds of motives people might have for being prejudiced."

3. "The fact that prejudice does exist is a thing you feel is unfortunate."

4. "Ignorance or no ignorance: it's terrifically unfair to the person who is the target of the prejudice. Is that it?"

5. "When people display their prejudices you recognize it as ignorance but you still feel that people ought to accept others at face value because of what prejudice can do to them."

J–*Client:* "And these guys where I work — they're really stupid. Boy, is that business ever run wrong. Why, my department is run by such a bunch of num-dums that it really makes me sick. — And when we get held up because things are set up wrong they just say — 'Well, we'll get a man who can get 'em out on time.' Well, they can't — nobody can because it's set up wrong. I went up to the boss last week and told him to give me my time and when he asked me why, I told him. He told me that he really wanted me to take over the department — he knew what was wrong — but that he couldn't very well because he hired me without telling the top men about my record. So his neck is out. Well, I couldn't take the job anyway. Mr. J—— who has the —— department is a pretty good guy even if he is dumb and besides he has a wife and some kids and I have nothing."

K–*Counselor:*

1. "On the one hand you'd like to see a bit more efficiency yet you find displacing a man distasteful."

2. "Looking at it one way, you'd like to take over but looking at it another way: no."
3. "Things are run so stupidly that no one could actually get the work out and when you pointed it out to the boss he indicated his confidence in you but you wouldn't really want to take the job because it would mean Mr. J— would lose his."
4. "Viewing it from the frame of reference of the efficiency of operation, you would like to accept the responsibility; but viewing it from a different frame of reference, the answer is 'no.'"
5. "That is, you just don't want to do anything that would hurt someone else."

One further comment can be made about the counselor's language and that is regarding the use of the same phrases over and over. A number of persons who have read the phonographically recorded interviews are struck by the counselor's apparently repetitious use of such phrases as "You feel —," "As I get it —," "In other words —," and "—, is that it?" There seems to be no clearcut evidence in the recordings, however, that the repetitiousness is as disturbing to the client as to the reader. The major criterion of the effectiveness of the language seems to reside more in the sincerity and spontaneity of the language than in its grammatical or rhetorical structure.

Before concluding this chapter on responding to the internal frame of reference, it may be well to discuss one further source of difficulty for the beginner. Most of us are so strongly accustomed to paying attention to the content of a respondent's remarks that learning to pay attention to the feeling or gist of the remarks is a somewhat difficult thing to do. To illustrate this point, let us consider the hypothetical example of the student who asks of a group of three people what time a given lecture is to be started. The first person replies, "At two o'clock." The second says, "Oh that thing! At two o'clock." The third says, "Oh gosh! At two o'clock. What time is it now?" Now, for the most part we do not remain detached from other people's responses. To the first person, who has responded in a matter of fact tone, the student is likely to reply, "Thank you" and move on. To the second person he is more apt to reply "Thanks" and wonder "What's wrong with the guy?" or "What's wrong with the lecture?" or "What's wrong with me?"

To the third person our student is more apt to forget to give thanks and to reply by giving the time. We just are not accustomed to detaching our own interests and observing that the first person seemed indifferent, the second depreciatory, and the third interested. The beginning counselor will learn more and more to appreciate the fact that feelings are not so evident from what the client says so much as from the way he says it, the phrasings he uses.

The following exercise is designed to present groups of hypothetical expressions in which the content will differ very little yet the feeling will differ markedly. You are to study each group and then attempt to formulate on a separate sheet of paper responses appropriate to each formulation of the client statement. Suggested responses are to be found at the end of the chapter.

EXERCISE 8

Response to Different Formulations of Similar Content

A–1. "I guess it's, in part, my fault. I just can't understand it in any other way. It doesn't make sense any other way, yet I don't see where."

A–2. "I guess it's my fault, in part, all right, even if I don't see where. It just wouldn't make sense in any other way. There are always two sides to these things."

A–3. "Oh I guess you could say I'm, in part, at fault. After all, there are always two sides to these things. But I'd sure like to know where."

B–1. "The biggest shock has worn off and I can face it now. I guess the thing to do is wait and watch my chance to get a new start."

B–2. "Well, the biggest part of the shock has worn off now. I guess all I can do is just wait and watch for another chance to start again — whatever that means."

B–3. "The biggest part of the shock has worn off, I guess. At least I can face it now. Just wait and watch and try not to fail again."

C–1. "I feel very inferior to *everybody*. I don't have *any* confidence."

C–2. "I just *seem* to feel inferior to everyone I know. It's *as if* I had no confidence at all."

C–3. "Boy, does that get me. I go around acting inferior to *everybody* just as if I didn't have *any* confidence."

D–1. "I guess I'm just dissatisfied with my folks. Now, that's a hell of a thing for a fellow to say about his folks!"

D–2. "I guess I'm just dissatisfied with my folks. Now, that's a hell of a thing for a fellow to have to say about his folks — but it's as simple as that."

D–3. "I guess I'm just dissatisfied with my folks. Now, that's a hell of a thing for a fellow to have to say about his folks — but it's more than true."

E–1. "I'm angry, all right! No use in denying that. Sometimes I just want to blow up and tear things all apart. It just can't last."

E–2. "There's no point in saying I'm not angry, because I am. And I'd like to blow up about it, too, but where would that get me?"

E–3. "There's no point in denying it makes me angry, because, by gosh, it does make me angry. Yeah, sometimes I get pretty peeved about it. And yet at other times I'm not too sure the provocation is really there."

❋   ❋   ❋   ❋   ❋

Exercise 6. Suggested scoring for identifications of base frame of reference.

2–*C*.		3–*C*.		4–*C*.		5–*C*.	
1.	Ex	1.	Ex	1.	Ex	1.	In
2.	In	2.	Ex	2.	Ex	2.	Ex
3.	Ex	3.	In	3.	In	3.	Ex
4.	Ex	4.	Ex	4.	Ex	4.	Ex

6–*C*.		7–*C*.		8–*C*.		9–*C*.	
1.	Ex	1.	Ex	1.	In	1.	Ex
2.	In	2.	Ex	2.	Ex	2.	Ex
3.	Ex	3.	In	3.	Ex	3.	In(?)
4.	Ex	4.	Ex	4.	Ex	4.	Ex

10–*C*.		11–*C*.	
1.	Ex	1.	Ex
2.	Ex	2.	Ex
3.	Ex	3.	In
4.	In	4.	Ex

Exercise 7. Suggested scoring for identifications of common errors of response.

B.		*C*.		*D*.		*E*.		*F*.	
1.	A	1.	D	1.	L	1.	C	1.	M
2.	M	2.	C	2.	D	2.	A	2.	L
3.	L	3.	A	3.	M	3.	D	3.	C
4.	D	4.	L	4.	C	4.	M	4.	A
5.	C	5.	M	5.	A	5.	L	5.	D

G.	1. C	H.	1. M	I.	1. A	J.	1. L	K.	1. D
	2. D		2. L		2. C		2. M		2. A
	3. L		3. D		3. M		3. D		3. C
	4. M		4. C		4. D		4. A		4. L
	5. A		5. A		5. L		5. C		5. M

Exercise 8. Suggested responses to different formulations of similar content.

A–1. "You feel it must be partly you but you don't see how."
A–2. "You feel pretty sure that it's partly you."
A–3. "You feel that it might be partly you but I gather you tend to doubt it."

B–1. "You feel it's pretty much a dead issue now and the future is the thing."
B–2. "I gather you feel it's pretty much a matter of resigning yourself to what the future may hold for you."
B–3. "You feel, then, that things are coming more under control, more within your ability to cope with them."

C–1. "Just at the very bottom, is that it?"
C–2. "That's the way you see yourself, is it, as seeming to be at the bottom of the heap?"
C–3. "It's pretty disturbing to you to see yourself acting that way, is that it?"

D–1. "You feel that it's wrong for you to feel that way."
D–2. "Even though it may be unpleasant, that's what it adds up to."
D–3. "Regardless of how it appears, your feeling about them is real. Is that it?"

E–1. "You feel just about as angry as you can feel; is that it?"
E–2. "Just not too sure that being angry will get you anywhere."
E–3. "Are you saying there that at least part of the time your anger may not be justified?"

Chapter

TYPICAL PROBLEMS IN

THE BEGINNING INTERVIEW

In this and the next chapter are presented a number of client statements. The reader is invited to try formulating responses to the feelings expressed. These expressions represent typical problems in two senses. Some are typical in that they represent expressions frequently met by the counselor; these are offered since for most readers there will be available but few cases for purposes of study and practice. Through these expressions a certain breadth of experience may be obtained vicariously. The other expressions are typical in that they are frequently difficult for the counselor. Problem areas of this type are offered for the vicarious experience which such material may also furnish.

By problem areas the writer means specifically areas of client expression which prompt the student or counselor to ask of himself, "Can I be of help here solely through close understanding? Shouldn't I do something else here? Dare I be consistent?" Such questioning as this has seemed to arise in almost every instance in which the content of the client's expression has distracted or seduced the counselor's attention away from the feeling involved. Two frequent forms of this distraction are the client's involving the counselor personally such as by asking his advice or his opinion and the client's raising of questions about the counseling process.

It is the writer's hypothesis that as the counselor becomes more and more capable of following the feeling, regardless of the content, he will find fewer and fewer reasons why he shouldn't try to follow the feeling.

The beginning interview presents certain problems to the counselor that are in part different from subsequent interviews. It is likely that the beginning interview will be more demanding of the counselor for several reasons. The counselor and client are new to each other and the relationship which is established at the outset will color a great deal of what follows. The counselor must be prepared to adapt himself to the mode of expression the client develops: the counselor is not going into the interview with a set routine. It is in the first interview that the client will begin to reveal himself. The counselor's reactions are correspondingly important. Errors in understanding the client may result in his hasty withdrawal. And usually it is in this interview that the client decides whether the counseling relationship is the method which he will use in his attempts to work out his difficulties. The exercises in this chapter will be devoted to problems which may arise in the opening of the beginning interview, in the client's first initial statements of difficulty and in the closing of the hour.

EXERCISE 9

In the exercise items presented below you will first be given the problem, that is, the situation or client response to which you must reply in some way. Analyze this problem carefully and then formulate the reply that you would make to it. Following each such problem is an analysis of the issue or issues involved as the writer sees them and suggestions for the type of reply which would fit the issues. At the end of the chapter are counselor replies formulated by the writer to which the student may wish to refer upon the completion of his own efforts.

A. Opening the beginning interview

1. The client is ushered into the counseling room and is seated. He then begins with: "Now that I'm here, it all seems so foolish

that I wonder why I came. I guess I don't really have a problem at all."

Issues. This is an apparent denial of troublesome concerns. It would be easy for the counselor to reassure the client some way by indicating that many clients feel silly when first beginning to speak to a counselor. To do so would be to deny the way in which the client feels, to say, in effect, that he shouldn't feel that way. Similarly, it would be easy to disregard the client's feeling by simply asking him to give you a little idea of what it was he wanted to speak about when he made the appointment. Such a response might easily lead the client to present a somewhat defensive, "watered-down" version of his concerns and might leave him feeling pressed. Paradoxical as it may seem, experience indicates that in such situations a full appreciation of a client's feelings will be followed on his part by some allusion to his concerns, the very thing which the counselor desires to see take place. The counselor's reply might well relate to the change in the man's feelings since making the appointment.

2. The client comes into the counseling room and is seated. He then starts, "I'd like to make it clear right at the outset that I'm not here because I'm crazy or neurotic or anything like that. I just heard that you people give advice on problems and I have a decision to make that I need advice on."

Issues. Here again we have a somewhat defensive person who is fearful of what the counselor may think about him. One temptation for the would-be non-directive counselor might be to "straighten the man out," to explain the nature of the service to him. There is no sound reason why the man should be "properly informed." He is already doing what the counselor wants him to do; he is expressing his attitudes in a clear-cut manner. The counselor cannot ask for more. A response might well be centered around the client's insistence that it is the decision to be made that brings him in rather than because he feels something is wrong with him.

3. After the client is seated he begins, "Just what are you? A doctor, a psychologist, a psychiatrist, a social worker, or just what?"

Issues. The client here seems quite concerned for some unknown reason as to the status of the counselor. Clients often have had previous experiences in seeking help that have left them very suspicious. Oftentimes, too, clients have a host of preconceived notions about what different activities are carried out under different professional titles. The counselor is certainly under the obligation to properly identify himself but is under no obligation to try to defend his professional affiliation nor to try to educate the client. The temptation may be strong for some people to be drawn into an argument with such a hostile client. It would seem only to identify one's status is to miss an opportunity of responding to the client's concern, even though the exact nature of the concern is unknown. In any event, the counselor might well expect an outburst of further hostility directed toward professional people in general or against some one group in particular. Or, the counselor might be prepared to undergo a systematic and aggressive grilling.

4. The client is seated and then begins, "I don't know how you go about all this. This is my first experience at something like this and I don't know quite how to start or what I am supposed to do."

Issues. This is the typical situation which often prompts the counselor to "structure," that is, to explain or define the interview process and relationship. There usually does not seem to be much of a purpose served by engaging in intellectual discussions. The clients are numerous who start off in this rhetorical manner. Obviously the client has things about which he wants to talk or he wouldn't be there. Just because he starts out by saying he doesn't know how to start doesn't mean he can't start. The fact is that he has started, he has already expressed an attitude to which the counselor can respond.

In most cases it would probably be quite satisfactory to reply something to the effect, "Well, would you like to start off by giving me some idea of why it was you wanted to see a counselor?" Normally this is sufficient to bring the topic of conversation around to the elements of concern to the client. Every so often the more defensive and dependent client will be unable to accept this, however, and may reply to the effect, "Yes, but I don't know just how to do it. Should I start with my childhood or what I'm doing now or just how?" It is the writer's judgment that the counselor response most likely to produce further expression and exploration will be a response to the feeling involved. In this case it would seem that the client is clearly implying that he or she has things of concern about which to talk but is uncertain as to where and how to begin. An understanding reply involving these two elements might readily be expected to result in some allusion to the concerns which brought the client in for help.

5. The client enters the office, is seated and waits for the counselor to start off. The counselor begins with, "Now then, Mr. J——, would you like to give me some idea of what it is that you wanted to talk about?" The client replies, "I can't hold a job. I've held fifteen jobs in the last five years. I worked for the D—— Auditing firm six months — no, seven months — well six and a half months. And for the B—— Construction Company for two months. I worked for the — (*client continues to list the firms and lengths of time employed.*) That's the way it's been."

Issues. In this client we see an example of an intellectual, historical presentation with little or no expression of feeling. We might speculate how he feels but the opportunity for projecting our own feelings onto the situation is great. Such summary presentations are not infrequently met. They seem to be characteristic of the client who is highly defensive and quite apprehensive about divulging how he feels. Such clients call for extreme care and delicacy especially since the counselor is bound to have feelings which would have been aroused by the events reported and therefore, in the absence of clearly stated client feelings, may project his own value system. In most cases of historical summaries, however, the client seems to be presenting the material with the general air of "This is the whole story," "This is my problem." The note of completeness may often be the cue for the counselor's response. The counselor may be forced to try to judge from the style of delivery how the client must feel in order to respond as he does. Time may give us the knowledge of how best to respond to such highly defensive persons who are, in effect, acting out the idea, "Do your damnedest but I know you can't do any better at this problem than I've already done." At the present time such persons are generally considered unlikely candidates for help from any approach. In any event, such clients seem to possess a remarkable capacity for side-tracking the counselor who tries to force a statement of feeling or who gets involved in the content of the response. The best reply, in the opinion of the writer, would be one which gets at the feeling behind the mode of presentation rather than the feeling which might be related to the events listed.

6. Client is brought into counselor's office. After seating himself begins: "Well, I don't really know why I'm here. I've been having trouble with my studies but I know why that is: I just haven't been buckling down to my studies. Anyway, the Dean said I'd have to come over here, so here I am."

Issues. It is easy to jump into a number of inferences regarding this client. Among them are: (1) the Dean has been inept at making a referral; (2) the student is defending himself by projecting the responsibility for his coming onto the Dean; (3) the client is right and he is faced with no more than a superficial situation; (4) the student may be faced with academic demands beyond his ability but is "covering-up." It is the presence of such a number of immediately available yet conflicting possibilities which may tempt the counselor-in-training to do just a little probing, even if no more than to utter a quizzical "Oh?" Another source of possible disruption to the counselor's intent to try to understand is the client's "dumping of responsibility" for the next move into the counselor's lap.

It does seem apparent that the client is trying to communicate that it was someone else's idea he should come in and not his own as he has knowledge of what he is doing. A response to these elements might be expected to facilitate further expression by the client.

7. The client comes into the office smiling and apparently interested and self-assured. The counselor leads off with: "All right, would you like to give me a little background in what it is that you wanted to discuss?" The client responds hastily with: "Oh, I don't have any problems, if that's what you mean. I just heard about this service you were offering and I thought I'd

drop in and see what it's all about — what it is you do here."
Issues. The beginning counselor, all set to really meet with a "real" case, may be sorely tempted to throw the client out. Or, the counselor may feel let down and drop his efforts to be consistent. Let him bear in mind that what the client has said may be quite true. One must ask, however, whether the counselor can really accept such an expression of curiosity as a "normal" or usual expression. Stranger defenses than apparent curiosity have been met in counseling situations. Assuming the behavior to be defensive, some therapists would recommend "breaking through" the defense with a statement such as, "Now look, nobody just comes in here out of curiosity alone. Go ahead. Tell me what it is that you wanted to talk about."

A response to the feeling being expressed would involve the juxtaposition of curiosity to felt need.

8. A not too unusual problem is the person who has the expectation that the counselor is not the one who deals with the problems with which the counselor actually hopes to deal. An example of such a client follows: "I have to make a decision whether to change my job or hold onto the risky deal I have now. I can't shake the feeling, however, that a lot of things are really in back of it, but they're personal problems — sex and worry and one thing and another — that a doctor, a psychiatrist should deal with."

Issues. Should the counselor attempt to communicate to the client that personal problems are the things with which the counselor hopes most to help? It seems quite likely that the counselor could readily stir up a discussion of the functions of the psychiatrist and the functions of the counselor and find himself suddenly, if not irrevocably, faced with the client's possible convictions — a course, which, if pursued, places the counselor in the position of having to "teach the client better," of denying the client's conception of this aspect of reality. An alternative for the counselor is the provision of an environment or atmosphere of understanding lacking in threat which would permit the client to discover for himself the possibility of exploring areas thought to be inappropriate. In this instance understanding might be fostered by responding to the immediate or pressing decision which seems to be blocked by the more personal issues. There is also the issue of whether the counselor feels that this is a violation of the client's integrity to so proceed. Possibly the counselor will feel that he should try to engineer a referral to someone who fits the client's concept of the "right" person. This is only one of the many areas in which the counselor must work out standards of professional conduct with which he can feel comfortable.

9. The client, after being seated, turns toward the counselor and begins: "Frankly, I'm quite worried about my five-year-old daughter. She's just gotten completely out of control and so I thought I'd better come in and see if I could get some help in dealing with her."

Issues. Such a statement as this provokes some deeply involved questions. Should the counselor endeavor to determine whether the child needs therapy rather than the client? Should the involvement of the other parent be investigated? Doesn't the counselor have the responsibility of determining here where his resources are most likely to be most beneficial? Is it right for the counselor to say to himself, "*This* is my client and I am here to help only him meet the situation"? Dare the counselor really trust the client to make the best decision of who is to receive help in such a situation? Where *does* the responsibility of the counselor lie? There are several facets to the situation which can feed the arguments pro and con for each of the issues raised. Are the parents overly concerned? Does a real behavior problem exist? Could there be organic involvements? Are the parents or parent projecting their own difficulties onto the child? Where does this seeming insistence on "control" arise? This one thing is certain: the parent is not only worried but is feeling pretty helpless. Possibly dealing with his feelings may be of real help.

10. The client is met at the appointed hour and ushered into the counselor's office. The counselor opens by saying, "I wonder if we might not start off with what it was that brought you here?" The client makes no reply but stares at the opposite wall with hands tensely clutched together, a flush spreading over his face, breathing quickly and deeply.

Issues. The counselor is, in an instance such as this, in something of a dilemma. Should he "break in" to encourage the client to begin or should he wait for the client to start in his own way? The counselor is faced with an expression of feeling: but just what feeling is being expressed may be far from apparent. The client may be strongly embarrassed now that he is in the situation that calls for revealing himself or facing himself responsibly. He may be overcome with panic, a strong fear that he may be about to reveal more than he wants to reveal. He may be overcome with the feelings of his problems. He may be blocked on how to start. He may be going through a real conflict as to whether he should speak out, whether he has the right to speak out his concerns. In short, there are a host of possible feelings which may be behind the expressive behavior.

It is not at all clear how such pauses can best be handled. Some counselors have evolved a general rule of allowing such an initial pause to continue for no more than a moment or two on the basis that the pressures being suffered by the client should not be added to by the additional burden of a continued and increasing pressure of feeling a responsibility for saying *something*. These counselors often respond in the vein: "I gather it's pretty hard to get started." There is, on hand, recorded evidence that indicates such a supportive response may do more damage than good. Where one client may appreciate the help in getting over the hump of starting, another client may deeply resent being pushed into making a statement before he is certain just what he wants to say and how he wants to say it.

The writer has on more than one occasion met the problem (especially during the earlier stages of his learning) by asking rather openly just what the client was experiencing at the moment; he did it by stating his uncertainty as to what the client was experiencing and asking if it could be this, this, or this. An example of such an endeavor to understand the client is, "I'm sorry, but I'm just not sure what it is that you're feeling here. Is it that it's hard to get started? That you're uncertain just where to start? That everything is in a jumble? Or . . . " Each possibility inquired into was an honest endeavor to try to be as nearly correct as possible in terms of the client's behavior. Often the clients would respond by communicating their feelings and the apparent impasse would be broken. At times the silence would continue.

One thing seems certain: a person under some pressure which blocks the expression of his concerns may welcome most heartily an *escape* into "rapport-establishing" social conversation. The question arises as to the helpfulness, either immediate or eventual, of the introduction of such a period of rapport-establishment. It is clearly supportive and is subject to all the doubts which may be associated with the direct use of supportive techniques in the interview. Many counselors and therapists will insist, however, that clients may have real needs for support at certain spots in the therapeutic process. Such insistence may well have grown out of repeated experiences — each experience having been accompanied by the assumption that the client did not have the strength to meet the situation, thus necessitating the counselor's intervention. Some day we may have experimental bases for evaluating such an assumption as being correct under certain conditions or possibly as being a socially shared autism.

B. Handling the initial statements of difficulty

1. "Well — I find that I'm troubled by doubts and uncertainties and things like that, although I don't know of any reason why I should be so concerned. Financially I'm well fixed. I'm very compatible with my husband; have two lovely children: I should be the happiest person in the world."

Issues. Quite typical is this initial problem formulation. The client expresses the form in which the difficulties present themselves: doubts and uncertainties. She also does the typical thing when she states she knows of no reasons why she should be so troubled. She then proceeds to give reasons why she shouldn't be troubled. Notice that finances, children, and husband are all placed completely out of range as problems to her. Experience has indicated to all therapists that these will be problem areas to her. It is this type of formulation which is easily identified as being defensive. The client is in a perfect position here to deny any suggestion, no matter how minute, the counselor might make to the effect that part of her problems will be found in these areas. Similarly, she has stated in categorical terms that she knows of no reasons why she should be troubled and this puts her in a position to deny any suggestion that she may have at least thought of *something* that might be called a reason. A non-challenging and understanding response to her feelings will involve two concepts: first, that she ought to be happy and second, that in the face of this her difficulties are quite puzzling.

2. "I've had a very unusual life. I don't feel very normal, but I want to feel that way."

Issues. This is a very broad type of statement. The counselor might be strongly tempted here to ask for a more specific formulation. One cannot tell what he means by "unusual" or "normal." It is clear that he feels different from others. It is also clear that he wishes to change. An understanding response would try to incorporate these feelings.

3. The client, after a few attempts to state his difficulties, responds, "I thought I'd have something to talk about — then it goes all around in circles. I was trying to think what I was going to say. Then coming here — doesn't work out."

Issues. This is an example of a response which can be quite challenging to a student. The client seems to be blocked, momentarily or otherwise. The counselor may be strongly tempted to offer just a little bit of support, just a little reassurance and encouragement to help the client get under way again. It seems so reasonable that encouragement should help here, too. And it may help him start. It seems so reasonable that encouragement in a small amount should do no harm. And it may not. But consider that in giving encouragement the counselor is evaluating the client as needing help, as being just a little bit weak. The counselor would also be denying the client's feelings, that is, the counselor would be saying, in effect, "You shouldn't feel that way," or "You needn't feel that way: everything is really all right." The fact that the client does feel incapable of going ahead at this point should not be confused with his actual capabilities. In addition to feeling confused and blocked, the client also feels that before he came he had some ideas of what he wanted to talk about. A response to the feeling involved would cover both feelings.

4. A middle-aged woman has opened the interview describing how lost she feels now that her only child is leaving home, how desperately she is seeking some way to fill the gap in her life, and how the upset is affecting her relations with her husband and friends. The counselor has been understanding her closely and the flow of feeling has been exceedingly rapid. Suddenly she changes this developmental flow of feeling and blurts out, "And if I don't have a problem, and if you don't want to go a bit farther than this, that's all right. There is no future — maybe when you're forty-eight years old you're supposed to climb on a shelf someplace and sit."

Issues. This is a difficult expression with which to deal. The client has directly involved the counselor by referring to what he might or might not want to do about continuing. She seems to be attempting to get the counselor to express in some way his evaluation of whether or not her situation is as hopelessly inevitable as she feels it may be. The counselor is in a neat dilemma. Should he express a reassuring, supportive evaluation he will be denying her feelings about the situation. Should he express a negative evaluation he will confirm her worst fears about the situation.

Such situations as these are best understood as rhetorical propositions. Obviously we can say that her remarks are an expression of a dependent need for external evaluation. That may be diagnostically helpful but it doesn't help us in understanding the feeling she has which prompts her to speak in the way she does. The questioning way in which she puts her feeling arises out of her feeling, "Are things as inevitable as they appear to be?" A response to feeling would confine itself to this.

The student may feel that the client has specifically asked for an evaluation from the counselor. In a sense that is true. It is true in the sense that she has so phrased her remarks as to *invite* an evaluation from the counselor. Direct requests for evaluation are usually more direct than this. And if it should turn out that even though rhetorically phrased the expression was intended as a direct request, the counselor will be enlightened in the response which follows. As a rule, however, the counselor will avoid undue intellectual involvement, if he responds to the feeling involved.

5. The same client as in the preceding excerpt goes on describing her difficulties for a few more comments and then states, "I could go on — there are some personal things — I don't see much point to it. . . . That's the general picture of the thing. I don't think they give a better picture. There's just nothing *there*. I've never felt *this* way before. Here's a perfectly good body just walking around with no place to go because I can't interest myself in a lot of little things that some women do. I'm interested in a lot of things that are really important, and yet there's no outlet for it."

Issues. This is an interesting and instructive response to study. This response involves the question of whether the counselor should try to respond to *all* of the feelings expressed or be selective. First, the client expresses her feeling that to continue is futile — but in a way that invites reassurance and support. Second, the client expresses her bitterness about her situation with finality: "There's just nothing there." Third, as she elucidates and elaborates this theme she makes a positive reference to being "interested in a lot of things that are really important" but then immediately denies the possible utility of such interests.

To what should the counselor respond? To all of the feelings? To a part? If to a part, to what part? In trying to find the answer let us bear in mind that in therapy we are trying to facilitate expression and exploration of attitudes. Had the first feeling been expressed alone, the feeling of futility with continuing the interview, we would have wanted to respond to it as a means of facilitating further expression. But she continued of her own accord. It is questionable whether a counselor's reference to this feeling would be helpful after she has left it behind. To respond to it at the end of her remark might well distract her from her present line of thought and feeling.

The counselor might feel it wise to respond to the depth of her bitterness when she seems to reach the bottom of negative self-evaluation in the remark, "There's just nothing *there*." But notice that she begins an exploration of this feeling: "I've never felt *this* way before." Again it seems questionable to respond to feeling when the result of the response would produce nothing better than the exploration which is taking place. The counselor may be

certain that the same negative self-evaluation will come up in
greater or lesser degree in many contexts to follow, sometimes as
a central theme and sometimes as a point of departure for further
"working through" activity.

Many counselors will jump at the positive self-reference feeling
that the positive side should be emphasized. The notion that therapy consists in "reinforcing by suggestion" the positive elements
in the picture is a notion of long standing but not of good standing. Coué developed the idea to an extensive degree. Other counselors may feel that the positive element should be emphasized not
for suggestive purposes but to point out to the client that a positive
element does exist and the situation is not as black as it seems.
This is actually the same essential supportive attitude with its con-
comitant negative evaluation of the client's capacities. Quite aside
from such factors as the psychological climate, probably the most
compelling evidence for the likely failure of an emphasis on the
positive reference lies in the client's own rejection of it.[1]

6. The client begins as he enters the door and turns to face the
counselor. At a rapid rate he pours out, "Well, I tell ya. Ya
got to help me with them V.A. docs, see. Jeeze, I go down
there and they say you ain't sick and alla time I'm about
doubled over wit cramps and I'm dizzy — vertigro or sumthin

---

[1] An anecdote which points up this perverse characteristic of the human
animal relates to a psychologically naïve doctor and a patient.
Patient: "You see, it's this way, doctor, I'm dead."
Doctor: "Is that so? Well, I can fix that. Now I want you to do just as I
say for thirty days and then come back to see me. Each morning and each
evening look at yourself squarely in the mirror and say three times, 'Dead
men don't bleed.' Got it straight?"
Patient: "OK, doctor. I understand."
Thirty days later the patient returned.
Doctor: "Well.   And how are you now?"
Patient: "I'm still dead, doctor."
Doctor: "Did you do as I told you?"
Patient: "Yes doctor. Twice a day I looked at myself squarely in the
mirror and repeated three times, 'Dead men don't bleed.'"
Doctor: "Now tell me. Do you believe that statement?"
Patient: "Why, yes, surely, doctor."
The doctor then takes a scalpel from a tray, grasps the patient by the fore-
arm and slashes his wrist.
The patient looks at the spurting blood, looks up at the doctor and blurts
out, "My God! Dead men *do* bleed!"

like that they call it — I was in a hospital for four months when I got my eardrum knocked out — a Jerry shell — we was pinned down by mortar fire and one of 'em got my ear and it's alla time runnin' and when the wind blows past my ear it makes me dizzy and I wanta vomit and all that, see. And my stomach — them docs keep tellin' me there's nuthin wrong wit my stomach, see, but I can't keep nuthin on my stomach — Ya can see how skinny I am. Yeah. Just look at me! Ya can see what kinda shape I'm in."

Issues. This type of outpouring may often constitute a problem to the counselor in that it immediately raises the issue of medical examination. Some counselors may wish to arrange for an examination before going further. Other counselors may be willing to accept the person since he has not come seeking medical help but help in getting medical attention (for ills which he reports the physicians do not find). An observation which seems to hold largely true for non-medical counselors is that in our culture people with psychosomatic symptoms seek the socially acceptable solution of consulting a physician long before admitting emotional involvements sufficiently to permit consulting with the non-medical counselor.

Aside from what steps the counselor decides to take here, it is still possible to respond to the man's feelings. It is obvious to see that he is trying to convey to the counselor that the ailments are real and the physicians are wrong.

7. The client comes into the room, is seated, lights a cigarette, and in response to the counselor's opening query as to what the client wished to talk about, replies, "Well, several things, I guess. But they all boil down to an unresolved Oedipus. At least that's what both the analysts I've been to have said, and I guess they're right. One of them saw me for six months and the second for a year and a half. They might have spotted the source of my troubles but they didn't do me a damn bit of good."

Issues. One issue which might well be considered here is the handling of the intellectualized problem statement. For the client to speak of his problem as an "unresolved Oedipus" is not at all communicative of his feelings about the things which concern him.

The counselor may expect to meet such labelings in either technical or nontechnical terminology. Such labeling may continue in typically defensive manner. If the use of such a label is defensive, pushing for elucidation is likely to be resisted. If the label is not used defensively, no probing is necessary as the client will develop the meaning the label has for him.

A second point of discussion concerns the reactions of the counselor to the client's negatively expressed attitude toward the practitioners of a different form of psychotherapy. We must see clearly that our responsibilities lie with the client, that it is the client who is seeking help and our reactions set the climate in which he can work. Should the counselor indicate in any way that he shares or condones or agrees with the client's negative feelings, it might well operate to deny positive feelings which the client actually holds but has not or cannot currently express. It might deny many gains which the client made during the course of his earlier experiences. Or, should the counselor indicate in any way a disagreement with the client's negative feelings, the disagreement might well operate to threaten the client in the immediate present.

Actually, the counselor is not so apt to take sides when the client has previously seen a practitioner whom the counselor presumes to be a qualified and ethical individual. When, however, the client reports he has seen or plans to see a person in whom the counselor has no faith the counselor is more apt to be subject to stress. Should he or should he not advise the client? It appears to the writer that the situation which exists in the immediate relationship between the counselor and client is not altered just because the counselor does not share the client's belief in the integrity of a third person. Moreover, to suggest to the client that a person in whom the client does believe or tends to believe is not worthy is to imply stupidity or ignorance on the client's part. The avoidance of such a step seems desirable. Finally, it might be said that the success of the counselor must depend upon his own skill rather than upon the lack of skill in someone else.

A third issue that arises in this example relates to the place of diagnosis in psychotherapy. It might be noted here that the client apparently has the diagnosis but not the insight. The counselor-in-training will come to recognize more and more that psychotherapy is not a matter of passing on to the client the diagnosis achieved by the therapist but is more a matter of a "corrective emotional experience" on the part of the client. One may be led to conjecture concerning the reputed efficacy of interpretations to clients. It is conceivable that the "insight" produced may not be as helpful as the resistance — resistance in a psychological climate that accepts the resistance.

An effort to see the situation in the same way as the client sees it would probably involve the ideas that the client feels relatively certain of the area in which his difficulties lie although his efforts to date to solve the difficulties appear fruitless.

8. The client, a young woman in her early twenties, for several minutes pours out a story of marital difficulties. She relates that all of her friends advised against the marriage; that her husband is clearly neurotic, won't work, is critical of everything she does; that she is probably neurotic, too, but not as much so as her husband; that the situation is getting desperate. During the outpouring she bounces a small baby on her lap. The baby is whimpering. She explains that it is the baby's feeding time. At the conclusion of her story she asks, " — Well, you can see the situation. It's a hell of a mess. Now just what should I do? Can I send him in here to see you? Can this service you offer help him? I mean, really? We've heard a lot about this non-directive counseling and I don't see how it can help but — just what should I do?"

Issues. It is not unusual for a client to present his or her situation in such a manner and it is not at all unusual for a beginning counselor to get rather confused by the number of different directions in which he might travel.

Some of the different things to which the counselor might find himself wanting to respond are: the client's dependency; the client's reference to herself as neurotic; the client's reasons for going into marriage against the advice of others; the doubtful attitude the client has taken toward the counselor's methods; the rejection of the husband; the client's apparent unreadiness to accept help for herself. It seems clear that the client feels the husband is the one who *really* needs the help. It seems likely that to respond to the other possibilities listed would only serve to establish a relation-ship with the client characterized by cross purposes. In view of the client's response it is doubtful that we can say she has come for help for herself beyond that of meeting the immediate prob-lem of getting her husband to behave quite differently. She is not asking for help with her own behavior.

The counselor is faced with the decision of accepting the woman as his client, accepting that the husband is really to be the client or expecting that both are to be clients.

First, what can the counselor do for the woman as a client in the immediate present? In view of the client's apparent lack of desire for self-help it may very well be that little or nothing can be done except to provide as understanding a situation as possible in the event that she may wish to seek self-help — now or at a later date. There is also the question of whether or not she should be urged to accept help for herself. Such a course of action would probably be taken by therapists as a last resort because of the enormous advantage which accrues when the client takes the step toward therapy by himself as well as because of the threat which accompanies such external evaluation of another's inner life. There are times when the counselor may clearly recognize need in another but be helpless to meet it beyond understanding it. In this situation the counselor might seek to understand the client's desire to see the husband changed rather than a desire for self-help.

Second, what can the counselor do to leave the door open for the husband to come in — without at the same time doing damage to the wife? It would seem on first consideration that it would be simply a matter of saying that of course the services are available to her husband. It would be unfortunate, however, if this were done in such a way as to allow the client to feel that the counselor agreed with her in the notion that the husband was the one who needed help. It is easy enough to surmise that the wife is in all likelihood constantly conveying to the husband her feelings that he is the guilty party. It is doubtful that she needs any help in this. Should her feelings be confirmed, the probabilities are that she would only intensify the pressure on him, thus materially de-creasing the chances of his coming in. On the other hand, to imply that her desire to have her husband come in is *her* problem (in the sense of its being a projection) would only be to threaten her and possibly to a harmful degree. It would seem best in answering about the husband to reply that the services are available to him should *he* care to come in. Some counselors go a step farther and point out that they don't have much luck with people who come in when they don't really want to. These counselors feel that this may help the referring person to orient himself to the motives of the one he would refer and to more realistically meet the situation. The point is a moot one.

9. In response to the counselor's opening query, the client begins: "I came today particularly because it was precipitated by a talk with my adviser. I'm in the School of Education. And the precipitating factor is my adjustment academically. And I think there are many factors involved in it; but that is why I came today, because he indicated so many things are dependent upon good grades, so to speak, that I thought I had better do something about it to help me along. And this is my second quarter here and I think I am still in the process of adjusting to the "great" institution. And I didn't do too badly last quarter, but it wasn't as well as I used to do. This is my fourth year of school. And, however, I felt I would do better this quarter, but I'm not, and I'm not studying at all. I feel — I thought I knew myself and my capacities. I feel that I'm not doing as well as I could. I think I know just about how far I can go, but I'm not doing as well as I should be able to. And it is so important now for anything and everything I do within the next few years. And I'd like some help; perhaps in helping me in my study habits particularly, you can help me get rid of what's blocking me and all."

Issues. This type of response may be particularly seductive to many counselors-in-training, especially where a part of their training has emphasized remedial exercises. The whole response is filled with content likely to draw attention away from the feeling expressed and the response ends with an invitation to center attention on the study habits symptom. Had the client been an office worker the complaint might well have revolved about her distribution of energies on the job. Had the client been a housewife, we might expect complaints centering on her handling of her household and social obligations. The feeling of not achieving up to capacity is a very commonly met feeling and the content, the vehicle on which the feeling rides, will vary according to each client's situation.

10. The client begins his initial problem statement as follows: "Well, they told me over at the Bureau of Guidance — I went there to take some tests to see if I couldn't find a job that suited me better than the lineman's job I'm on now, you know, Illinois Bell — well, they gave me this bunch of tests (*pulls out a form showing the profile of test scores*) and I was low on this — (*looks at form*) — Emotional Stability test — so — they told me I'd better come over here and get whatever it is straightened out. (*Momentary pause.*) Just what do they mean by — or what is meant by 'emotional stability' anyway? I don't get it."

Issues. This problem statement is a typical defensive formulation. The client speaks of "emotional stability" as a thing which exists apart from himself as a person much as one might speak of a bad heart or a bad liver. If he is to make progress, he must come to accept and express his own feelings as his own feelings, something within himself rather than external to himself. The counselor might well feel that the question the man poses provides an opportunity to "structure" or in some way to teach the man what he must do to help himself.

There are two possible factors which would militate against such a step. First is the matter of his probable reaction to being further faced with the implication that something is wrong with him. For the counselor to "structure" or to respond in such a way as to try to point out to the man what all is involved and what he might do to help himself is only to demonstrate the counselor's conclusion that there is something wrong with the client. The client has indicated some recognition and acceptance by coming in but indicates a good deal of rejection of difficulty by his "externalization" of the situation.

The second factor which stands in opposition to a "structuring" or teaching response is the movement toward internalization already apparent in this one response. He moves from "*they* found this" and "*they* told me to come" to "*I* want to know what they mean." The counselor hopes to facilitate the client's consideration of his own (not other people's) feelings about his situation and clearly the man has expressed a concern of his own.

If defenses are presumed to be behavioral organizations which the client is incapable of reorganizing, then it would seem reasonable for the counselor to utilize some device for producing the reorganization for the client. If defenses are presumed to be present behavioral organizations which, while purposive and functional, are less immutable than characteristic at a given moment, the counselor may feel more free to attend to the client's struggle to make sense of his situation. The client in this example seems to be struggling to achieve some satisfactory formulation of what "they" have said about him and how he views himself.

C. Closing the beginning interview

1. The counselor has just responded to the client's last comment relative to her questioning attitude toward the significance for her of pregnancy. A slight pause ensues, at which point the counselor says, "I see that our time is up, perhaps we should stop for today. Would you like to come back?"

The client replies, "Yes, I think so. Will this help? Of course I know that you can't say, but do you think I will get a sense of calm out of it?"

Issues. Such requests for reassurance are not at all uncommon and many clients have been willing to return even in the face of considerable reassurance given by counselors. Obviously the counselor cannot guarantee the client the results desired. Moreover, there is no assurance for the counselor that the client's demands or desires in the way of outcomes are at all obtainable or reasonable.

Because the counselor cannot give an out-and-out guarantee and because he feels the pressure of the client's need for reassurance, he may succumb to an indirect method of supporting the client. He may, for example, begin to relate the statistical probabilities of successful outcome. He may relate instances of success with other clients. He may comment reassuringly on the effort with which the client has tackled the problem during the interview, implying that such efforts might well yield success.

The giving of reassurance by the counselor, however, may not be accompanied by the acceptance of reassurance on the part of the client. Wanting the client to feel reassured and implementing that want through supportive comments cannot guarantee the client's feeling reassured. Moreover, there is a real question of whether the course of therapy is not retarded when the energizing discomfort is reduced. A more serious question arises when one considers the possible consequences of having implied a successful outcome to a client who does not achieve it. It is quite reasonable to expect that the client's doubts about himself would only be increased as the result of failure in the face of what was supposed to be success. A third question arises when one stops to realize the dependency the counselor invites through reassurance at such a point and the opportunity he misses of fostering independence in the client. Still a fourth question can be raised against reassurance here. The deeply dependent client may not be able to accept the amount of reassurance a counselor is willing to give and may continue to press the counselor for more and more, with the counselor ending up trying to put the client off and the client feeling rejected rather than reassured. Through reassurance the counselor may find himself in a poor position with a client who is set to prove that the counselor can do nothing for him. Such a client can engage the counselor in a battle of wits, always jumping into the loophole the counselor has left for himself. In these battles the winner is always the client.

It is so obvious as to be painful that the client in this response is expressing hope that a sense of calm and inner peace will come out of the counseling. The counselor in this case responded to this hope. The client affirmed the counselor's response and the counselor followed with, "OK. I'll see you on Tuesday."

It seems appropriate at this point to remark that a great deal of successful movement in therapy can be judged by what doesn't happen. Of all the mis-movement that could have taken place at this point in the interview none did.

2. A young man of twenty has just expressed his concern over the direction his art work has taken and the morbid element which has entered it. The time set for the interview elapses and the counselor speaks, "Well, I see our time is about up. And when would you like to come back in again?"

Client: "Uh, well, when are you free? — and then I could work that out probably a little easier."

Issues. This situation appears to be entirely innocuous. It appears that the client is merely asking what times the counselor has open. This seems especially understandable when it is known that the client works and is not free to come at just any hour. Notice, however, that through this reply the client has not accepted the responsibility for stating when he would like to return, thus leaving the counselor in darkness. One might say that for the counselor to be cautious here is for him to be over-cautious, that for the client to express himself thus is perfectly reasonable and polite. This may or may not be so. We can, however, bear in mind that a less dependent person would more likely have spoken out for what he wanted and then have expressed the willingness to adjust the hour. A counselor does not foster dependency in a client in one overwhelming moment. Dependency is fostered in little steps. This could be one of them. The counselor in this case replied in such a way as to indicate that the client's wishes came first as he, the counselor, could be free most hours.

3. The client, a man of thirty-two, has experienced a great deal of difficulty in expressing his concerns until just before the end of the interview period. At a late point he begins to talk quite openly of things which concern him deeply. He is obviously not ready to stop. The counselor breaks in to say that the time is up.

Client: "What? Already? I've got so much more I want to say and I'm finally able for the first time to actually say it. Look, can't I have just a few minutes more?"

Issues. There are two issues involved here: (1) should the counselor have broken in to call time, and (2) should the counselor give the client the extra time he asks for?

A number of reasons have been advanced for setting and keeping a limit on the length of the interview hour. Among them are the following. A definite stopping point gives the client an additional factor for which he must accept responsibility — he must accept this limitation on his ability to manipulate his environment. A definite stopping point tends to prevent the development of anxiety which might ensue in the face of an uncertain stopping point. A definite stopping point provides him with a known period which he is free to use as he sees fit and avoids the possible arousal of guilt feelings when he is uncertain as to whether he is imposing on the counselor's time.

The writer prefers to think of the matter of time limits in terms of the attitudes of the counselor in setting, in altering or in any dealing with the limits — the attitudes of the counselor and the psychological climate they provide. First and foremost will be the division of attitude on the issue of whether the client can really be responsible for himself or whether he must be manipulated by the counselor. If the counselor holds the former attitude, he will perceive no need for not calling time on the client; the client, having been responsible for himself so far, is not suddenly a different being. If the counselor holds the latter attitude and perceives a need for manipulation of the termination point, he must decide what is best for the client. The former attitude provides a climate which embodies implications of responsibility, independence and capability. The latter attitude provides a climate embodying implications of dependence, inability and incapacity for responsibility.

It seems clear that the problems surrounding the decision of whether or not to call time on the client apply also to whether or not to extend the time. One issue which arises should the counselor decide not to extend the time is the possible effect upon the client. A refusal to extend may arouse hostility and feelings of rejection on the part of the client. Moreover, many counselors refuse to conduct themselves in a closed, rigid manner adhering to one answer only. One way of meeting the dual criteria of respecting the client's integrity and yet remaining flexible when the client asks for more time (and the counselor is free to give the extra time) is for the counselor to enter into a new time contract with the client and then continue the interview. Should the counselor not have the free time, the response he makes might well touch on the client's keenness to continue, incorporate an apology for the disappointment he may feel and raise the question of when he might like to return. Here, as in all other parts of the relationship with the client, sincerity of the counselor is at a premium.

4. The client, a young married woman of twenty-five, has spent the interview period in struggling to decide whether she really wants or needs counseling and to decide whether she really does or does not have a problem. It is clear to the counselor that the woman is confused, dependent and in a position for which counseling could be of real aid to her. When the counselor indicates the hour is up and asks her wishes about another appointment she replies, "Well, do you think I should come back again? Do you think I've got a real problem here — I'm neurotic or something? I'd be willing to come back, if you think it will help any."

Issues. There are three basic positions which can be taken by the counselor in regard to the dependency of the client's behavior: (1) the counselor may feel she should come back and express his feeling accordingly; (2) the counselor may feel she should come back but withhold direct expression of this feeling; and (3) the counselor may honestly not know whether coming back is or is not to the client's best interests.

As the counselor-in-training progresses in clinical work, both in diagnostic training and in interviewing experience, he is going to become more and more aware of "pathology" on all sides of him, he will come to see much "normal" behavior as serving defensive functions. These things he will begin to see in his friends, his relatives, his co-workers, the incidental acquaintance, and even the man at the counter of the soda fountain. The trainee may well reach the conclusion that if everybody, including himself, doesn't *need* some psychotherapy he could at least *use* some. In short, much of the trainee's experience will furnish him a basis for responding to the client in the example above as being in need of or being in a position to use further help. The counselor may feel it his professional obligation to give an honest answer to the client.

At the same time that the counselor is becoming increasingly aware of the "needs" which exist in others he will become increasingly aware that the presence of a "need" in a person is not necessarily accompanied by an acceptance or awareness of that "need." He will also become acutely aware that pointing out "needs" to a client does not assure acceptance by the client. On the basis of such knowledge, born out of textbooks but "really" learned by nearly every counselor through experience, the counselor may choose to withhold the expression of his opinion regarding the client's "needs" lest the client be more apt to resist and break off the relationship.

What do we hope to achieve through counseling and psychotherapy? Is it not to help the client to become more and more independent of the judgments of others as to how he should act and more and more dependent upon himself, the lessons of his own experiences? Some will feel strongly that this can be done only if the client is willing and able to surrender a measure of his independence until the unknown determinants of his behavior can be brought to light and under control. Others will feel strongly that such a notion is probably faulty in its assumptions about the resources of the human personality to achieve greater independence of others and greater dependence on self without temporary surrender of independence during the uncovering of unknown behavior determinants. If this latter assumption is correct, or to the extent that it is correct, the time for tapping the client's resources is now. The question becomes not one of whether the client should return or whether the client would likely profit by returning but rather a question of what can be done at this moment to help the client mobilize the resources at his command. An attempt to foster independence at this moment (for the client in the example) might well be through an effort to convey understanding of her feelings of confusion and feelings of inability to decide for herself what she wants or needs to do.

5. A young woman in nursing training has been referred to the counselor by the training institution because of consistent resistance to supervision. The hour has been spent by the client going over the injustices which she feels have been heaped upon her and how it seems to be a continuation of the same situation she experienced in her home life. As the counselor

indicates that the time is up and asks what she would like to do about another appointment, the young woman replies, "You know, I don't think I need to come back. I think I see what the problem is now — for the first time in my life I think I see. (*Slight pause.*) No, I don't think I'll be back. Thanks so much for your time. I think you've really given me something."

Issues. How much real help can a person get from a single contact? Does the counselor have a responsibility to encourage a client to work through problems to clearly recognized solutions?

One situation which every therapist must face is the matter of who is to decide when the interviews should terminate: the counselor, the client, or both. If one assumes when he accepts a client for therapy that he takes on an obligation to see the client through to his, the therapist's, satisfaction, it is likely that he would feel it necessary to ask the client above to return. If one assumes that his job is limited to providing a situation which a client can use as desired, then he takes on no obligation to judge or think for the client. Every counselor must decide toward which assumption he leans for here, as in the great majority of the issues in psychotherapy there can be no real compromise, no real eclecticism. Either one accepts responsibility for the client or one accepts responsibility only for himself and the situation he can create. The therapist may compromise with his own feelings in such a situation as this by explaining to the client that if she should decide in the future to come in again she would be free to do so. Although subtle, such a counselor response seems clearly to be based upon the assumption that the client probably has more to work through. A counselor who is really willing to permit the client to use the situation as the client wishes would be willing to accept the client's decision as it is made and respond to the client's feeling of clarity and control over her situation.

6. At the end of the hour when the counselor asks the client, a young man of about twenty-five, what he would like to do about another appointment the client replies, "*I* don't know. I kinda get the feeling that you must be thinking, 'Why is he coming in here taking up my time? He hasn't got any real problem. Why doesn't he take his little, trivial concerns and leave me alone to work with people who really need help.'"

Issues. This is one of the clearer examples of an invitation to support. Should the counselor meet the expressed need? Many counselors might well feel that the client should be given encouragement here, that the client should be led to feel that he is worthy of the help the therapist can give. Such a feeling of worthiness might well be desirable for the client to possess. However, possibly he wouldn't be in for help if he did feel worthy. Assuming that it is desirable that he not feel unworthy of the counselor's help, there is still the question of the counselor's conduct most likely to foster the change. To offer reassurance even in a subtle form is in effect to deny the client's feelings. Were the client to face his feelings directly it might well lead to their changing. A non-supportive, non-denying effort to understand the client's feelings would involve the client's struggle with his feelings of unworthiness in the form they take for him at this moment, namely, the struggle to decide whether or not his problems which seem so important to him are "really" important.

In the case from which this example was taken the client repeated this expression during the second and third interviews. At the opening of the fourth interview he announced proudly that he knew now what he had been trying to do. He went on to state that he had been endeavoring to get the counselor to offer reassurance, to say, in effect, that of course the counselor was interested in working with him. Should the counselor have offered any reassurance, he continued, then he could be friends with the counselor but could have no real trust in the counselor because obviously anyone who thought him worthy was stupid. The client's apparently innocuous bid for reassurance had turned into a very live issue which served as a springboard for a deeper exploration into his motivational life.

7. In this example the client, a man of 42, has spent the major portion of the hour in relating events about which he is troubled but with little reference to how he feels about them and with the general air, "Here they are. You fix 'em up!" When time is called and he is asked what he wishes to do about another appointment, he replies, "Now look! I've told you about all these things and all you do is just listen. That's okay, I guess: you're

supposed to know what you're doing — *but* — what I want to know is this — what good is just talking about all this going to do?"

Issues. Here is a response which can be interpreted to have elements of hostility, resistance, need for information, non-readiness for therapy, uncertainty and/or possibly other things as well.

If we view the client more or less as a reacting machine which is to be manipulated by setting before it the proper stimulus patterns against which to react, then we must calculate how to respond to the client at this point. On the other hand, if we view the client as an autonomous system capable of self-direction and self-alteration when given an environment which does not seek to press him in any direction, then possibly the most effective response will be to try to understand the expressed uncertainty the client feels with the counseling method as an attack upon his problems.

Probably one of the most difficult things for a counselor to learn is to face away from the immediate goal he would like to see approached. Certainly we all want to see our clients have sufficient understanding and faith in the methods we use, regardless of what the methods are, to carry them through whatever the therapeutic process is. We are all quite certain that it is usually impossible to convey much if any understanding through descriptions alone. An understanding and faith in the therapeutic process comes to clients through the experiences they have with the therapeutic situation. We are forced, then, to restrain ourselves from a direct approach. We must provide experiences for the client from which the client can learn what therapy is like. This learning to do something else is a common task for all therapists. It does not seem reasonable to assume that the final answer to the necessity for an indirect approach is always to be found in the client as "resistance." Resistance is not a thing: you can't paint it, you can't weigh out a pound of it, you can't put it on the floor and stumble over it. Resistance is a name which identifies a complex phenomenon but does not describe it. How much of resistance will eventually be described in terms of threat and defense, how much in terms of reaction to perceptual or conceptual inconsistencies, how much in terms of motivational conflict, or how much in other terms is difficult to guess. It has been suggested that a substantial part of the resistance found in therapy may be a product of the psychological atmosphere provided for the client rather than a product of the client's psychological operations per se.

8. The client, a young housewife of about twenty-five, replies to the counselor's question regarding another appointment by saying, "Well, no. I don't see any reason why I should — ah — what I'm trying to say is that I can't see that you're doing anything for me. I'm not completely unsophisticated about these things and I've given you several opportunities — or rather — invitations to give your slant — view on these things — well, specific points where I feel confused. I certainly don't expect you to come out with any world-shaking answers nor do I even expect you to be able to give me any specific answers to any of these questions I have — but by gosh I did expect you to at least think with me once in a while. — Ah — and since you don't seem inclined to help me I — ah — I see no reason to return. (*Slight pause.*) That is unless you have — unless you feel that I've got it all wrong or something."

Issues. Here, as in the consideration of any single client response unit, the reader may feel frustrated with not having more information concerning the client and what has preceded the response under consideration. Many readers will feel that to consider the single response is a procedure so atomistic as to be of doubtful value. Such a notion may well be correct. As yet no experimental evidence is available on which to base an evaluation of any given unit of consideration as most helpful. In the opinion of the writer the judgment one makes as to the most helpful or meaningful unit of client performance is more a function of the judge's attitudes and conceptions of personality and therapeutic process than it is a function of the client's performance per se. If the counselor feels the client must be "seen through," must be known for what he is rather than for what he sees himself to be, then it is only reasonable to expect that the counselor should wish to consider larger samples of the client's performance, samples large enough to "give the client away." On the other hand, if the judge feels understanding the client as the client sees the immediate situation is the desired state of affairs, it is questionable whether larger units of client performance will always be helpful. Larger units of consideration may well expose the counselor to the client's inconsistencies (at least they should, providing the counselor is minimally sensitive) and being thus exposed the counselor may be subject to confusion as to the client's meaning at the immediate moment. This can be considered as a hazard for the counselor and yet it is one which he must face. As an interview or series of interviews progresses the counselor will be exposed to additional knowledge about the client whether he likes it or not. One skill a counselor may develop is to use this additional knowledge not to see beyond or through the client but to see more clearly with the client.

There are two more issues which might be raised in connection with the example: (a) what *can* be done with a client who is all but leaving the interview relationship as is this client and (b) how much responsibility should the counselor feel for each client who comes to him for help?

Sooner or later the counselor must come to accept that not all clients will carry through with a complete therapeutic experience. Some clients are going to terminate at the end of the first interview. On first consideration this may strike the reader as being bad, as being evidence of failure. Maybe this interpretation of events is the best but it is not the only possible interpretation which is open to consideration. We tend to think of the work we do as being successful only to the extent that a client works through his situation both extensively and intensively. Quite apart and almost as if it were unrelated to our work we also think of the client's readiness for therapy. Clearly, very little is known as to how a readiness for self-examination comes about in an individual. Possibly many clients who terminate in the early stages of the interview series are not engaged in seeking therapy but are engaged in becoming ready for therapy, in reaching a sufficiently clear conception of their situation and their own desire to receive help that they can go ahead. Possibly one of the most helpful things a counselor can do is clearly to leave the decision in the hands of the client as to whether or not to continue. Paradoxical as it may seem, experience indicates that when counselors feel free of having to make the decisions for the clients, feel free of having to encourage the clients in any way and feel free to accept the clients' decisions no matter which way they go, more clients feel free to continue and do continue. In a sense this should not seem at all paradoxical since the presence of encouragement or urging is an expression of the counselor's judgment that the client does need help, that there is something wrong with him. It is difficult to conceive of the client who would not be threatened by such a judgment. Possibly, then, what we should do with a terminating client is to accept him as he is. Possibly, too, we should not accept responsibility for the client but accept responsibility for the one thing we can control, the psychological climate we provide for him.

The notion that premature termination may represent a successful step forward for the client even though the counselor may feel it to have indicated failure gains additional credibility when attention is turned to what happens to clients subsequent to such terminations. A number of such clients return at a later date. At this later time they seem to be much more "ready" to turn their attention to their own feelings. A number of such clients return for help at a later date but to proponents of other therapeutic approaches. The writer has known of a number of such cases where persons apparently unable to utilize client-centered therapy subsequently entered into psychoanalytic therapy and were quite successful. The writer is also familiar with an even greater number of clients who were unsuccessful in a psychoanalytic relationship but who, at later dates, were successful in a client-centered therapeutic relationship. The concept of "psychotherapeutic readiness" cannot be disregarded entirely nor dismissed as not falling within the scope of the counselor's possible contribution to a client.

9. A woman of forty has spent the hour in what seems to have been a more or less usual process of recounting her difficulties with some superficial examination into them. When asked if she wishes to return, she replies, "Why yes, I would. I think by now you should have a pretty fair notion of my situation — I can't think of anything I've left out — of importance, anyway — and so, yes, — ah — now I want to come back and get some answers, get the answers to what I should do. Same time next week? Do you have that time open? — it's best for me."

Issues. What should the counselor do here? Should he disregard the material about getting "the answers" in the hope that the client will not present such a demand at the next interview? Should he structure; explain the therapeutic relationship and how it is not a matter of the counselor's supplying "answers"? Should he reflect the client's feeling that she has done her part and now it's the counselor's turn? Should the counselor "go along" with her and plan to deal with the situation next time? Should the counselor respond in such a way as to encourage the client's attitude of expecting the counselor to provide "the answers"? Should he discourage the attitude toward "the answers" but encourage her to return?

Most therapists, if not all, would agree that it is extremely unlikely that she will get "the answers" in the following session. Does this mean, then, that the counselor has an obligation to convey this information to the client? Many therapists will respond in the affirmative. It would seem quite reasonable that an affirmative response should be made on the basis that clients should not be misled, that counselors should seek to be honest in their dealings with clients. In the writer's opinion the issue at hand is really not one of honesty or dishonesty with the client. The therapist here is dealing with a dependency reaction. It seems entirely unlikely that the therapist would be prompted to point out to a client the unreality of dependent expectations with respect to some other person or event. It is when dependent reactions involve the counselor directly that he is often led into feeling that "this situation is different." How different is it in the life of the client? Why should dependency on the counselor be conceived as different from dependency on someone else? Possibly responding to the expressed feeling will bring the feeling more clearly into focus where the client can struggle with it directly. Possibly the client will terminate.

10. In this example the client is a young man of about twenty-five. The interview has proceeded rather quietly until at the close of the first interview the client suddenly sobs out, "God! I don't know whether I want to come back or not. I'm telling you this is terrible! I feel that if I go into this any further I'm going to find something so horrible about myself that it

will damage my personality beyond repair — for all time —
that I'll never recover. I feel like I'm on the edge of a precipice — just one more step and down I go — and by God I don't
want to end up in a hospital — I don't want to."

Issues. When a counselor is suddenly faced with feelings as strong
as these, delivered by a person feeling extremely pressed and
panic-stricken, the counselor may find his own autonomic nervous
system is in splendid functioning order. Even though the client
is not making a bid for reassurance the counselor may hasten to
offer reassurance or at least he may want very much to do so.
Counselors are threatenable, too, and can be thrust into impulsive
behavior by their own emotional reactions. Assuming, however,
that the counselor is in control of his reactions, there is the problem of whether or not to attempt to lighten the client's load. The
literature in psychology seems to be consistent in observing that
denial of feeling and repression of feeling is more likely to do
harm to the personality than is expression and acceptance of the
feeling. It would seem more reasonable that the counselor's energies be directed toward facilitating the client's expression and acceptance of the dread he feels than that the counselor's energies
be directed toward suppressing or denying the client's feelings.
How one sides on this issue will be related to how much trust
one feels can be placed in the capacity of the client to deal with
his own situation.

❋   ❋   ❋   ❋   ❋

Exercise 9. Suggested formulations of responses.

A–1. "That is, the concerns that brought you here don't seem quite
so great now that you're here. Is that it?"

A–2. "It's the difficulty you're meeting with this decision rather than
the feeling something is wrong that is bringing you here."

A–3. "I'm a ——— . I take it that it's important to you in some way
to know this."

A–4. "You have some things that you want to talk over but you feel
uncertain as to how to begin, is that it?"

A–5. "That's the problem, is it, just one lost job after another?"

A–6. "If I understand you correctly, then, you feel the Dean has
misjudged the situation: that you're pretty well aware of what's
going on."

A–7. "I see. It's curiosity that brings you rather than something that is of concern to you."

A–8. "In other words, you have this immediate decision pressing on you yet these more personal things seem to be standing right in the way."

A–9. "I gather you feel the situation has gone so far you just feel helpless in the face of it."

A–10. (No suggestions.)

B–1. "You feel you have every reason to be content, and that makes it very puzzling why you should be troubled as you are."

B–2. "You don't feel like others, but you would like to change."

B–3. "Now that you're here you feel confused in trying to bring out the things which you planned to talk about, is that it?"

B–4. "I gather you feel deeply concerned as to whether the future is as inevitable as it appears."

B–5. "Your interest is there and your health is there, but where to use them constructively, that's what has you stumped."

B–6. "They tell you there's nothing wrong with you but you feel you're really sick for sure."

B–7. "In other words, even though you haven't gotten the help you wanted you do feel fairly sure where your difficulties may lie."

B–8. "It's not for yourself that you've come for help, but more that you're groping for *some* way to get your husband straightened out — is that it?"

B–9. "You're just not stacking up to what you felt surely you could and should do: is that it?"

B–10. "That is, they've suggested there may be some emotional difficulty, but I gather you're not at all sure as to just how it fits in with you."

C–1. "I gather that that sense of inner peace and calm is what you would really hope might come out of these interviews."

C–2. "Well, that would depend in part on you. I could work in *most* times."

C–3. "Yes, I believe so. (*Looks at appointment book.*) We can go for another ——— minutes. Would that be satisfactory?"
(*Alternative, in the event of no available time.*)
"I gather you *are* quite keen to continue right now but I'm afraid I'll have to disappoint you. What would you like to do about another appointment?"

C–4. "There's real confusion there — is that it — and you just feel you can't decide within yourself what you want or should do."

C–5. "I see. In other words you feel the situation is sufficiently clear to you now that you can swing it yourself."

C–6. "*You* feel them to be important but — *are* they? Is that the question?"

C–7. "You feel pretty uncertain as to whether this is the way to tackle these things."

C–8. "As far as *you* are concerned, then, you feel pretty certain that this is not going to help — but not completely certain — is that it?"

C–9. "I gather you feel that you've done your part and from here on it's up to me? Yes. Same time next week is fine."

C–10. "It's terrifying for you to think of going ahead."

Chapter VI

TYPICAL PROBLEMS IN THE

MIDDLE AND CLOSING PHASES

It is clear that unless the beginning interview is successfully handled the counselor may have no reason to be concerned with the problems of subsequent interviews. The problems which arise in later interviews are different from the problems of the first interview only in the matter of degree, not in kind. Each interview must be opened. In each interview the client deals with the current status of his problem situation. Each interview must be closed. The same elements will be present which will lead some therapists to support, to probe, to interpret or to evaluate and other therapists to understand.

As subsequent interviews progress the problems concerning which counselors must make decisions grow in complexity and subtlety. The continuing relationship will introduce such factors as familiarity, which may block the therapist's vision at points and lead him into a social role and away from the role of therapist. The continuing relationship may lead the counselor into an identification with the difficulties of the client and result in the therapist's taking steps that he would never think of taking in a beginning interview. We may muster logical reasons on all sides to support such inconsistencies in therapist behavior. In time such reasoning must be validated against the fact that in therapy as in any other learning situation we are dealing with lawful processes, processes which are not capricious and inconsistent. We must be careful not

123

to assume that because learning takes place in the client our actions as counselors caused that learning process to occur. It seems more profitable to hypothesize that as the learning process takes place our actions influence it in direction, in speed, and in content. An interpretation to a client may appear to speed insight yet retard the learning of independence.

The exercises which follow will most certainly not communicate all the subtleties which go into therapeutic interviewing. The hope is that the exercises will provide at least a suggestion of the directions and degrees in which subtleties can exist.

In considering the beginning interview it seemed excusable to break down the problems into those connected with opening the interview, the initial statement of difficulty and closing the interview. In considering subsequent interviews the writer does not feel it to be excusable to adopt any categorization as very meaningful. In accordance with this notion the exercises which follow will not be given any special order. Problems will be presented which relate to openings, closings, negative feelings, positive feelings, ambivalences, strong expressions, indirect expressions or any other type of situation regardless of where it might have occurred in the interview.

1. In this example the client is a young man of twenty-four. Three days earlier he had been interviewed for the first time and had asked for an appointment at 9:00 A.M. on this day. It is now 8:45 and the client comes in, visibly disturbed and upset. The counselor is standing in the hall conversing with another counselor. The client approaches with quick steps and blurts out, "Can I see you right now? I've just got to see you right away!"

Issues. The central issue in such a situation is whether the counselor will see the client immediately or have the client wait the fifteen minutes until his scheduled time. Restated, the question might be phrased, "Will the counselor meet the expressed need of the client or will he seek to avoid meeting that need?"

Many counselors on viewing a situation such as this feel that one must either meet the client's need or reject the client, that *not* to meet the client's expressed need *is* to reject the client. Paradoxical as it may appear other counselors feel that *to* meet the client's need is to reject the client. Obviously both can't be right. In the land of paradoxes, psychotherapy, both can be right though opposed. The counselor who feels he must meet the need of the client or reject him is apparently perceiving the dependent need of the client and acting so as not to reject it. The counselor who feels that to meet the dependent need is to reject the client apparently is perceiving as more important the autonomy need of the client and acting in such a way as not to reject it.

It is the writer's opinion that one of the most pernicious and deleterious tendencies which has characterized the thinking of psychotherapists is the tendency to perceive people in psychological difficulties as basically helpless, as incapable of reordering their lives without outside guidance. It is almost as if psychotherapists were incapable of seeing the constructive forces within the troubled person. No matter how negatively this tendency among therapists might be evaluated, it is quite understandable how they might be led in that direction. Clients or patients do not tend to speak of their strengths during the interviews. They speak of their inadequacies, their lacks of strength. They may go to extreme lengths in vociferous denials of any strength or in expression of terrifying fears of having no strengths. Are we to be seduced by their verbalizations into disregarding the strength they are demonstrating in even daring to tackle their troublesome conditions?

If the therapist seeks to establish a dependency relationship, he may well wish to take advantage of the opportunity offered by the client's feeling of urgent need. On the other hand, if the therapist seeks to use this as a small but yet a real opportunity to help the client depend more upon his own strength than upon the counselor's, he may well reflect the client's feelings of urgency but ask the client to wait until the appointed time.

Earlier there was discussed a situation in which the client asked for more time at the conclusion of an interview. There as here is the question of how honestly can the counselor ask the client to wait. If the therapist clearly has other pressing duties, it would seem that he would not be dishonest nor playing a role in asking the client to wait. If he has work he had planned to do but which could wait, the situation becomes ambiguous and the therapist will have to fall back upon what he is willing to do. If he has nothing to legitimately occupy him, asking the client to wait would seem either dishonest or clearly judgmental regarding what is best for the client. In such a case the counselor might wish to ask the client if he would like to start his "hour" now.

Problems of early arrival as a dependent demand will face the counselor from time to time. The setting given in this example (a fifteen-minute period) was chosen because it is neither gross enough nor inconsequential enough to force all counselors to agree in what they would do. The counselor must reach a decision at some point, however. If he would accede to seeing the client fifteen minutes early, why not accede to the client who arrives early by sixteen minutes, by seventeen, by eighteen, by nineteen, by — ? Where does one stop?

2. The client, a hospitalized patient on an open ward, arrived about fifteen minutes late for the twenty-first interview in the series. He had arrived late several times before.

Client: "Late again."
Counselor: (*Adjusts volume level of recording machine.*) "That's all right."
Client: "We had a pretty lively session today. (*Client refers to group-therapy session which precedes his individual session.*) There were six of us there. I mean they did. I didn't speak very much — as usual."
Counselor: "One of those prolonged sessions again, huh?"
Client: "Yeah. (*Pause*) I don't seem to have much to say today."

Issues. Here the counselor has made two errors, errors he probably would not have made in a beginning interview. The problems of opening this interview, however, are no different from opening a beginning interview.

The client starts off with the expression of a feeling. In this case it is not clear just what feeling is being expressed in the client's "Late again." If we were able to see him and hear him say it, possibly we could agree as to what he was saying. The counselor's error comes in treating the patient in a social rather than a therapeutic manner. The therapist attempts to indicate directly to the client that his lateness is not being held against him. Acceptance rather than condemnation could have been equally well expressed had the counselor endeavored to respond directly to the client's feelings as expressed. Even if the counselor had not caught the feeling, it was not of evident help to play the social role. Possibly a flow of feeling could have been tapped had the counselor stuck to his therapy.

Some readers may be thinking at this point that the significant element in the client's lateness is the evidence it bears of probable hostility toward the counselor. Without arguing the accuracy of the diagnostic inference there is, nevertheless, a great deal of room for arguing about the therapeutic efficacy of a direct use of the inference in an interpretation to the client.

The second error the therapist made was in responding to the client's second remark in terms of his, the counselor's own feelings about "prolonged" sessions. Possibly this is being hard on the counselor. It might be that he was responding to a faulty "adding up" of the client's expression and the elements of the total situation: (1) the client had been in a group therapy session, (2) the session presumably had gone overtime, (3) the client was late; ergo, the session was a prolonged one. What the counselor failed to respond to was the client's allusion to the "pretty lively session" in which "I didn't speak very much — ." Possibly had the counselor responded to the client's feeling that even though he hadn't participated much he was really interested in what went on, the client may very well have brought out in discussion what had been of such interest to him. As it was, the client didn't feel he had much to say.

In addition to the questions raised about the counselor's playing of a social role, there is a question of what is to be done when a client reaches an apparent impasse expressed in the terms, "I don't seem to have much to say today." Should a topic be suggested by the therapist? Should the client be offered encouragement? Should the counselor offer to terminate the hour? Should the counselor "structure," that is, define the client's role in the relationship? Should the therapist attempt to reflect the client's feeling of "nothing to say"? Should the therapist just wait and say nothing?

Let us first consider the possibilities which would exist were we to respond to the content, the subject matter of the words he uses.

He has said, in effect, that he has little to say. If that is accepted as a fact rather than a feeling, the implication would be that to spend further time is probably fruitless. This notion can be discarded. It is obvious that the client must have a great deal to consider or he would not still be hospitalized.

Perceiving the client's expression as a feeling of having little to say, however, does not automatically suggest how the therapist should respond. The counselor might moralize with the client by indicating in his reply that the client shouldn't feel that way, that of course he has plenty to talk about. The counselor might interpret the client's feeling as signifying resistance (especially in the light of his lateness) and respond in such a way as to try to lead the client to consider this possibility in his behavior. The counselor might decide to probe for some material, knowing that the client's expression is only a feeling and not a fact. The therapist might hasten to respond in such a way as to try to reassure the client that it is perfectly all right for him to feel that way and possibly he wants to quit for the day. The therapist may decide that the client has a "need" to be met here, a "need" for not going ahead at the moment and the therapist may act to fulfill that need (thereby disregarding a possible "need" to go ahead which is more indirectly expressed). The therapist may simply endeavor to convey his understanding and acceptance of the client's feeling and leave with the client the responsibility of going ahead or stopping. If the counselor really is willing to leave the responsibility unequivocably with the client, at least the client will have only his own feelings to battle with in deciding whether to leave or stay.

3. The client in this example is an undergraduate student. In the second interview he states, "Well, I felt that for the last year and a half when I first came to this school, I didn't have that incentive, that goal, goal to seek, so I more or less — I did my work, but with no particular end in mind, just merely to get through the school, get my degree. My degree was the end and it didn't seem particularly, uh, well, didn't seem particularly, much of an incentive that I didn't know exactly what I was going into. Well I looked over the courses and I finally decided what I liked best and what I could do best in and I still don't

know. I'll probably have to take vocational guidance to make sure and see what they tell me; and if they corroborate my own likes and my own plans why I'll go right ahead. At any rate I'd like to see what they have to say."

Issues. The first issue which arises is whether or not the counselor should refer the client to a vocational adviser or vocational guidance agency where tests might be procured. Another facet of the issue is whether the counselor might decide to give the tests himself, presuming, of course, that he has adequate facilities at hand.

If the goal of the therapeutic experience which the therapist seeks to provide for the client is the goal of providing better answers to the client's problems, then surely any answers that offer promise should be investigated. On the other hand, if the goal the therapist seeks is the reduction of the factors within the client which make problems for the client, the therapist may view answer-giving as only reinforcing the problem-making processes. Again we are faced with the basic decision of whether or not we should endeavor to meet the expressed needs of the client.

It is interesting to note that the client reports that he selected — "what I liked best and what I could do best in —," " — and if they corroborate my own likes and my own plans why I'll go right ahead." Isn't the problem here that for reasons as yet unknown the client seems unable to be certain of what he is certain he likes and can do best in? Why the uncertainty of such certainty? What part is being played by the feeling that he can be certain of himself only from outside corroboration?

4. The same client goes on later in the interview to discuss some of his actions into which he had gained an element of insight. "Mhm. I'm even, I'm just amazed at the way I can fool myself, that way. And, uh, I thought about it, and I thought that maybe there was something seriously wrong with my personality, maybe some, well these conversations these — the good me and the bad one, so called, they tend — at one time I was very worried about whether I was completely a schizoid personality. I wasn't worried about it seriously. I don't worry about —."

Issues. Many a beginning counselor may decide that when the client begins to talk of a "schizoid personality" the time has come to make a referral or at least to give serious consideration to such a course of action. As obvious as it may seem, we must bear in mind that technical terminology is increasingly finding its way into the language of the layman. It is not at all unusual to find such a term as part of the language behavior of a college student. The use of the term does not assure the presence of the condition to which the term refers.

In the interviews from which this recorded excerpt was taken the counselor was apparently impressed with the marked discomfiture being experienced by the client as he discussed the situation which led him to bring up, tentatively, and rapidly reject his fears of a serious personality disorder. The counselor responded with "A really valid situation (*referring to the situation described by the client just before his present remark*) which made you raise that question, disturbing as it might be." Should the counselor have forced, in a sense, the client to face that the question is disturbing to him when the client has clearly hastened to add, " — I wasn't worried about it seriously. I don't worry about — "? Here is a real issue in therapy: do you really let the client go at his own pace or do you try to "lead him on"?

Another question we might bring up is whether the counselor should seek to name for the client the emotional or affective state being experienced by the client. In his reply above the counselor did respond by labeling the client's affective experience of the moment even though the client had verbally sought to deny it.

A response which deals more completely with what the client is experiencing and perceiving would involve not only the disturbing nature of the question which had arisen in the client's mind but would further involve the client's present expression of its no longer being of such great concern.

Let us suppose for the moment that the client is really quite concerned about whether or not his behavior is indicative of a serious disorder. Let us suppose further that the client is quite aware that he is side-stepping an open expression of his concern by his " — I wasn't worried about it seriously — " statement. What is the therapist's task here? The counselor can endeavor to force an admission, to force the client, as it were, to face himself. This hardly seems justifiable, if we grant at the outset that the client already recognizes what he is doing. One way to view the situation is to ask whether there is anything to be gained by leaving the client intact at such a point and further to ask whether there is anything to be gained by stripping the client's defense from him. Many a counselor might well ask of himself if there are needs of his own that are met only when the client openly admits what the therapist can deduce. Another way to view the situation is to ask whether the client gains more from making a step forward himself or from having the therapist make it for him.

5. Near the close of an interview a client responds, "Now the nature of next week's visit will be not so much to uncover my own problem — I might do some of that I suppose — but be more or less a report actually on what I am doing to solve these problems, I think."

Issues. At first glance this client-response does not seem to provoke any question at all. The client is merely expressing the notion that next week instead of exploring he wants to bring things up to date as to what he is doing about his problems. There seems to be nothing startling about this. It is given as a rather clear cut statement which, in effect, terminates this interview through announcement of plans for the next. The whole thing seems quite innocuous. "Signing off" statements may very often be quite innocuous. Very often at such a point the counselor may change from the role of a therapist to a social role. It is at such a point that the counselor's attitudes may show because his role is altered.

A second factor may be involved here as well. Notice that the client has referred to the interview process, how the hour is to be spent. This can be seductive for the therapist, especially if the therapist is feeling somewhat uncertain as to whether the client is spending his time as profitably as possible or whether the client really understands that he is free to use the time as he sees fit. The counselor might well be tempted to structure here, to reassure the client that: "Yes. Sure. Fine. That's right. You do what you want to do here." He might word it with less betrayal of his attitude as follows: "Mhm. Okay, well, consider the time yours to use as you want and do the things you feel will be most helpful to you." In one sense this would appear quite superfluous as the client is engaged in doing what the counselor is urging.

One further comment is that clients are very well noted for not following out the plans they make for the use of following hours — when left to themselves to decide. Is this good, or is this bad? It would suggest that planning for the client what should be taken up in a subsequent interview may not fit in with the topical movement most "natural" to the client.

6. In a still later interview the same client as above goes on to say: "I'm getting places. I'm making definite progress. In fact many of my, in fact many of my, uh, roommates have remarked that they have seen me going to classes and nearly dropped dead from amazement (*laughs*) and it's given me quite a glow of inward satisfaction that they would talk that way. They would say, 'What's the matter, you're going back on us, finally going to classes.' They regard it as a high sin over there. And that attitude, I might add, is part of the reason why I don't go to classes, too; because it's considered smart, it's considered wise not to go to classes, but to stay home and loaf or study, never get anywhere, if you go to classes. And I found that not to be true."

Issues. This illustration is introduced because it presents a number of different feelings being presented simultaneously and thereby presents the issue of to what feeling, feelings, composite of feelings or combination of feelings should the therapist respond. Here are the obvious feelings in the order in which they occur. (1) I'm making progress. (2) Even other people notice my progress. (3) It is quite satisfying. (4) They put a certain amount of pressure on me. (5) I tried to respond to the pressure of their attitudes. (6) I feel they are clearly wrong.

When a counselor is seeking for certain cues in the response of a client, cues which will lead him to something "deeper," it is easy to understand that one of these feelings might well be perceived as *the* significant feeling. Such a set on the counselor's part should be expected to lead him into missing the pattern, the configuration of feelings and their total meaning. To see in the client's response such a list of feelings as is suggested above is very much to see a human being as (1) a head, (2) two arms, (3) a torso, and (4) two legs. Just as children apparently so perceive people, as evidenced from the juxtaposition of the bodily members in children's drawings, so will most beginners perceive the parts of client responses without perceiving the relationship. That will not mean that a relationship does not exist.

Were we to rephrase the client's remark in such a way as to fill in the unspoken but inherent relationship we might get something like this: "I'm making progress. For this I have two lines of evidence: first, other people notice the change (which gives me a lot of satisfaction); and second, I have been able to overcome the pressure of their attitudes and go ahead with what I think is right." In attempting to convey understanding of the client's remark to the client the counselor would give central play to the client's conviction of his making progress. Just how the rest of the material might be handled could easily vary within a wide range without destroying the communication. Several possibilities are offered at the end of the chapter.

Many readers will recognize in this client's response the type of "documented" claim of progress that clinicians feel is valid, the type of claim with supportive evidence that would be extremely difficult for a client to fabricate. On the basis that a forward step, no matter how faltering, should be met with a positive reward, many therapists would feel that some sort of praise or encouragement might well be in order here. In addition to the fact that a growing body of experimental evidence suggests that reward and punishment do not operate in learning as for centuries people thought they did (and wanted them to), there is the immediate fact that the client's feeling of progress may change to a feeling of no progress. Moreover, the feeling may change to a *conviction* of no progress and then the counselor who has offered praise or encouragement — and thereby implied his own conviction that the client has progressed — may be in an awkward position. On such a cross a counselor can be crucified. If he maintains his original position, he must disagree with the client. If he changes to now agree with the client, the client may lose faith. With the investment some clients will have in maintaining that they do not need help or can't be helped, the offering of rewards can be risky. Another way to look at it, of course, is that since the therapist acted in good faith the real responsibility lies in the client and his resistance.

7. In this illustration the client, a young woman in her middle twenties, has started off the third and last interview with the feeling of nothing to say. We shall reproduce a few excerpts from the recording and then proceed to the issues which the counselor's handling of the situation raises.

Cl 1: (*laughing*) "This gets worse every time to get started. I think I'm about all talked out now."

Co 1: "It's harder each time you try to begin, huh?"

Cl 2: (*pause*) "I don't know . . . (*long pause*). I guess that maybe this had better be the last time. I don't have enough things to talk about."

Co 2: "You feel you . . . you feel you don't have so much need to discuss things, is that what you mean?"

Cl 3: "Yeah. Yes. I've talked about them so much in the last week or so, and you know, more than usual, or something, and they're getting rather dull now, and uninteresting."

Co 3: "Um hmm. It seems to you that they change in meaning to you as you discuss them more, is that what you mean?"

Cl 4: "Well . . . no . . . not in meaning, exactly . . . in interest anyway." (*pause*)

A few responses later the interview continues:

Cl 9: "I'm being uncooperative. (*pause*) I honestly can't think of anything to say." (*pause*)

Co 9: "You've sort of come to the place where you have to think up something to say, is that it?"

Cl 10: "Uh huh. This is only the third time too, isn't it . . . There! See, they must not be as important as I thought they were. (*pause*) I honestly can't think of anything to say."

Co 10: "You're not real sure what it is . . . you might have just pushed them aside for a while, huh."

Cl 11: "If that's the case, then it isn't good, because then they'll just keep coming up . . . later."

Co 11: "You don't want to just push 'em down because you feel they might crop up again."

Cl 12: "Um hmm. (*pause*) But I don't know what to do about them, anyways."

Issues. Most of us could probably agree that the direction being taken by the client is not one calculated to strengthen the relationship between client and therapist nor one calculated to be of much help to the client in fostering a further exploration of the problems confronting her. The first issue before us is why she has taken this direction.

One view we may take is from an external frame of reference. What seems to be operating within the client? What "dynamics" seem evident? In Cl 1 we might posit an element of resistance to exploration of problems, bearing in mind that the client may also be rejecting the therapist as well. In Cl 2 we might posit further evidence of an internal resistance and have even more confidence in the notion of feeling toward the counselor by reason of the client's threat to terminate the contacts. From Cl 3 we might be more strongly convinced than ever of strong feeling against the therapist. The client's description of her problems as "dull now, and uninteresting" could well be a thinly veiled description of the counselor, not the problems. Similarly, we might judge Cl 9 as indicating a feeling within the client that the *counselor* is uncooperative. From Cl 9 we could also infer internal resistance by reasoning that the client has released some of her hostility toward the counselor and, following the pause, speaks now for herself. The content of Cl 10 would seem to constitute a defense for the counselor's consumption arising out of internal resistance. The aggressive manner of presentation in Cl 10 would further suggest hostility toward the counselor. Especially after the reasonableness of Cl 11, Cl 12 would suggest once more the hypothesis of internal resistance, a degree of unwillingness to face her problems, as a strong causative factor in the client's behavior.

A second view we may take is from an internal frame of reference: how closely the counselor was able to sense it and convey understanding. In Cl 1 the client expresses not only the feeling that it's harder each time to begin but the feeling that maybe she's said about all she has to say. The therapist's response in Co 1 was only half complete. In Cl 2 the client expresses in new words the feeling that maybe she's said all she has to say. The counselor clearly misses this feeling (which if it were true in fact would mean the end of the contacts) and strives to guess what reason lies behind her expression about terminating. She has offered as a reason the lack of things to talk about. The counselor has construed this to mean no feeling of a need to tackle her problems further. The client's agreement at the start of Cl 3 is not supported in the remainder of her statement. The latter part of the statement appears to be more of an attempt to find reasons which will fit in with the counselor's statement rather than a real expression of a felt lack of need. The counselor once again fails in Co 3 to stick with the client. Here he has missed the notion of the problems as dull, uninteresting and boring and has brought in the observation of the change in meaning. In Cl 4 the client has to correct the counselor and point out that it is not the meaning that has changed but the significance of the problems or the interest in the problems. In Co 9 the counselor misses again. He brings into the conversation an inference to the effect, "If you can't think of anything to say, then you'd have to make up things to say." The client has not expressed this notion, but deftly uses it against the counselor in Cl 10. In Co 10 the counselor seems to be clearly putting ideas before the client. She has certainly not expressed the notion that she may be pushing things aside. From Cl 11 we learn that the client is aware of the consequences of not facing her problems — if not facing them is what she is doing. The counselor demonstrates in Co 11 that he clearly understands the feeling he has suggested to her. The client reacts to the threat by still further denial of inner resources to deal with the problems.

From these two analyses we get two different conclusions as to what has contributed to the client's movement in a fruitless direction. On the one hand we may posit internal resistance to the problems and hostility toward the counselor. On the other hand we may posit consistent misunderstanding and subtle threat.

8. This excerpt is from a phonographic recording of a young woman who sought help because of marital difficulties. The response given here took place about twenty minutes after the interview began. "Uh huh. (*pause*) That and the fact that he doesn't read and doesn't particularly enjoy it. And then also another reason would be that, well, I mean he has to be important; of course, we all do, but I think more so because he . . . oh, I can just see it from his mother and his brothers, so, well, his family spoiled both him and his brother, just terribly. And again, his parents were older when he was born, I think his father was in his forties or so when he was born, and uh, I

think one big disadvantage of having your children so late, you're sort of, your other interests don't mean so much to you then. Things like going out, going to dances, and going to the theatre and you turn all your attention on your children. And I think that's very bad in a number of ways, and I think in this case it was because his family just worshipped those two kids, and just spoiled them in every possible way — just made them think they were the most important people in the world and that everything they did was right. And I can see it in both, both my husband and his brother. They are very much that way. I mean, they, they pretty much consider themselves, first."

Issues. This is a type of response which may throw the counselor off the track in his efforts to respond by reflecting the client's feelings. The client presents a lot of material which describes the husband and how he acts. The client does not speak directly of her own feelings toward the husband and how he acts. To what feelings should we respond? The husband's or the client's? If the client's feelings, then how do we sense them? We can depend, in part, on preceding statements to give a context. Preceding statements cannot always be depended upon, however, since expressions will not always be related directly to what has gone before. One way of getting a context for a statement such as this is to ask "How must the client feel toward the situation to talk of it thus?"

In the recording the counselor replied, "Got to have a feeling of importance." This response relates to the husband's feelings. As to the client's feelings we notice that she expresses herself negatively toward the husband and describes a host of factors which have contributed to the husband's behavior. Her description conveys the notion that even though the husband couldn't help developing as he did, nevertheless his behavior is blameworthy.

It might be well to take up here the problem of replying to client responses which are perceived by the counselor as expressions of resentment. Some therapists would be quick to perceive this client's statement as evidence that she resents her husband. Careful reading of the response will show such an inference to be unjustified. She has not expressed herself against her husband but against certain aspects of her husband's behavior. She may come to express resentment toward him as a person and again she may not. To present her with the notion that she resents him as a person now may only lead to defensive behavior on her part. Diagnostic perceptiveness in such an instance as this client response may lead the therapist into an over-statement from the client's frame of reference.

9. Later in the same interview as above the following sequence took place.

Co: "This new realization of how strong his need for importance was led you to believe that, has led you to see, that you really weren't achieving much satisfaction from the marriage situation."

Cl: "No, I realized that before, but I resented it more, I think because I didn't realize, I mean I wasn't thinking so much in terms of his needs, too, which I am now, a little. I can see how strong his needs are, and he has to find satisfaction for them, too, and before I think I was blaming him more because I wasn't thinking of it in terms of uh, his real needs, I was just thinking, oh, I don't know what a contrasting statement would be but not as something that he really needed, but just as something (*Co:* Just was, huh?) yea, just the way he was."

Co: "So that sort of now realizing this you can accept that situation a little bit easier, is that what you mean?"

Cl: "Yes. But granted that he is that way, I've got to work out some way for myself."

Co: "Saying there, that accepting the full strength of his need, then where are you going to get your satisfaction, huh?"

Cl: "Uh huh (*pause*) (*looking at her hands*) I've gotten so nervous just talking about it, I can't really think clearly now." (*pause*)

Issues. This sequence was selected because it brings up the problem of what the therapist should do when the client is making splendid progress along a fruitful line and then suddenly begins to pay attention to his or her own emotional reactions.

Several avenues of response are open to the counselor. He may wish to probe or push further into why her reaction to the material is so upsetting. He may wish to teach her, possibly pointing out that her nervousness is a good index of the importance to her of the material with which she is dealing. The therapist may wish to reassure her by some appropriate, sympathetic remark to the effect that therapy is not always easy. The therapist may wish to simply disregard her comment and treat it only as an aside remark. In such a case he may reply only to the preceding material. The therapist may wish to understand what she is feeling at the moment. In such a case he may be expected to respond to the feeling that even to think about the situation and what she can do about it is somewhat upsetting to her.

In the recorded interview from which this material was taken the therapist did respond to the client's feeling. The subsequent movement was typical. Having faced the problem the client moved to an expression of incapability of dealing with it. It is this coming to grips with one's inner attitudes such as helplessness that seems to result in their changing.

Co: "Sort of just thinking about the situation and facing it in here is not . . . sort of gets you upset a little bit, huh?"

Cl: "Yes. I've gone over everything so many times in my mind, and it's — and I get upset just thinking about it by myself."

Co: "You've done a lot of working on this problem yourself."

Cl: "Uh huh. But I feel that I can't straighten it out for myself. I don't know why it is, I guess it's that same business of saying, well, this could be the reason or that could be the reason and which is the real reason and I know I rationalize a great deal, and I think of something and I think, well, now am I rationalizing or is this what's really true. And I rationalize so effectively that often I don't know myself." (*laughs*)

10. In this recorded excerpt the client starts off the second interview, "Well, it's hard to know where to start, because I think I can relax a little more today, I was thinking about last time, and (*laugh*) I realize I wasn't utilizing the counseling situation at all. I mean I was so, I was very defensive, wasn't I? I mean I felt that."

Issues. Counselors expect clients to be defensive, especially in the first interview. We can even interpret the client's reference to her past defensiveness as a defense against starting on her problems even now. Further, we can interpret her shift from "I was so, I was very defensive, wasn't I?" to "I mean I felt that" as a defense against a possible therapist judgment in agreement. It is also possible to conjecture as to the dynamics of need-fulfillment which lead the client to make a negative statement about herself. It is also possible to view the client as feeling that last time she was defensive somewhat to her own detriment but not feeling so driven today. Responding on such a basis may leave the client feeling understood rather than challenged.

11. This same client at a later time expresses feelings which are not at all uncommonly met in therapy. (*pause*) "I sort of keep coming back to the idea that this is all so silly when there are so many people with real problems. I mean I feel it must seem silly to you and it seems silly to me. I don't see any sense in feeling, oh, the way I do about things. I mean, there are so many people with real problems, like a lot of fellows I talked to during the war when we had to send dependency discharges, oh, they lost their business and their wives and everything. I mean people who really had something the matter and here I am just stewing about myself. And, oh, I don't know, I thought, well, what's the use of thinking more about myself because that's the whole trouble anyhow."

Issues. Nearly all clients, if not all people, can find someone against whom they can compare themselves with the consequent feeling of making a mountain out of a mole hill in the difficulties which they themselves face. Feelings such as these may be viewed from different angles. Assuming that perceptions are end products of motivational processes, are purposively determined, they have little meaning in themselves except as signposts pointing to motives. In this instance such a motive might be the need for reassurance, the need to deprecate one's self, or the need to escape from the reality and pain of facing one's self. Assuming that perceptions constitute the boundaries within which behavior is limited and that these boundaries are relative to the setting in which they are placed, such feelings as we are describing here have their significance as descriptions of the person's reality.

Clinical experience has repeatedly yielded the observation that such feelings as we are dealing with here are not uniform but change from one time to another. Taking this fact alone there is a real issue regarding the psychological consequences of the therapist's acting in a way as to either side with the feelings or side against them. If the therapist takes a stand with the feelings expressed at this moment, it is likely that he shall have reduced the freedom of the client to present a different or contrary feeling. If the therapist takes a stand against the feelings expressed, it is likely that the client will have available a portion of the therapist's values toward which he can move dependently or from which he can move aggressively. An effort to understand the feeling as a feeling which the client has does not so entangle the therapist or the client.

To so many people it will seem ridiculous to attempt an understanding of the client's feelings. Logically it would seem that the client should reply in the affirmative and then stop. Many counselors feel that somehow or other there must be something added by the therapist with each response or the client will come to a halt. On the contrary, however, this does not seem to be the case when the responsibility for what is to be done in the interview is left clearly with the client. Much more likely is it that the client will move into a further exploration of the factors underlying the expressed attitude. Typical is the movement which occurred in this case when the counselor responded by reflecting the client's feelings. The client moved in the next response to the very thing many counselors would presume could be "uncovered" only by the therapist. "I mean it seems so silly. It irritates me to death, but, that I stew the way I do. Objectively there's no reason, really. I guess that goes back to the common idea, you say, oh it's all in your mind and wasn't a problem really. So I suppose, and then I was wondering after I went home last time, how much I really want to change, since I realize I'm getting satisfaction out of the feelings of resentment that I have. I think I must. And I don't really think I want to give them up." Then two responses later she continued: "Uh huh. I think I must feel some inadequacy in respect to my husband and I think that I'm, I mean my way of getting back at him for making me feel that way is to sort of resent him and think 'Well I wish I hadn't married you anyhow'." (laughs)

12. At still a later point in the interview process the young woman whose responses we've been following had come to an impasse

as to what to say. She had just expressed the feeling that she ought to quit thinking so much about herself, that thinking about herself is the source of her trouble: but, how to avoid it.

Co: "Sort of saying that consciously you realize that thinking about yourself isn't too good and yet it's awfully hard not to do that."

Cl: "Awfully. And I suppose it's something I've pretty much always done. I don't know why. (*pause*) I don't know how to get away from it, I mean I don't know whether, whether getting at the causes wouldn't help me to get away from it or what. Probably it started in the home situation where, well, where, probably first in relation to my mother. I don't know whether that's worthwhile going back over that. For a long time I've accepted the idea that, uh, oh, that my mother didn't really approve of me, I mean she, she was one of five sisters and I was the girl and my brother was the boy, and naturally she preferred him, which is recognized by everybody but herself I think. I know my grandmother a long time ago, I remember she said, 'Well, you just have to get used to the idea that mothers always like their sons better anyhow.' And then she is quite, she places quite a value on social things, people; and as I told you I was more interested in being by myself and in reading, things like that. She was constantly getting after me about that. So I suppose she started all these feelings. I mean the relationship with her. I know I never felt secure with her, never felt that she approved of me in any way. But I've been conscious of that for a long time and I've pretty well accepted it, as just the way things were."

Issues. It is not at all uncommon for clients to bring out such material as this and to report it as "*pretty well accepted.*" What is the counselor to do when the client begins to explore into an area of probable significance and then cuts it off as unimportant? Should the counselor attempt to contrast in some way the manner in which she reacts toward her husband and her feelings about never being able to please her mother? The counselor might choose to overemphasize to a slight degree the client's statement of having accepted the situation with her mother in the expectation that she will bring out her resentment of it. Here, as in nearly every instance, the counselor is faced with making the decision of whether the client is capable of moving ahead on her own or whether she must have help from the outside or can use external guidance because it is quicker.

13. In one last excerpt from this recorded case the following exchange took place.

Cl: "Uh hum. And another thing that I've always done, I guess arising again from the home or from a very early age, I know I've learned to keep my feelings to myself pretty much, anyhow, how I really think and felt about things. For instance in my attempts to get along with other people I never, I never was really acting me, I was always acting what they were . . . I mean what I thought I should be in terms of the situation, (*Co:* Uh huh.) and never what I really wanted to be. And I've been, I know I was conscious of that quite early. And, I think again that that goes back to when I was very young. I remember one Christmas when I was, we moved in 1930 it was, well it couldn't have, it was earlier, when I was five or six when my, uh, parents gave me something for Christmas that they thought was just what I wanted and really it wasn't, and I remember being conscious that I mustn't show disappointment, that I must act as if I was pleased. And I'm sure they couldn't have told me that, I mean I'm sure I really remember and it couldn't have been when I was any older than six. And I remember feeling very strongly that they wanted to please me and thought they were and that I must act as if I were, and not let them know what I really felt. And that's always been pretty much my reaction. I mean I just try to act as I think I'm supposed to in a situation, rather than the way I really want to. And I catch myself doing it in conversation now, lots of times, so I might almost be called non-directive, because instead of giving my own opinion sometimes, well particularly with people who, with, I don't really like too well or have too much respect for, I find myself just reflecting their opinions right back to them, or you know, instead of putting forth any of my own, I just sort of restate theirs when I'm talking to them. So I'm. . . ."

Co: (*interrupts.*) "Then in the, many of the aspects of your real self you have kept hidden from others and just shown them (*Cl:* That's right) the self that, uh, (*Cl:* That I thought they'd approve of.) you thought they'd approve of."

Cl: "Uh huh, that's right. (*pause*) And I suppose again that could come from a constant disapproval of my mother. I mean whenever I did have a real feeling or thought or something that I would tell to her, she would think of some reason why it wasn't a good one, almost always. So I just . . . in order to protect myself, to keep from being hurt."

Issues. In these statements is contained insightful material. The client has been able to go back into childhood situations and relate her present feelings to possible causative factors. It would appear to be a perfect set-up for the therapist to raise the question, "And maybe, too, you have to keep your real feelings hidden from your husband for fear he'll disapprove." Such a question may be a perfectly correct interpretation. This does not mean that the client's reaction to it will be the most constructive possible reaction.

Let us stop for the moment to consider how a person may feel when he is presented with an interpretation of his own behavior. Suppose for the moment that you are in an argument with someone on a point about which you feel strongly. Your opponent is verbally a more facile individual than you are and the argument starts going against you on the logical side yet you can't shake the notion that in spite of all his arguments he just doesn't see your side, you can't shake the notion that you are right. As you continue to press your point you select more and more tenuous illustrations and make broader and broader generalizations. You are doing your best to get him to see at what you're driving. Suddenly he says, "Now you're getting defensive." He may be perfectly correct: but do you like it? It is unlikely that you will respond by thanking him profusely for giving you insight into yourself. Later you may come to agree with him yet at some cost to your own feeling of integrity.

Not all interpretations, however, will be received with hostility. The client may well be very grateful and stimulated by the insight a therapist can provide through interpretation. In a sense, it is very much like the gratefulness and stimulation experienced by a student in the classroom as the expert gives him insight. There can be no argument but that it can be helpful. There can, however, be argument as to whether the client's and the student's development of insight on their own is not more helpful. A common illustration of this is in the experience of almost every teacher. Most teachers feel that they really don't know enough to teach but that their own teachers did. Possibly the experience of being taught, the experience of being in a situation where someone else knew the answers better and demonstrated it, is conducive to the engendering of a feeling of superiority in others. If it is at all possible that a client can gain his own insights, it might well be that for the client to gain the insights on his own will foster a feeling of inner competence. Most therapists, I think, would agree that the more the client can do for himself the better off he will be.

14. In this phonographic excerpt the client, a young man in his early twenties, has come for but three interviews. In the last interview he develops the notion that the things which have been of concern to him are all specific events in the past about which he can do nothing, and which have resulted in the development of a "father complex." He continues.

Cl: "They don't exactly call for a plan of action. So therefore, there's not much I could do about that." (*pause*)

Co: "Those things don't lend themselves to any action on your part."

Cl: "I don't know what to do about having a father complex. I used to think it was a father complex. I don't know whether it is, or not. Except I sort of enjoy having it, I guess."

Co: "You're not just exactly sure what your relationship there is, but it is satisfying in many ways, huh?"

Cl: "Except that it keeps me immature."

Co: "It is satisfying, still that's one thing that might be holding back your growth to maturity."

Cl: "But I don't want to give it up."

Co: "You're sure of that."

Issues. Frequently clients report liking their symptoms in spite of the discomfort entailed. Simultaneously they may recognize such behavior as avoiding the facing of what lies beneath the symptoms. This type of situation provokes the question of whether or not the counselor will seek to hold the client for the client's own good but against his conscious or unconscious will. It is almost a certainty that if therapists were able to be uniformly effective in holding a client through such a negative period until he was able to carry on with his desires for help, all therapists would employ the suitable means. The facts are, however, that no such suitable means seem to exist, or if they do exist, they are not widely known. Clinic records are all too filled with entries to the effect that such and such a person terminated appointments against advice or failed to appear for an appointment and did not respond to letters of inquiry.

There is a growing body of clinical experience (some of it painful to the therapists) which suggests that just because a client terminates or interrupts the contacts with a therapist it is not necessarily bad. One line of evidence is in the growing number of persons who, when unsuccessful in achieving a satisfactory solution to their problems with one therapist or a therapist of a given point of view, shift to another therapist or to a therapist of a different persuasion. All too unfortunately are those situations seized upon as evidence to the new therapist that *the first* therapist was ignorant, incompetent, and guilty of unethical conduct. In this highly unstructured field of counseling and psychotherapy there is usually very adequate reason for any therapist to feel insecure. The defensive behavior is nevertheless regrettable even though understandable.

A second line of evidence which suggests that the counselor may be doing the client a real service not to pressure him into continuing when he feels he doesn't want to do so is in the reports of clients who interrupted therapy yet returned some time later to again take up counseling. A number of such clients have reported that the experience of being left in a position of responsibility for themselves freed them to return for their own purposes rather than for the purposes of others through which their earlier appearances had been motivated. Others have reported that the early contact or contacts had started them to really thinking about themselves and had brought to them the realization that in the final analysis they would have to be the ones who did something about themselves. Other reports are made, too, but these are enough to suggest that the whole field of "counseling — readiness" is a field of which we know but very little. Obviously what is needed is a complete set of recordings on all clients and the good will of other disciplines in the field of therapy which would encourage research on failure cases.

Each counselor must face for himself the decision of whether he will try to hold the client or whether he will make the client's leaving an experience which will not traumatize or threaten him but will leave the door open for his return to the counselor or to some other therapist from whom the client may find the help he is seeking.

Again, clients often bring up the notion of terminating in the same way as they bring up any other feeling or attitude. There would seem to be no logical reason to presume that an attitude on this subject is a lawfully different phenomenon than an attitude on any other subject. Many efforts to hold clients may appear to therapists to be successful when what may have occurred is no more than a change of attitude by reason of factors internal to the client rather than by reason of counselor activity. There is the possibility that acceptance and understanding in such instances may hasten or at least not retard such an alteration in the client's feelings nor leave the client feeling that there is something about terminating which is bad.

15. The client in this, a second interview, is a middle-aged woman whose only child has left home, precipitating deep feelings of purposelessness in the client. She has come for help expecting to be told what to do. Throughout the first interview she tried to shift responsibility to the counselor. The second interview begins as follows:

Co: "Well, where do you want to start in this morning?"
Cl: "Gosh, I wonder. I can't think of anything to ask. What I told you before . . . to get into what I told you before in detail works me up to sort of an emotional jag and uh, from my point of view I don't see any particular object to it."
Co: "Uh, going into it really uh, gets you a bit upset, is that it?"
Cl: "It certainly does. Maybe there's some line which you'd like to pursue. I'd be glad to answer any questions if there —— ."

Issues. There have been references in earlier examples to the handling of dependency. Rather than continue or repeat the references to these issues it is the intent here to consider the issues involved in phrasing the response to the client's last remark. It is presumed that the counselor will endeavor to understand the client's remark and to convey that understanding to the client, that the counselor will not seek to probe, support, evaluate, interpret or disregard the client's expression. The issue then resolves itself into whether the client's response is more accurately perceived as a request for the counselor to take over or more accurately perceived as an expression of a feeling that it would be easier on her if she didn't have to take the lead.

The distinction just made may seem rather superficial. Experience indicates however that it is not so superficial since the consequences of the two views are sufficiently often different to warrant being considered. A response which treats a request or apparent request at "face value," that is, which treats the request as a request, will almost always involve some reference to the counselor. The counselor in this particular case responded, "You'd be glad for me to take the lead. You feel as though you're sort of played out." As is quite typical when therapists point their fingers at themselves in this way the client replied, "That's it. Yes." The counselor then found himself holding the responsibility for the next response. Had the counselor not responded to the inference of the client's remark, the inference that she wanted him to take the lead, but had continued to respond to her feelings as expressed not implied the result very likely would have been different. The second sentence of his reply by itself would have kept the focus of attention on her feelings and more likely would have resulted in continued expression and exploration.

We might rephrase the issue by posing the question: when is a question or request really a question or request and when is it a rhetorical form of assertion? Let us suppose for the moment that you are working on a quiz in a class and turn to the instructor to say, "Oh boy, this is a toughie, isn't it?" It is very unlikely that he will perceive your statement as a request for information on the degree of toughness inherent in the test. On the other hand, as you begin counseling it is very likely you will usually perceive as a direct request for information or for your opinion a situation in which the client says something to this effect: "Well, I've been thinking that maybe I ought to take some vocational tests to see what they say about all this. Don't you think so?"

The discussion on this topic would be patently incomplete were it not pointed out that such attempts to get the therapist to take responsibility may persist over an extended period of time and interviews. Especially for the beginning counselor this can be a source of great pressure to either "structure" the interview, explain to the client how he is supposed to act, or to give the opinion or information the client appears to be asking for. There will be occasions, too, in which the client is directly asking for something. In such instances, however, the request will nearly always be put quite directly and will not be confused with an expression that is accessible to being viewed as rhetorical assertion. To treat a direct request as a rhetorical assertion may result in the client's feeling rejected although experience indicates that more often the consequences will be the same as if the request were clearly rhetorical. How one counselor handled several direct requests is reproduced below. They are reproduced here to demonstrate the point that in places there may be no set answer as to what to do, that in the final analysis the counselor must count on himself. These excerpts are from two successive interviews. Their original numbers are retained so as to give the reader an idea of the times in the interviews at which they appeared.

Co 47: "You feel you've tried so hard to live up to a lot of these standards that others have talked about and so on, that you're really not quite sure where you live."

Cl 48: "That's right. Does it seem as bad to you as it does to me?"

Co 48: "You wonder if it could seem as bad to anybody else as it does to you."

             ❊   ❊   ❊   ❊

Co 62: "You feel that if you keep on as you're going, you will burn yourself out."

Cl 63: "Yes. (*long pause. . . .*) What do you think I should do?"

Co 63: "Well, I think, I think the kind of thing you are doing, that is, I think if we can explore this enough, the kind of thing you're doing right here, that if we can explore it deeply enough, I think we'll find the answers. I don't pretend to know them now; you don't know them now; but I think we can find them."

Cl 64: "Do you really? You have to go to class over there." (*end of hour*)

             ❊   ❊   ❊   ❊

Co 110: "So maybe they're not really contradictory."

Cl 110: "No, I guess they're mutually re-enforcing. (*laughter*) What would you say to do?"

Co 111: "You feel, really, that you'd like me to (*Cl:* Yes.) try to say something. And I suppose that the one thing that I could say I don't even know that you'll believe. That is, that I'm trying to understand how this whole situation feels to you because I think as you explore your way through it, that as I understand what it is you're exploring through, then we could arrive. But when you ask, 'What should I do?' I suppose you're asking about exams, primarily, or at least partially. Is that part of it?"

      ❋   ❋   ❋   ❋   ❋

Cl 119: "Yes. As soon as I sit down and study and say, 'Now, I must take an exam in April for something — it's so automatic, it's such a bad habit, whereas if I knew I weren't going to take an exam, even the next quarter, knowing I wasn't getting credit for the last quarter, I wouldn't be able to take next quarter's exams, because I might have gone over the (*word lost*) or something I don't know. It seems so sadistic to place blockages in your way, doesn't it? I mean actually that's the, that's a little pathological."

Co 120: "In other words, it seems a little foolish to put a rope so that you can trip over it."

Cl 120: "You think I should, *don't* you?"

Co 121: "You feel quite sure you know what I think about it."

Many readers probably will have felt by this time that the concern over direct questions and requests is an over-concern with consistency (or an over-concern with rigidity). What occurs as the interview continues exemplifies the type of insight and emotional experience which clients can develop at early stages in therapy and which lead many counselors to feel strongly that consistency must have a more potent effect than it would appear to have on logical grounds or on most theoretical grounds.

Cl 129: "I guess it's the old argument of change by revolution or evolution. I just don't know which stage is better. Whether completely to turn over and not take these exams, for instance, and not, and break ties with home and all the other things that we were talking about the other day, or whether to just have the same things and try to achieve in that. Like having your cake and eating it too, I guess."

Co 130: "You're not sure what would be the effective method."

Cl 130: "No. In the short term or in the long term . . . again, the future . . . That's why I would like you to tell me what to do, so I could at least do the opposite. (*laughter*) I wouldn't though, really I wouldn't."

Co 131: "You realize there could be some satisfaction in doing something different from what you might be told."

Cl 131: "Not really. If you told me, there wouldn't be, because I really would do whatever you told me."

Co 132: "You feel a little puzzled that I don't try to throw the scales one way or the other."

Cl 132: "No, I don't feel puzzled because I know that you want me to work it out, but I don't feel I can work it out any further."

Co 133: "You feel as though you're sort of stumped."

Cl 133: "M-hm. (*pause*) Probably the unconscious me wants to place the burden on you."

Co 134: "Might be a kind of desire to shift the load to somebody else, eh?"

Cl 134: "I hope it isn't. I hope it isn't."

16. The client, a young unmarried woman, in a late interview in the series, has been dealing with the feeling that the counselor ought to participate in the therapy by providing guidance and interpretation. She has known of a young man who has been in therapy conducted in an interpretive, guiding manner and has seen the success that he has obviously achieved. It has puzzled, concerned and angered her that the counselor does not proceed as did the other therapist and in a manner that she had expected when she first came in. In the process of expressing these feelings she speaks as follows: "Yeah. And he accepted it. I mean, he — seems to me he got him there a lot quicker. Well, anyhow, what — I mean, my idea when I came in — well, this should be very simple. All I have to do is straighten out my thinking, I mean, all the — I can really do it. But I'm doing it in a very slow and confused fashion. And I want to speed it up. It shouldn't take very long. It should be very simple. I think another aspect of that, you know what I said about everybody's a little bit neurotic and I have a few things that are blocking or impeding me and what I want to do — . But I don't know, it seems to me that it's a pretty serious. . . . I mean, you shy away from those words, neurotic and maladjusted. You know, I mean you think a neurosis is a horrible thing. And yet I think actually (*pause*) actually I have a pretty serious problem, which I wouldn't admit to my-self or to you before."

Issues. Among the goals of therapy is the goal of helping the client to face himself, to face his judgments about himself which he has previously denied to consciousness. Some therapists feel that this is possible only through or most efficiently through the guidance of the therapist. Client performance such as is reproduced above is evidence to other therapists that therapist-guidance is not necessary. In any event, whether the client achieves a degree of self-facing by himself or by the instrumentation of the therapist, there remains the issue of how the therapist will respond to this step ahead.

In the excerpt above the client has come to face the feeling that her situation is serious. Her newly revealed feeling gives us ample understanding of her desire to have the counselor take the lead and relieve her of the fearful task of facing her own feelings directly or at least delay the process of facing them. When the client does face a deep and disturbing feeling of this sort the counselor is faced with the decision of what to do. Some counselors will feel that the blow should be softened or that the anxiety which may be expected to follow should be somewhat allayed. These counselors may feel that the client doesn't have the strength to face herself directly or that the anxiety aroused may be destructive. Such judgments by the counselor would prompt support of some type. In other words, the counselor may believe as does the client that the situation *is* serious and consequently act accordingly. Such a confirmation by the therapist may help the client to view her feeling as fact.

In response to such a facing of self as is exemplified in the excerpt some therapists may feel that the client should be praised or rewarded, that the client should be led to view her forward step as a "good" thing. Such action seems appropriate if the therapist judges that the client can't learn but must be taught how to use the therapeutic situation. Still other therapists would feel that the client needs neither instruction nor support but is in reality capable of accepting the feelings she has been able to uncover by herself and that the progress which will follow facing herself will teach her the benefits of getting in touch with her own feelings. These therapists might seek to face with the client her facing of herself.

17. In the closing session of a three interview case judged by the

therapist as largely unsuccessful the following sequence of events occurred and is reproduced as it took place throughout the interview.

Cl: "Well, I've been thinking over what I've been saying here and I think that I will stop with today. And, oh — Because the more I've been talking the more I've been thinking, well, I come up with an answer like, 'So what?' I really haven't accomplished anything except putting down into words and, uh, convincing myself that what I'm doing is all right. And uh. . . . ."

Co: "That is, it doesn't seem to give you any more answer than you'd already come to, is that. . . . ."

Cl: "Well, the only answer I've got so far is that what I'm doing is what I want to do and, uh, that's reason enough to do it and, uh, as long as I can go on that way and it doesn't bother me any more than it is right now, I think that's what I'll do, just keep on, and, uh, unless, if I come to some great problem. I don't see where, uh, where I can gain anything more by coming in, at the present, anyway."

        ✳   ✳   ✳   ✳

Co: "As far as continuing any more with *our* contacts there isn't sufficient value that you can see to them, that is, it serves no purpose of yours."

Cl: "No, now, no. Yeah, I've gotten out of it what I think I needed. I had a chance to put into words what I've been thinking and by doing so it helped me out some, and it got me to thinking in a little different line than I had done before, so I just reached the conclusion that's satisfactory for the time being . . . ."

Co: "Yet you'd like to leave the door open in the event that you change your mind."

Cl: "Yeah, I would like that, but I'll go ahead and see how things turn out. I've come to the conclusion that I, that it isn't, my ideas aren't based on a neurosis and that I think helped me as much as anything."

Co: "M-hm. That is, you've drawn reassurance from the situation, that it's solid thinking and not neurotic thinking."

Cl: "Yeah and that is one question I was going to ask you, you've had experience along this type in here or else you wouldn't be here, it didn't, my talk and all didn't have a basic neurotic background to it, to *you*, did they?"

Co: "Are you saying there that you are not *really sure* yourself."

Cl: "I'm sure myself, but whether, but whether it is based on *some* neurotic tendencies, well that would be all right, it doesn't matter too much, but I would like an outside opinion. That will help also to clarify, or else if I, if you said that it was neurotic why then, uh, I'd probably continue on and see, but for myself I can't see it, and that's not, that's subjective of course — "

* * * *

Cl: " —, because I can't, I can't even pick out a philosopher that I can follow straight through, I can't uh, I hold them in the same position that I hold churches, so I've got, I've had to build for myself all my ideals, and they are all subjective and uh, I know subjective ideals aren't, don't have much basis, and they could fall — *quick.*"

Co: "Sometimes the structure is not sufficiently sound and once starting to collapse, uh, it would be with frightening rapidity."

Cl: "Yeah — but if I know that I've got, that I'm sound so far, why uh I'm satisfied and I think that I am."

Co: "You feel pretty sure on that, uh, that aspect of it."

Cl: "I haven't put into words everything I've thought here, that's impossible. I can't, in three or four hours put down all your beliefs and your reasons, so maybe it's somewhat vague, but I think I've given an idea, uh, at least."

Co: "That is, a sufficient sample to — "

Cl: "Yeah, and uh, so that I think that just winds up my part of it, anyway."

Co: "Mm hm. That is, that unless I have something more that I want to say — why you feel that as far as you are concerned that you got what you came for."

Cl: "So — that's *that.*"

Co: All right, we'll leave it on that basis, then, and uh, uh, should you desire at any other time to come in, I mean, if anything else occurs to you that you would like to talk over, why fine, if not, fine."

Cl: "And then — You haven't anything more to say for yourself?"

Issues. Here there seems to be but one central issue, the issue of consistency, and the problems which go with it. From all one can see in the excerpt (and in the total recording as well) the client did not come to grips with the elements of his situation but apparently achieved a conviction that all was well.

In the face of such a situation the counselor must struggle within himself to decide whether he should remain consistent and see the client leave or vary his approach in an attempt to hold the client. Many therapists will feel strongly that to continue in a consistent manner is in reality to be rigid. On the other hand, many therapists will feel that to vary one's approach is to demonstrate a vacillation which invites further manipulation at the hands of the client.

One argument which appeals to those who would favor variability is the notion that you can't help the client who doesn't return to be helped. In contrast with this argument is the notion that an experience with a thoroughly consistent situation may have deep effects upon the client. Some day there may be experimental evidence which will give us clues as to which of these notions is the more likely valid one. It would seem most important for the beginning counselor to recognize that the strength of his own conviction as to which of these notions is more likely correct will not insure that actions based upon the notion of his choice will produce the results he desires.

During the course of an interview the counselor cannot be certain that the client's announcements of intentions to terminate will be followed by termination. There is no more reason for the therapist to "believe" such an announcement than there is reason for him to "believe" that the client is now clear in his thinking. Correspondingly, we may expect that the client subsequently can become just as dissatisfied with a decision to terminate as with a decision that all is well.

18. One situation may arise in almost any interview. That situation is a prolonged pause.

Issues. To the beginner a pause can be very puzzling. Until experience has been gained the would-be counselor often may be unable to make reasonable inferences as to the nature of the pause and consequently base his actions on fright, not fact. Following are a number of possible inferences which the beginner may wish to bear in mind.

Let us first presume that a client is actively engaging in the expression and exploration of his situation. Everything seems to be going along according to expectations. A pause at such a point may arise for such diverse reasons as: (a) the client is searching for the right words to express his next thoughts; (b) the client is trying to muster up courage to present a new and painful topic; (c) the client is ruminating over what he has just brought out; (d) the client is continuing in his exploratory processes but without verbalization; (e) the client is blocked and can't think of what to say next; (f) the client is doing nothing more than resting from the emotional strain of the preceding moments.

The issue which arises for the therapist is whether he will interrupt the pause or wait for the client to continue. Since the therapist wants to do what is best for the client, the therapist must judge whether intervention of some sort will break in on a constructive client activity, will support the client over a rough spot that would be more helpful if faced, or provoke the client into an activity before he is ready to face it. In general, it seems reasonable to think the client should be left the responsibility of going ahead when the client is taking responsibility for having paused in the first place, when the pause represents a responsible expression of the client's attitude.

When, however, the pause represents an action or lack of action which is forced onto the client by the relationship between client and therapist, there may be a great deal of question in the counselor's mind as to what step to take. The client may be pausing because (a) he feels largely misunderstood by the therapist or because (b) he fears condemnation by the therapist. It may be that (c) the client is angry with the counselor and seeks to force responsibility onto the counselor. Another possibility is that (d) the client is expecting the counselor to lead the interview and is waiting for the counselor to go ahead. The counselor may be faced with (e) a client who comes to the interview only to prove that he needs no help and, in effect, is challenging the therapist to try to prove otherwise.

In such negative situations as are presented in the preceding paragraph the therapist is thrown back into the problem of deciding whether he will seek only to understand the client, to do his best to view the situation as the client views it and to communicate his understanding to the client, or whether he will attempt to use some device or other to get the client going. Unfortunately there are no frequency data from which we can draw assurance that consistency of understanding is either more often or less often followed by satisfactory continuance of the interview than when some course of action is taken. The counselor for a number of years to come will be forced back upon deciding whether he wishes to take on a type of responsibility comparable to that taken in medicine and consequently view the person as a patient presenting himself for treatment, or whether he wishes to take on a type of responsibility comparable to that taken in legal practice and consequently view the person as a client coming for consultation on personal problems.

19. A young woman, twenty years old, makes this statement: "Yes, and I asked her — well, it just happens that she isn't a good-looking girl, in fact some might say that she is rather homely, but she has a sister that is very, very pretty, and she's about two years older than she is, and very popular. And I asked her whether she had ever felt as though she was jealous of her in any way and she said, 'No,' she never had. And it seemed that this girl always went around with very good-looking girls, and she said she was never conscious of feeling as though she was inferior to them, and she never had any doubt feelings and I thought that was so unlike me. I felt awful. I mean, she felt genuinely — she didn't even have to fight against it. She just didn't have it in her."

(Note: Try to reflect the feeling here before reading the comment which follows.)

Issues. This example is simply one of technique per se. Whose feelings would you reflect, the client's or the feelings of the girl to whom the client refers?

20. The same client at a different point in therapy makes the following statement: (*Laughs*) "Yeah. That's right. Well, actually I let fear just dominate me, that's the whole point. It was just a great big fear, because if a teacher didn't like me or I didn't think I could go ahead it was just a fear right there that I couldn't make good. And if somebody said something about me I think of the past mistakes or something and I think well, if they knew about that then they'd realize that I wouldn't live up to it or something like that. I won't let my-

self progress. That's the whole thing. I'm just dead set against myself."

Issues. This statement exemplifies an insightful response. In considering the conditions which might govern the type of reply the counselor chooses to make we might turn our attention to the psychological climates different responses are likely to provide for the client.

Let us presume for the moment that the counselor, for some reason or other, feels that it is desirable at this point to approve the client's reaction, to assure the client that the step taken in insight is a good thing. This is, in effect, to say to the client that after all she is not, in the final analysis, capable of handling her own affairs; that she must have the way pointed out for her very much as we presume is the need for the child; that she is praiseworthy when she does these good things.

Let us presume now the counselor feels that the client should not rest on her laurels at this point but should push ahead to something deeper, something more significant. This is to say again that she is, in part, incapable of handling her own affairs and must be guided from without to the correct viewpoint. It is also to say that she is incompetent and superficial, that her feelings of achievement and insight aren't "really" significant.

Finally, let us presume the counselor feels the client has achieved something for herself and the counselor seeks only to understand her feeling about it. This would appear to say to the client that she is a person capable of handling her own situation and a person worthy of being respected, not led.

Whether a person is capable of being responsible for himself or herself is a moot question. Many people feel one way or the other. Bear in mind that these are feelings, too.

Suggested Responses

1. (*a*) (Presuming the counselor must ask the client to wait.)
     "I gather you feel this is something that just can't wait? Is that it? There is something that I must attend to right at this moment but I'll be back by 8:30 or sooner, if possible."
   (*b*) (Presuming the counselor is not otherwise occupied.)
     "This is something you feel can't wait, is that it? If you'd

like, then, we might start now. That would give us until
9:15."

2. (*a*) "Feel somehow it's not right to be late, is that it?"
  (*b*) "Pretty interested even though you didn't get in very much."
  (*c*) "Not so much on your mind today."

3. "That is, you've picked out the things that you felt were the best
bets but you've been uncertain within yourself and still are, as to
whether or not you're really on the right track."

4. "In other words it brought up the question of seriousness but it
wasn't something that really worried you."

5. "You want more to consider what you are *doing* about them — is
that it?"

6. (*a*) "So you feel you're really getting ahead."
  (*b*) "That's the way the evidence points, then, to real progress."
  (*c*) "As you see their reactions and your own ability to brush their
attitudes aside it means to you that you're getting ahead."
  (*d*) "More and more able to do what *you* see as right than what
they suggest."

7. Co 1. "Harder to start and maybe, too, you've said about all there
is to say."
  Co 2. "You feel that maybe there's just not enough to work on to
warrant further contacts, is that it?"
  Co 3. "Getting just plain tired of messing with them."
  Co 4. "I see. They just don't demand your attention as they did."
  Co 9. "Feel you should bring up something but you just can't
think of what you could bring up — is that it?"
  Co 10. "Maybe you had just over-emphasized their importance."
  Co 11. "And that you wouldn't want."
  Co 12. "Just stumped."

8. "So that even though these characteristics were more or less forced
on him by his life, you tend to resent them — is that it?"

9. (See the response given by the therapist in the excerpt at the end
of the example.)

10. "I gather that you feel you were a little too defensive last time, kinda blocked yourself, but not as pushed today."

11. "That is, when you compare your situation with the situations you've seen others face, it makes you wonder if you aren't over-emphasizing the importance of things."

12. "So that you've come to feel that not being accepted for what you are is just one of those things that you have to face, is that it?"

13. "In other words you were driven into it for self protection."

14. (See counselor's responses as presented in the example.)

15. "That is, you feel it would be easier on you if you didn't have to lead off yourself, is that it?"

16. "You'd gone along just as if the situation were simple but you've come to a point where you just have to admit you feel the situation to be anything but simple."

17. (Sometimes there doesn't seem to be any answer except that which the counselor in the situation feels is the best thing he can do for the client.)

18. (See 17.)

19. "You could scarcely understand how she could be *not* jealous and *not* inferior."

20. "You feel that if you're looking for the real obstacle to progress, you can look in a mirror."

Chapter

SOME SPECIAL PROBLEMS IN

COUNSELING

From time to time questions are put to therapists that do not relate specifically to the subject matter of the interview yet relate significantly to how the counselor operates. They are the "What do you do when ── ?" questions. We shall consider a number of them here because the issues they raise can be as complex and as puzzling as specific interview issues.

"What do you do when a friend or a relative wants to come to you for counseling?" The mark of the novice is his willingness to exercise his training on his friends, acquaintances and relatives with indiscriminate abandon. This seems to hold true whether the novice is training in vocational guidance procedures with consequent references to job-demands and opportunities, whether the novice is training in psychoanalytic procedures with consequent references to unconscious forces, unconscious patterns, superego mechanisms and ego structure, whether the novice is training in Individual Psychology with consequent references to life-style and purposive behavior, or whether the novice is training in non-directive procedures with consequent attitude reflection. Sooner or later the would-be-therapist, or someone close to him in therapeutic training, finds that his invitations to some person to speak of his problem result in that person's going far beyond the responsibility the trainee is willing to take. Many counselors as a result

161

of such experiences have concluded that dealing with any persons known to them is to be avoided.

On quite a different basis many therapists have reached the same conclusion. These therapists feel that no person can operate effectively as a brother or friend during one hour and the next hour operate effectively as a therapist. Much has been said about the therapist's feelings coloring his own perceptions under such circumstances.

A third basis on which therapists tend to reject working with someone closely associated with them is that the obligations they undertake as therapists may hamper their freedom to be themselves at other times.

These three reasons, unacceptable degree of responsibility, possible personal involvement, and limitation on freedom, are the major reasons advanced which point in the direction of not working with relatives or close associates. These bases are not the only ones from which this question may be viewed, however. This seems especially true when the therapist does not hold himself responsible for the conduct of the client either in or out of the interview situation. It seems to the writer that this may very well be the central issue. To the extent that the counselor does hold himself responsible for standards of conduct outside of the interview he is in a less favorable position to help the client. Put in another way, the more the counselor is responsible for a person's standard of conduct outside of therapy the more difficult it may be for the client to be free and self-responsible during the therapy hours.

Consideration of the client must be involved even further in seeking an answer to our question. When psychotherapeutic efforts were in their earlier stages the public knew little or nothing about them. Today Freud is a household word. Psychoanalysis is the topic for cartoons even in the most popular magazines. Dreams are seldom considered portents of things to come but as indicators of unconscious conflicts. Even the concepts of transference and displacement are not unknown to readers of best selling novels. In brief, clients may be much more sophisticated in a valid way with a consequent increase in the effectiveness with which they can utilize the interview situation. This clearly seems to be the case in non-directively conducted therapeutic contacts. Whether it holds true for analytic situations in which transference is encouraged and is handled quite differently the writer is not qualified to say or judge.

The degree of skill the therapist possesses and his feelings of security in the answer he reaches seems to be one variable in the answers which have been worked out to our question. A second variable is the degree to which the counselor is really able to let the client be responsible for his own standards of conduct. A third variable is that of the client and his attitudes about seeing someone else or the availability of another counselor.

Presuming that the counselor has decided that he will give a negative answer to the client's request to be seen in therapy, there remains the question of how the counselor will handle the situation. Being turned away may be a traumatic experience to the client. It may serve to reinforce his feelings of loss of integration and helplessness. Or it may serve as evidence to him that he is foolish in thinking that he needs help. The counselor will probably desire to avoid unhelpful implications. Some counselors will feel that the most effective thing they can do is to indicate their negative decision openly and honestly and at the same time to use the opportunity to help the would-be-client to define more clearly his felt need for assistance. It is not at all clear how helpful it is to the would-be-client for the counselor to present all of his reasons for not seeing the individual. Much of the material the applicant might be unlikely to understand. It seems reasonable, however, that the counselor could communicate to the client knowledge of other therapists who are available, some notion of what to expect from the therapists, and some notion of how the therapeutic situation might be approached most profitably.

What do you do when you want to refer a client? This question is but one which can be asked about referrals. Another important question relates to *when* does the counselor refer a client. In the discussion on the preceding pages we have considered one situation in which the therapist has referred a client, a client whom the therapist is unwilling to see due to the closeness of the two parties. This referral was made because of an attitude held by the counselor. The counselor may also wish to refer a client when he feels the situation which the client presents is too complicated for the training the counselor has had. The therapist may also wish to refer the client when the therapist feels there are elements involved with which his training does not fit him to deal.

It is easy for any writer to lay down a group of rules for therapists to follow, especially for the non-medical therapist to follow. I shall not attempt to do this for two definite reasons. First is that most of the rules do not stem from what is most helpful therapeutically but from social-legal-medical issues and these issues are not decided for us by nature but by man, with all the consequent variations in interpretation. Second is that rules are easy to understand in the abstract but so often very difficult to apply in practice. To give rules is to give the student a false sense of certainty that he knows what he should do when he gets there.

To the writer it seems more profitable to consider the conditions which form the context in which the question of referral is likely to arise. Since non-medical therapists are constantly informed that they work under a Sword of Damocles, the threat of organic involvement in the client's situation, one might expect to have reason for frequent referral to medical practitioners. The opposite seems to be the case, however. The writer is not personally aware at the time of writing of any clients with physical complaints who have presented themselves to non-medical therapists for psychotherapy without having previously consulted at least one or more physicians or psychiatrists or were currently under the care of a physician, with the exception of a few persons who sought a counselor first because their fears of what a physician might find were so overwhelming as to constitute a block to their seeking medical examination. Experience suggests at the present time that it will be only infrequently the non-medical counselor will have occasion to refer the client to the physician, that all but the exceptional case will be self-referring or will seek aid from the counselor in facing the medical consultation. These facts do not carry the implication that the non-medical therapist should be lax in his obligation to refer the client who presents a non-psychological problem but they do carry the implication that the counselor should not hasten to join the ranks of those who have failed to be of help to the client. It would seem that as the years go on and psychotherapy becomes a more widely accepted part of our culture we might expect an increase in the number of individuals who present themselves to psychotherapists without prior medical consultation. At the same time, we might expect an increase in the number of individuals who present themselves for psychotherapy while undergoing medical treatment. Might we not further expect that just as non-medical therapists become increasingly involved in working in conjunction with medical people the reverse will also come true and psychological counseling will become an important part of treating serious illnesses or other organic disturbances.

Even though the most smoke and fire have arisen at the borderlands of psychological counseling and medicine, in practice the question of whether or not to refer a client arises much more frequently when the counselor feels he is failing. Each therapist, medical or non-medical, must work out his own salvation here. He can blame the client or patient, he can find reasons in the circumstances of the situation, or he can look into his own handling of the case and seek to profit by and not just accept his errors. There are at least three immediately available avenues to self examination: phonographic recordings, consultation with another counselor, and bringing another counselor into the interviews. These will be discussed in some detail at a later point.

Should the therapist feel that referral is desirable he must make decisions of the following kinds. Is the referral something he feels desirable but not necessary? Is the situation such that the counselor will not continue to see the client at all? Will the counselor continue to see the client only if the referral is effected and the other professional person is willing? To what extent is the referral desired by the therapist because of his own anxieties? To what extent is the referral a matter of referring a competent person or a matter of getting an incompetent to a place where he can be cared for? To what extent is the damage the act of referring may do the client a necessary evil?

If the counselor has thought through such questions as are suggested above and conducts himself honestly in accordance with the answers he reaches, it is least likely that he will do damage and most likely that the referral will be accepted. This is clearly a place where play-acting and role-taking are most likely to be harmful.

In the preceding paragraphs the matter of referral has been limited to the notion of the transferring of responsibility for conducting the therapeutic situation. Much has been written on the problems of referral of clients not for therapy but for supplementary aid from other community resources. While referral for supplementary aid will in many situations be demanded by the organization in which the therapist works and by the nature of the situation the client faces, we must bear in mind that such referrals may not be therapeutic. Rather than thinking of such manipulation of the client, even though necessary, as therapeutic it may be more profitable to think of it as part of the situation external to the therapeutic relationship and prepare to deal with the client's attitudes relative to the referrals. It may be profitable also to deal with clients' requests for referral as attitudes which when properly handled may yield therapeutic gains.

What do you do when a friend or relative inquires about your client? Here again medical-legal-social problems may be involved which will force the counselor to feel he must divulge information given to him by the client. There can be no question that therapy is best served only where the client is completely and unequivocably protected in what he discusses. The client must feel secure. If the counselor does operate in a situation in which he may be forced to divulge material, he will serve his client best by making such a fact known at the outset and what he may be called upon to divulge. Some counselors have taken the stand that they will under no circumstances divulge information without the specific consent of the client. Because questions can be asked of a counselor in such ways that he cannot be certain of how to handle them, many counselors direct all inquiries to the client himself. In the case of written inquiries the replies may be worked out by counselor and client together.

What do you do when a referring authority or agency inquires about the client? This is a variation on the preceding question but involves the same basic therapeutic issue of confidence. One possible method is to inform the authority or agency that the client did appear and since the relationship is strictly confidential no information can be divulged, but, if the authority or agency wishes, the client will be informed of the inquiry. Often the authority or agency will seek only an evaluation of progress. Even if the counselor feels certain that he can make such an evaluation, there is still the question of the extent to which divulging that evaluation consists in a violation of the client's integrity. The counselor may wish only to indicate that the client is still coming in and is working on the problem or that the client has terminated the contacts with or without apparent satisfaction. It seems reasonable to expect in an institutional setting the client may anticipate that what he says will be a matter of record. In such situations it is likely the client will think of the therapist as one of a group of trustworthy people. Even then the therapist may be requested to not reveal certain items. The therapist must then decide whether or not to be honest or play a role of being a therapist.

In considering the matter of divulging information we have discussed only situations in which the client's identity was known to others. When the client's identity is clearly protected by the conditions under which the counselor speaks of the interview material, it is difficult to conceive of its constituting a violation of the client's integrity.

What do you do when you want to record an interview? One of the factors which many counselors feel will interfere with getting a recording of an interview is that the client is likely to be apprehensive about the presence of the equipment and about the eventual use to which the interview material is put. Experience has indicated that when the counselor is secure in his own feelings, when the counselor has decided in his own mind just how he will use the material and how he will not use the material, when the counselor is completely willing to discuss this with the client and feels that he is not going to violate the client's integrity, then very few clients express unwillingness to be recorded. The facts of a well thought out recording program are not the elements which seem to disturb clients. The counselor's apprehension and anxiety do, however, seem to be very important variables. The biggest block to recording is the therapist. Much less frequently than might otherwise be thought will the therapist find clients unwilling.

In an effort to meet the issue of obtaining recordings and also of interviewing under conditions of observation without violation of the client's integrity counselors are coming more and more to the position that these processes should be clear to the client so that he will know with what he is dealing. Consequently, many counselors now refuse to do secret recording and insist that the equipment be in full view during its operation. Similarly, counselors are coming to feel that the one-way screen is no longer appropriate and that observers should be so placed that the client may view them if he wishes. Such conditions permit the client to be in control of his own integrity. Although many readers will feel that such conditions will hamper the course of therapy, experience has not indicated that such expectations will be borne out.

What do you do when the client hits a problem area which is also a problem area to you, the counselor? There may be no answer to such a question as this. If the client's difficulties are so close to those of the counselor as to arouse the counselor's anxieties it is possible the counselor will not be at his best. He may become less sensitive to the feelings expressed by the client and may read some of his own feelings into the client's expression. He may tend to shy away from responding to the client closely. The counselor may wish to take up these problems in a therapeutic situation of his own. In any event it seems less likely that the counselor will be of harm to the client, if the counselor continues to pursue a disciplined course of action in accordance with his training and does not depart from it because of momentary pressures.

What do you do when a client interrupts his counseling with no further communication to you? The issues involved in this problem were discussed in connection with examples brought up in Chapters V and VI. The reason for bringing it up again is that it clearly represents one important type of situation in which the client can hit a counselor's tender spot, a spot which is a problem to the counselor. None of us like to feel we fail. This is especially true when the apparent failure is directly connected with our professional efforts. When a client fails to appear for an appointment and makes no effort to communicate with the counselor regarding why he no longer appears, the implication of counselor failure is present. Almost invariably the situation is complicated by the expectations of the community and the expectations of one's fellow workers or supervisors as well as one's own professional aspirations. It is often difficult for counselors to refrain from trying to circumvent apparent failure in one way or another. In most instances the steps taken are not clearly thought out and are steps which the counselor would be less likely to defend as sound therapeutically — except, of course, as a last resort. The implication here is not that the counselor should not try to draw a client back but that his efforts should be well thought out on other than emotional grounds. It seems reasonable to expect that if truly careful thought is given to them the results of the steps will be more readily apprehended by the counselor to his own educational benefit.

What do you do when you want to follow-up a client to see how he has progressed? Obviously one area of great importance to an evaluation of the results of therapy is the follow-up interview. Important as it is for our purposes we must be cautious of its effects upon the clients. It would be undesirable were the follow-up interview so conducted as to imply to the client that the counselor felt the client might need more help. It would also be undesirable were the follow-up so conducted as to force the client to consider situations which he did not want to consider. In brief, it would seem undesirable to introduce elements of threat into the follow-up interview. On the contrary, every effort might well be made to minimize the threat. One step in this direction is to ask the client before he terminates counseling if he would be willing to be interviewed again at a later date as a part of the counselor's own efforts to improve the services he offers. A second step might well be the handling of the follow-up interview in such a way the door is left open for the client who wishes further interviews but also in such a way the clients are not brought to feel they should come in for further interviews.

What do you do when the client brings up humorous situations in the interview? This question has often been a puzzling one to students, especially when they are trying to fit everything they do in the interview into a technique pattern. One thing which no technique discussion can ever convey is how to be relaxed and natural in an interview. Should the client be speaking of something humorous and trying to communicate the humor to the therapist, the therapist would have to be insensitive, tense, or preoccupied not to join in the humor. On the other hand, a client may be speaking of a humorous situation but trying to communicate to the counselor some aspect of the situation which is far from humorous. To respond to the humor might be quite inappropriate. Some counselors do not feel it at all harmful to introduce their own humor into an interview but certainly not at the expense of the client nor when it would appear to be inappropriate to the client's feeling tone. Probably the most significant aspect of the expression of humor is in the attitude which lies behind it, the thing which the counselor expresses through humor. Is it an attempt to reassure the client? Is it a means of reassuring the counselor? Is it an attempt to get the client to favor the counselor more?

What do you do when there is an interruption of the interview by a phone call or a knock at the door? This type of situation is one which raises the issue of the extent to which the counselor is willing to make himself completely available to the client during the scheduled time period. Most counselors seek to avoid all interruptions by posting a "Do Not Disturb" sign on the office door and by having someone else answer the telephone. When these are not possible steps, many counselors prefer to inform the client at the outset of the hour that an interruption may occur.

What do you do when the client wants to give you a gift? Clients will express gratitude in many ways. One way is through the giving of presents to the counselor. They may express their thanks only verbally. Whether the gratitude is expressed verbally or materially the most important issue would seem to be the feeling expressed and the counselor's handling of that feeling. If the therapist drops into a social role and responds by giving welcome for the thanks or by giving thanks for the gift, he misses what might be a valuable opportunity for therapeutic gain in the client. The therapist cannot be certain, except on some theoretical grounds, as to what lies behind the gift or other expression of gratitude. The therapist, however, can meet the expression of gratitude as he does the expression of any other attitude as well as doing the socially conventional thing.

SOME APPROACHES TO

INTERVIEW ANALYSIS

In the preceding chapters the major effort has been directed toward issues which are of importance in determining what the student will do as a therapist in the interview situation. This, however, is not the only meaningful learning activity. Much can be learned through close study of phonographic interviews and attempts to analyze them. This chapter will be devoted to the consideration of a number of different analyses of interview material, not for the results which came from the studies but to introduce the student to some of the ways that interview material has been approached. While the studies considered for the most part have been systematic research endeavors, it is hoped that the student will be stimulated to try on a smaller scale the same activities or variations of them for the highly valuable learning experiences they offer. For the student to learn only the elements of a method and the current thinking accompanying it is not enough. Indoctrination approaches sterility. The reason that the student should give a substantial proportion of his energies to studying interviews is to enable him to form reasonable judgments about the effects of his interview behavior and as quickly as possible assume the status of an independent thinker who draws his evaluations from his own experiences rather than from what the book has to say.

The analyses of interview material may proceed in two fundamental ways. They may be directed toward trying to determine whether what has happened in an interview is good, bad or at some point in between. They may be directed toward trying to determine what happened, what processes were at work, what laws of nature were in operation. Because therapy is a process of social significance there can be no doubt of society's interest in and right to know the relative effectiveness of a given therapeutic approach. At the same time one can easily appreciate that if all efforts are concerned with evaluation and none devoted to seeking understanding of the lawful operations involved, little advancement is to be expected in the learning of the student who spends his major efforts in seeking to evaluate the effectiveness of his present work. It seems more profitable for him to seek to determine ever and ever more clearly what is happening that has psychological significance. As he does so, the likelihood increases that he will be able to control the processes in the directions he deems desirable. It is also more likely that he will have an increasingly better notion of desirable directions.

The whole story is not told in the dichotomy between the directions of evaluation and of discovery for in trying to follow the path toward discovery there is a pitfall. In viewing the phenomena of the operations of natural law it is possible to take either of two positions. We may take the position that the most profitable approach to understanding new areas of data is to bring to them concepts which we already have developed and try to understand the new areas in terms of the established concepts. We may take the opposing position that the most profitable approach to understanding new areas of data is to work with the data closely and to seek concepts which suggest themselves from the relationships which can be observed in the data. These new concepts can then be compared with established concepts. The pitfall, in the writer's opinion, lies in approaching data with established concepts, for in this approach there is all too often an acceptance by the investigator of the validity of the concepts which he brings to the data and all too often the data are rejected and the concepts retained. Present day conceptions of the nature of the physical universe were certainly not achieved by trying to translate all observations into the early Greek concepts of earth, air, fire and water. Freud's conceptions of personality structure and operation were certainly not achieved by trying to translate the observations he made into the philosophical and religious concepts of behavioral determinants existent in his day.

The dichotomy which is found in psychotherapeutic research also extends to the learning of psychotherapy. The learning activities which appear to be most profitable are those in which the student develops from his own experience hypotheses as to what happens in psychotherapy and then proceeds to test them in his own experience. This is not written to encourage unlicensed and haphazard messing around with someone else's life. It is written to encourage carefully thought out and responsible testing of hypotheses. It is the writer's conviction that what is known about psychotherapy in both theory and practice is as yet quite primitive and consequently any effort toward indoctrination rather than controlled exploration is criminal.

The reader who seeks to learn "the technique of non-directive or client-centered therapy" will never find that for which he is looking. There is no "non-directive technique." Experience has suggested the hypothesis that reorganization of the disturbed personality will take place more readily when external intervention is at a minimum and self-exploration is at a maximum. We may speak of this as the non-directive or client-centered hypothesis. The hypothesis has persisted over a period of time but the procedures or techniques which have been used in an attempt to implement or try out the hypothesis have changed and will change. One procedure which currently seems to be the most effective yet evolved is that of understanding the client from an internal frame of reference. This is not unique as a procedure at all. Every individual may use this procedure in communicating with others each day. What is unique in client-centered therapy is the consistency of use of understanding in the effort to implement the non-directive hypothesis. Each client who is seen furnishes new experiences from which judgments of effectiveness of methods and judgments of the validity of the hypothesis may be drawn. At the same time that the data become available for evaluational judgments the data become available for inferences as to the psychological factors at work in the personalities of counselor and client and the relationship between them.

In the paragraphs which follow there will be presented a few of the many efforts made in approaching the data of the phonographically recorded therapeutic interviews. This material represents far from a complete coverage. It is illustrative of efforts made to achieve concepts and understanding directly from the data. These illustrations are limited to those which the writer has had an opportunity to see in development or to discuss with the investigator.

One of the earliest attempts to report observations made of nondirective, phonographically recorded interviews was by Rogers.[1] " — What happens? What goes on over a period of contacts? What does the counselor do? The client? I shall try to put quite briefly, in somewhat oversimplified form, the different steps in the process, as I have seen them occur many times, — " The steps he listed are reproduced below, but without the illustrative material accompanying their description in the original paper.

1. The individual comes for help.
2. The helping situation is usually defined.
3. The counselor encourages free expression of feeling in regard to the problem.
4. The counselor accepts, recognizes, and clarifies these negative feelings.
5. When the individual's negative feelings have been quite fully expressed, they are followed by the faint and tentative expressions of the positive impulses which make for growth.
6. The counselor accepts and recognizes the positive feelings which are expressed, in the same manner in which he has accepted and recognized the negative feeling. — And in this type of situation, insight and self-understanding come bubbling through spontaneously.
7. This insight, this understanding of the self and acceptance of the self is the next important aspect of the whole process. It provides the basis on which the individual can go ahead to new levels of integration.
8. Intermingled with this process of insight — is a process of clarification of possible decisions, possible courses of action.
9. Then comes one of the fascinating aspects of such therapy, the initiation of minute, but highly significant positive actions.

[1] Rogers, Carl R., *Some Newer Concepts of Psychotherapy.* A lecture given at the University of Minnesota, December 11, 1940.

10. There is — a development of further insight — more complete and accurate self-understanding as the individual gains courage to see more deeply into his own actions.
11. There is increasingly integrated positive action on the part of the client.
12. There is a feeling of decreasing need for help, and a recognition on the part of the client that the relationship must end.

This exposition of Rogers' has significance in that it represents a first type of step in approaching new data, a tentative description of relationships among the data of observation, the evaluation of the hypothesis. The student is encouraged to formulate his own tentative description of what he sees in his own work.

Rogers' presentation of his description in common terminology emphasizes the closeness of the observations to the data and the lack of a tendency to impose existing notions onto the data. The introduction of descriptive technical terminology into a formulation of the relationships, however, would not necessarily force the data to the concepts and may increase communication as well as suggest areas of comparability between different areas of research endeavor. The next formulation is one made recently by the writer and is intended to describe the data observed in non-directive interviews in terminology which might be used by an observer of a complex learning situation. Such a formulation as this may serve to stimulate thinking as to the possibilities of using learning concepts as explanatory concepts in therapy and to suggest that therapeutic material may constitute a rich field of data against which the learning theorist may check his hypotheses.

1. The client initially engages in the expression of attitudes, usually negative, but often ambivalent or positive. (a) The loci of these attitudes are usually external to self: the client usually refers to symptoms and problematic events as things which are happening to him rather than as phenomena which are in large part of his own making. (b) The attitudes are generally expressed defensively; they are so expressed that they can be easily and rapidly altered or reinforced should their expression be met by rejection or denial from the therapist; and the form in which they are put usually is not wholly negative when re-

lated to self but may characteristically involve some protection of positive self-evaluation.[1]

2. In the presence of a non-evaluating psychological climate [2] the client begins to engage more and more freely in a continued expression of attitudes and to engage in exploration of the significances attributed to the elements of the problem situation. This type of activity appears to be quite comparable with the early manipulative activity characteristic in experimental learning situations.

3. When the client's attitude manipulations are met by the therapist's response to the figure-ground relationship being experienced by the client, two effects appear to be initiated. (a) One of the effects is an emphasizing of the figure-ground relationship which results in a clearer contrast of what is assigned to figure and what to ground. (b) A second effect is an enhancement of the press within the client for completion of understanding (*gestalt druck*). This enhancement seems due not only to the clarification of perception but also due to the ongoingness of the manipulative activity and the lack of distraction or disruption which might result from a therapist response that called for consideration of a different figure-ground relationship.

4. As the manipulation of attitudes continues there is a bringing into perceptual juxtaposition, simultaneous or temporally sequential, of memories, concepts, evaluations or other such elements of the problem situation which must eventually be recognized as related, if insight is to appear, but which at the moment may be perceived as unrelated. This seems comparable to the phenomenon or phenomena underlying latent learning.

5. As the manipulation of attitudes continues there is an increasing movement from ground into figure of self-referrent evaluations with a consequent increase in discrimination between the evaluations of self and the life experiences which provoked

[1] The student may be interested in trying to understand how a seriously depressed patient's statement, "I am completely worthless," can be thought of as defensive.

[2] The term "psychological climate" is used here in the sense it was given in Chapter III.

or accompanied the self-evaluations. As the discrimination increases the stability of the earlier figure-ground structure decreases and more elements are permitted to enter and form a new structure.

6. In the presence of the more complete figure, new evaluations emerge and this attitudinal reorganization is accompanied by appropriately corresponding changes in the client's behavior.
7. Throughout the course of therapy the client is exposed to the psychological climate provided by the counselor or therapist. This climate provides the same opportunities for the client to learn to evaluate himself as were provided in his earlier experiences outside of therapy.
8. As new figure-ground relationships are formed, previously learned behavior patterns incongruent with the earlier attitudes but congruent with the altered attitudes begin to appear and much behavior which had earlier been expressed defensively now appears in less guarded ways.
9. As self-re-evaluation and insight proceed, the client experiences a decreasing need for help. At the point where, in the client's current situation, events which previously had evoked negative self-evaluation to an acutely uncomfortable degree no longer redintegrate such evaluations, the client terminates the contacts.

Such descriptions as are represented in the two foregoing formulations of the course of therapy can be helpful in the qualitative factors which they suggest. When qualitative factors are approached quantitatively there emerge estimates of validity and often new hypotheses as well.

One early attempt at quantification was made by the writer.[1] It is discussed here because it serves to illustrate further the notion that the study of data can proceed largely through hypotheses suggested by the data themselves. It was the writer's desire to compare the counseling procedures used by therapists of different points of view. Nowhere in the literature available at that time were there clear-cut descriptions of how therapists proceeded within any point of view. All that was available consisted in a

[1] Porter, E. H., Jr., "The Development and Evaluation of Counseling Interview Procedures," *Educational and Psychological Measurement*, vol. 3, 1942, pp. 105–126, 215–238.

description of goals and sub-goals of the therapeutic sequence. The counselor was informed that he was to establish rapport, but he was not told how to do it. He was informed that he was to set the stage for the development of the client's problem but was not told how to set it. He was informed that warmth and understanding were desirable, but again he was not told how to implement these concepts. In brief, each point of view had definite notions of what was to be accomplished but no instructions were available as to procedures. The feeling was common that counseling or psychotherapy was an art and not a skill. The literature expressed this feeling rather clearly although usually implicitly.

Since there were no clear-cut criteria available in the literature as to just what constituted guidance interview procedures, directive procedures, non-directive procedures, or analytic procedures, the writer turned to phonographic recordings of interviews. By studying the individual counselor responses certain relationships began to suggest themselves. Through the process of grouping and regrouping responses which seemed to be implementations of the same procedures a series of categories were finally settled upon and described briefly. These categories are reproduced below. In the research, each counselor response was assigned to one of the categories, thus making quantification of qualitative differences possible and permitting comparisons of counselor procedures from one interviewer to the next and from one interview to the next. The use of the coding system shown permitted each counselor response to be identified on a typescript, thus making it possible to determine where judges agreed and disagreed on specific points.

Defining the Interview Situation
(1a) Defines in terms of diagnostic/remedial purposes, procedures, etc.
(1b) Defines in terms of client responsibility for directing the interview/reaching decisions, etc.
      (1u) (Unclassifiable)
Bringing Out and Developing the Problem Situation
Uses lead which:
(2a) Forces choosing and developing of topic upon client
(2b) Indicates topic but leaves development to client
(2c) Indicates topic and delimits development to confirmation, negation, or the supplying of specific items of information
      (2u) (Unclassifiable)

Developing the Client's Insight and Understanding
Responds in such a way as to indicate:
(3a) Recognition of subject content or implied subject content
(3b) Recognition of expression of feeling or attitude in immediately preceding verbal response(s).
(3c) Interpretation or recognition of feeling or attitude not expressed in immediately preceding verbal response(s).
(3d) Identifies a problem, source of difficulty, condition needing correction, etc., through test interpretation, evaluative remarks, etc.
(3e) Interprets test results *but not* as indicating a problem, source of difficulty, etc.
(3f) Expresses approval, disapproval, shock, or other personal reaction in regard to the client (but not to identify a problem).
(3u) (Unclassifiable)
(4) Explains, discusses, or gives information related to the problem or treatment.

Sponsoring Client Activity / Fostering Decision Making
Proposes client activity:
(5a) Directly or through questioning technique
(5b) In response to question of what to do.
Influences the making of a decision by:
(5c) Marshalling and evaluating evidence, expressing personal opinion, persuading pro or con.
(5d) Indicates decision is up to client
(5e) Indicates acceptance or approval of decision
(5f) Reassures
(5u) (Unclassifiable)
(I) Irrelevant
(OU) Otherwise unclassifiable

The check-list reproduced above represents an effort *not* to impose concepts external to the data upon the data. Every effort was made to describe each procedure as a procedure without reference to whether it might be considered good, bad or indifferent from any one's point of view, whether it might be considered directive, non-directive, analytic or any other external categorization. In other words, the check-list was designed to determine what the data would show about themselves. Another check-list, one designed by Snyder,[1] represents what would appear to be an

[1] Snyder, William U., "An investigation of the nature of non-directive psychotherapy," *Journal of General Psychology*, vol. 53, 1945, pp. 193–223.

undesirable tendency to introduce concepts external to the data. Inspection of his "Definitions of Counselor Categories" reproduced below will reveal that the significance of a given counselor response is automatically determined by its inclusion in a given category. The counselor response automatically is deemed directive, non-directive, somewhere between the two, or as incidental. There are no reasons why we should presume that one response is a "sheep" and another a "goat." Research efforts of this type may seriously hamper investigation by their implicit assumption that the nature of the data with which they deal do fall into certain previously determined qualities. This is a variation of the trap of trying to explain the physical universe in terms of earth, air, fire and water.

DEFINITIONS OF COUNSELOR CATEGORIES

Lead-taking Categories. (Those which seem to determine the direction of the interviews; which indicate what the client should be talking about.)

    Structuring. Remarks which define the counseling situation. Remarks indicating the purposes the interview may be expected to accomplish, or the responsibilities of both individuals; i.e., telling "What we can do here." Also includes remarks setting the time and limits of the interview, but not those relating to the end of the interview. Would include "You can have just an hour," but wouldn't include "I see we've come to the end of the hour."

    Forcing client to choose and develop topic. Includes all efforts of the counselor to place responsibility for the direction of the interview upon the client. For example: "What shall we talk about today?" or "Well, how do *you* feel about it?"

    Directive question; specific types of questions. Asking an outright question which requires the giving of a factual answer. It does not include interrogative statements which are merely designed to redefine, clarify, or describe a feeling. It would include "What do you think of that?" "How old are you?" "Do they resent the fact that you are not aggressively going out after jobs?" It would not include "And you aren't too happy about it?" or "It's rather unpleasant for you, is that right?", particularly when such questions follow somewhat similar statements.

Non-directive leads and questions. Statements which encourage the client to state the problem further. This excludes leads that would greatly limit the client in what he could bring out about the problem or his feelings regarding it. It would include "Tell me more about it" or "Would you like to tell me how you feel about it?" or "How are you today?" (asked in a general sense). In general this type of lead is one that encourages a statement without limiting the nature of the response except in a very general way, as in "Tell me more about it."

Non-Directive Response-To-Feeling Categories. (Those which seem to attempt to restate a feeling that the client has expressed, but not to interpret nor offer advice, criticism, or suggestions.)

Simple acceptance. "Yes," "M-hmm," "I see," "That's right" (If not answering questions or similar responses. Must not imply approval or criticism.)

Restatement of content or problem. A simple repeating of what the client has said without any efforts to organize, clarify, or interpret it, or any effort to show that the counselor is appreciating the feeling of the client's statement by understanding it. The wording need not be identical with that of the client.

Clarification or recognition of feeling. A statement by the counselor which puts the client's feeling or affective tone in somewhat clearer or more recognizable form. "It makes you feel very much annoyed," "You love your mother but you resent her telling you what to do," "I think sometimes you wish you'd never been born."

Semi-Directive Response-To-Feeling Category. (Those responses which are interpretive in character.)

Interpretation. Responses in which the counselor points out patterns and relationships in the material presented. This category is always used when causation is implied or indicated. "You do this because . . ." If the counselor attempts, even vaguely to say "why" the client does or feels something, it is considered interpretation. "Perhaps you are revealing feelings of inferiority." "When people feel frustrated they often act the way you do." "There's your problem."

Directive "Counseling" Categories. (Categories of responses which imply a relationship in which the counselor attempts to change the immediate ideas of the client, or to influence his attitude toward them.)

Approval and encouragement. "That's fine." "You've covered a lot

of ground today." "You bet." Any statement which lends emotional support or approval to the client's insecurity.

Giving information or explanation. Answers to any questions about
the nature of psychology, or any other informational material;
anything which is recognized as a generally established fact; any
personal information about the counselor.

Proposing client activity. Any statements which imply that the
client should take any sort of action.

Persuasion. Attempts to convince the client that he should accept
the counselor's point of view. "Don't you think it would be
better that way, now?"

Disapproval and criticism. "You need to get hold of yourself."

Minor Categories. (Those responses which do not seem to be related to the principal problem of the client.)

Ending of the contact. Any responses dealing with the bringing to
a close of contact, or with the setting of a time for a future
contact.

Ending of the series. Responses relating to the bringing to a close a
series of interviews, or to the beginning of the client's feeling
that he does not need further counseling.

Friendly discussion. Material unrelated to the client's problem and
serving only the purpose of establishing good rapport between
client and counselor.

Unclassified. Any response which cannot be classified in one of the
above categories.

A yet different approach to raw data was that made by Curran [1]
who studied intensively the twenty interviews of a single case and
reported his analysis of: (1) the interview content, that is, the
negative emotional responses, positive emotional responses, insight
responses, and choice responses; (2) the course of insight in the
solving of the problem areas; and (3) the relationship between the
areas of the problems and the development of insight.

The intensive study of a single case leaves much to be desired
as to the validity of the concepts evolved and yet such an effort
may yield fruitful hypotheses for further study. The amount of
learning that a student can achieve through intensive consideration of a total case is great indeed. He may not come out with

[1] Curran, Charles A., *Personality Factors in Counseling.* Grune and Stratton,
1945.

any answers but he must certainly increase the scope of his vision.

Raimy[1] made a study which represents quite a different use of interview data. Raimy was interested in studying the person's concept of himself, the way the person sees himself with his own eyes. Psychotherapeutic interviews were judged to be an excellent source of data since a major proportion of the interview content would be devoted to self-referrent material and because in successful cases the self-concept could be expected to undergo a change. A study such as Raimy's, while contributing in large part to theoretical considerations of the self-concept, nevertheless contributed to a better understanding of what transpires during the course of therapy. Raimy analyzed interviews for the references clients made to themselves which could be classified as:

P — Positive; a favoring attitude toward self,

N — Negative; a disapproving attitude toward self,

A — Ambiguous; manifest self-reference but too vague to classify,

Av — Ambivalent; conflicting positive and negative attitudes toward self, and

Q — Non-rhetorical questions.

A recent study which again illustrates going directly to the data is the study made by Hogan[2] in which he studied phonographically recorded interviews and after numerous trials evolved an operational definition of defensive behavior which permitted quantification of this aspect of interview material. The essential point here is that Hogan's definition is dependent upon the *verifiable* performance of the client in the interview rather than upon *interpretations* of the performance and inferences as to the operation of forces not directly observed.

In analyzing a number of interviews Hogan felt that he could see two aspects of the client's self. One aspect was the self as perceiver, knower, experiencer, behaver. This aspect is represented

---

[1] Raimy, Victor C., "The Self-Concept as a Factor in Counseling and Personality Organization," Ph.D. thesis, Ohio State University Library, 1943.

[2] Hogan, Richard, "The Development of a Measure of Client Defensiveness in a Counseling Relationship," Ph.D. dissertation, University of Chicago, 1948.

by such client statements as: "I am doing that just for the satisfaction in it," "I could see how he felt," "I know that that is so," and "I feel pretty bitter about it." The second aspect was the self as perceived, the client's awareness of the concepts, beliefs, ideals, values and attitudes pertaining to self. This aspect is represented by such statements as: "I want to do the best I can," "I guess I just give up too fast," "At least I can get along well with others," "At times I'm a pretty aggressive person," and "I'm just not the kind of person who gets angry."

Utilizing these two concepts of *self-as-perceiver* and *self-as-perceived* Hogan proceeded to analyze interview material for instances in which clients reported perceiving things which were incongruent with or in conflict with what they felt to be true about themselves. Some examples of such incongruencies are: the young man who wants to succeed in school yet finds himself not studying; the young woman who wants to get married yet finds herself driving off all overtures from men; and the man who prides himself on his control over his temper yet finds himself quite angry with his wife. Hogan described defensive behavior as behavior in which the client proceeds to deny in some way the validity of his experience and to cling to the notion about himself. Non-defensive behavior was described as behavior in which the client accepts his experiences and alters his notions about himself or at least does not deny the validity of the experience. The young man who wants to succeed in school may defensively offer false reasons for his not studying or he may face the fact that he is not studying and may seek to discover why not.

For the student who attempts to analyze interview material from Hogan's point of view there may be rewards both in understanding more clearly the concept of defensiveness and in becoming more acute in awareness of the client's viewpoint in a therapeutic interview.

Stock [1] approached interview material to study the demonstrable relationship in attitudes of the client toward himself, others, rela-

---

[1] Stock, Dorothy, "An Investigation into the Interrelations between the Self-Concept and Feelings Directed Toward Other Persons and Groups," M.A. thesis, University of Chicago, 1948.

tionships with others and others' attitudes toward himself. She undertook to identify client attitudes as:

++ Positive expression with high emotion
+ Positive expression with intellectual emphasis
± Ambivalent expression
− Negative expression with intellectual emphasis
− − Negative expression with high emotion
O Objective expression with no feeling evident

In addition, attitudes not toward self but toward others, the relationships with others and toward others' attitudes toward self were further classified as:

(1) Personal; e.g. wife, husband, mother
(2) Social; e.g. friends, schoolmates, business
(3) Impersonal; e.g. dresses of people, people on street
(4) Counselor; e.g. counselor, counseling situation or process
(x) Incidental and extraneous remarks
(n) Agreement with counselor or correction of counselor response
(p) Past attitudes referred to which do not reveal present attitudes

Hoffman [1] had noted that in initial interviews clients often reported behavior that was immature and for which the client disclaimed responsibility while in later interviews of more successful cases behavior of greater maturity was reported and clients tended to accept responsibility for the behavior. Using Raimy's system for classifying responses as positive, negative, and ambivalent, Hoffman sought to compare the attitudes and the maturity of reported behavior as interviews progressed. The maturity scale used was as follows:

(c) The individual is behaving with little or no control over his environment; he is immature and not responsible,
(b) The individual is exercising moderate control over his environment; he is manifesting some maturity and some responsible action, and

[1] Hoffman, A. Edward, "An Investigation of the Relationship Between Attitudinal Changes and Reported Overt Behavioral Changes," M.A. thesis, University of Chicago, 1948.

(a) The individual is behaving with a good deal of self-direction, maturity and responsibility.

Steele[1] and Wolfson[2] were interested in trying to determine whether "successful" and "unsuccessful" cases varied in how the clients perceived elements of their problem situations. Specifically, they sought to compare the clients' perceptions of:

(1) The *agent of solution*; whom or what was perceived as a source of help in solving a problem or problems

(2) The *causes*; the reasons stated, or clearly implied, which were perceived as the reason or reasons for the behavior in relation to the problem or problems

(3) The *means*; the method or way perceived as to reaching the goal, and

(4) The *goals*; something which is desired to be, to do, or to have.

Each reference to one of these elements was further classified according to the degree of certainty expressed by the client. These degrees of certainty were judged to be evidenced by expressions indicating the client:

(a) does not know or perceive the cause, means or goal;

(b) perceives the possibility of the cause, means or goal; and

(c) perceives with certainty the cause, means or goal.

Rather than continue with other studies which are suggestive of methods of approaching the analysis of interview protocols, it may be helpful to present a "check-list" of items which the student might use in analyzing case materials for a more systematic coverage. Again it is emphasized that students should not expect to get ready answers to the host of questions which plague them regarding therapy. The answers keep changing as the therapist grows more experienced. This chapter is devoted to some of the readily available ways of increasing the student's experience. No brief is made for any particular kind of analysis of interviews. It is strongly hoped that as rapidly as possible the student will abandon

[1] Steele, Betty, "The Amount of Exploration into Causes, Means, Goals, and Agent: A Comparison of Successful and Unsuccessful Cases in Client-Centered Therapy," M.A. thesis, University of Chicago, 1948.

[2] Wolfson, Kate S., "Clients' Explorations of Their Problems During Client-Centered Therapy," M.A. thesis, University of Chicago, 1949.

the crutches which are offered here and move toward making analyses on his own. Under no circumstances are any of the approaches to analysis of interviews to be memorized. They are presented as materials about which to think. Where they do not satisfy the student, let the student alter them. It is as a basis of departure that the following "check-list" is presented.

Interview Analysis Check List

A. Concerning the Client

1. List the significant feelings expressed by the client.
2. Indicate why you feel each instance is significant.
3. Analyze each reason given in "2" above and indicate whether your thinking is in the internal or external frame of reference.
4. If you feel there are any of the feelings listed under "1" above which should be handled differently from the others, indicate your reasoning for such handling.
5. Analyze your reasoning in "4" above for thinking in the internal and external frames of reference.
6. Write out what you imagine the client would be likely to reply in response to the handling you recommend in "4" above.
7. For each feeling listed under "1" above write out what you would consider an adequate "reflection."
8. Are there expressions by the client that you just don't understand?
9. List any evidences of progress made by the client.
10. List any evidences of progress having been blocked.

B. Concerning the Counselor

1. List the significant feelings expressed by the counselor.
2. Indicate why you feel each instance is significant.
3. Would you have handled any part (not covered in section A) of the interview differently? Indicate how you would have replied and your reasoning for it.
4. Analyze your reasoning in "3" above for thinking in the internal and external frames of reference.
5. Are there instances of counselor responses where you just don't understand what he is doing?

C. Concerning the Relationship

1. How would you characterize the relationship between the counselor and client?
2. What type of psychological climate has been set for the client? Give instances to support your thinking.
3. If possible, find instances where the counselor's attitudes have been (a) probing, (b) interpretive, (c) understanding, (d) evaluative, and (e) supportive. Describe the behavior in which the client engages following each type of counselor attitude.
4. Note any instances in which the relationship has broken down. Attempt to account for this on the basis of the counselor's behavior and on the basis of the client's personality organization.
5. Analyze the "social" chit-chat that may appear in the interview for what may be taking place between counselor and client.

D. Concerning Miscellaneous Issues

1. What problem or problems does this particular case pose?
2. Can you mention any material of a similar nature where the handling was different?
3. What material in this case has implications for you as to personality theory?
4. Note any new notions which you may have developed for a minor or major research approach to the data.
5. What theoretical writing do you feel could be brought profitably into consideration of the case?

Chapter IX

COUNSELING PROCEDURES

POST-TEST

The test material presented here is divided into two parts. Part I will be a twenty-item free response test, that is, twenty consecutive client responses will be given to which the reader may respond. In the appendix on page 206 there are responses against which the reader may compare his own replies. Part II will consist in a selection of twenty passages taken from the cases presented in Snyder's *Casebook of Non-Directive Counseling.*[1] These selections are to be analyzed in accordance with the directions given. In Appendix B, page 207, there are presented notations of elements of significance that might be expected to appear in the reader's analyses. Cases are drawn from this source so that the reader may refer to the whole cases or other parts of the cases as desired.

It is felt that the multiple choice type of item begins to lose significance as larger and more complex units of interviews are taken into consideration. For this reason the items in Part II are in essay form.

[1] Snyder, William U., *Casebook of Non-Directive Counseling.* Boston: Houghton Mifflin Company, 1947.

Part I. Free Response to Attitudes [1]

Instructions. In this part of the test you are presented with twenty consecutive responses made by a twenty-one-year-old veteran. On a separate sheet of paper write out your formulation of a "reflection" of the feeling involved.

Take each response in turn. Do not read ahead.

1. How do you do? My name is Jones, John Jones. The Training Officer said that he thought I ought to come to see you.
2. You see, he says that he thinks I've got an inferiority complex; that I don't dig into my work. He keeps saying that I don't take initiative even when I can do a job well. What do you think about that?
3. I'd like to talk it over with you if you think it would really help me.
4. This may take quite a while. How much time can I take?
5. Well, you see, — I know that I'm loafing on the job just as well as the Training Officer knows it. I think that he tries to do what is right but I think that a good part of my loafing is his fault.
6. It's the way that Training Officer upsets me. He makes me mad with his always checking up on me.
7. He keeps throwing in my face that if I don't get on the ball this is my last chance for job training under the V.A. program.
8. I can't lose this income. I was out of work for a long time and I just got married here a couple of months ago. I just don't know what I'd do if I got cut off.
9. I like this on-the-job training. I've always wanted to do cabinet making. I've got a flair for it. This stuff is really right down my alley.

---

[1] This test as given is a slight modification of a test developed by Douglas D. Blocksma for use in a short-term training program described in Blocksma, D. D., and Porter, E. H., Jr., "A Short-term Training Program in Client-Centered Counseling." *Journal of Consulting Psychology*, 1947, vol. 11, pp. 55–60.

10. (*15-second pause*) You know, that Training Officer sure does remind me of my older brother!

11. He's the brother next to me — older — there's four of us — a brother — a sister, and then this one — he's just a year older than I am. He was always so bossy. Dad would give us a job to do together and my brother would always try to run it. (*Pause*) But that's neither here nor there. What I've got to figure out is how to quit loafing. Going to lose this job if I'm not careful.

12. I've got to make good on this job — that's for *sure*. It's really a swell chance. I've always wanted to be a cabinet maker just like I told you. It's so darn much fun working with my hands and seeing what I can make — seeing the results right there — and besides — cabinet makers are always in demand — and they make a good living too.

13. Let's look at it this way (*Pause*) and this hurts to talk about. (*Pause*) I don't know why the Training Officer should affect me this way. I get so mixed up when he's watching me work I usually drop my hammer or my file or gouge the wood with the chisel or plane or something. I get so shaky that I just have to quit and do something else no matter how silly it might seem.

14. It's *all* so silly that he affects me that way. You must know why I'd react that way. Can you tell me?

15. (*Pause*) I've thought a lot about this and I'm not at all sure that my brother is responsible for all this. After mother died, when I was five, my brother had to help take care of me — he had to tell me what to do lots of times — I was kind of a screwball and he always had to do the real planning. My high school counselor once told me that my brother was the cause of my lack of effort in school — but — I'm not so sure it was so much my brother.

16. I guess this talk is supposed to help me — but I don't see that it's helping me any.

17. Even though I haven't settled anything I really think that I can manage to keep from losing out on this job. I don't think I need to talk about it any further.

18. Maybe talking with you has helped. I think I see the answer

now — but I don't especially want to go into it all — it's too personal.

19. One thing I forgot to tell you is that the Training Officer has already put through papers with my boss to have me fired, if I don't get on the ball in the next two weeks.

20. I certainly want to thank you for this. And I hope I haven't caused you any inconvenience. You'll probably have to work late now just because I shot off my big mouth and wasted all your time.

Part II.   Counselor Attitude, Frame of Reference and Psychological Climate

Instructions. On a separate sheet of paper describe for each of the following counselor-client exchanges (a) the counselor's attitude, (b) the frame of reference in which the counselor operates and (c) the psychological climate which seems to be established by the counselor's actions.

21

Cl: "—— Well, I've sort of hit a hump. Occasionally I come to a point where I don't know what to say next. There's a lot I'd like to say but I can't get it out."

Co: "M-hm. You shouldn't feel that you need to be under tension to talk all of the time. That's the way one might feel in a social conversation, but here it's different. Any time you'd like to stop and collect your thoughts, go ahead and do so. It won't need to be embarrassing to you, because I will understand that you're just doing a bit of organizing."

22

Cl: (Pause) "Isn't one thing about me I like. Can't even like my own fingernails. They're not smooth like yours. They've got ridges running all down them. My fingers are long yet they're — they're long and they're — yet look stubby, gnarled, and cut. My skin's all flucked up. That's just my hands alone. My knuckles look screwy. I'm just a little jerk. Of course I can wear gloves, and I can counteract my being small and underweight and undersize by clothes. In fact I can wear a hat to cover up this crumpled hair. It won't look nice when it's combed and it won't look nice when it's mussed. It isn't curly — it isn't curly enough so that it will stay put and it isn't straight enough so that it will stay put. It always looks half shot. Of course, I can wear a hat for that. But that leaves one part of me uncovered, between my hat brim and my collar."

Co: "M-hm. That's pretty terrible, isn't it?" (*Smiles*)

Cl: "Yeah. I wish I was like my brother. He's dark just as the rest of the family is. Me — I'm light — puny. He's heavier-built than I am, too. Guess I was just made up of odds and ends. I'm too darn light. I don't like my face. I don't like my eyebrows and my eyes. Bloodshot, little cow-eyes. I hate my pimple chin and I detest the way my face is lopsided. One side is so much different from the other. One side, the chin bones stick out further and the jaw bones are more pronounced. My mouth isn't right. Even when I smile, I don't smile the way other people do. I tried and I can't. When other people smile, their mouths go up — mine goes down. It's me; backward in everything. I'm clumsy as the devil."

Co: "You feel sort of sorry for yourself, isn't that right?"

Cl: "Yes, self-pity, that's me. Sure, I know I pity myself, but I got something to pity. If there were two of me I would punch myself right in the nose just for the fun of it."

Co: "M-hmn."

Cl: "Sometimes I get so disgusted with myself!"

Co: "Sometimes you feel somewhat ashamed of yourself for pointing out all those physical inadequacies, right?"

23

Cl: "Yes, the people are too worried about what you're thinking about *them* to be thinking about you. That's what I've found out so far. So I don't worry about that any more. I haven't completely gotten rid of it, but I believe after awhile if I work on it a little more and keep telling myself that no one's worrying about me it'll be better. It's the last two days that I've tried that system. You can't advance a theory on just two days' work."

Co: "That's right. You feel that that worry is letting up a little bit and that with further experimentation it should — "

24

Cl: "I find that I've kept a lot of childhood worries. They seem childish afterwards. But, boy, how big they seem before you get the answer!"

Co: "M-hm."

Cl: "One of the biggest things I'll ever obtain is confidence. I don't have confidence of my own judgments." (*Pause*)

Co: "M-hm. You traced that back somewhat last time, didn't you?"

25

Cl: "Yes, the kids at home didn't seem to be. To some of those kids it's just as casual as shaking hands, except that it took longer. In fact, some of them might even be classed as street-walkers. There are two spots in town where any night of the week you can find several cars parked. That's disgusting."

Co: "Sex is a pretty horrible thing, because it's so strong."

Cl: "So strong, and plainly an animal instinct. You can't resist it even though it does seem to ruin your character. It's a strong impulse that you've gotta accept even though you don't like it."

Co: "You feel the most fortunate person would be the one who could put it out of his life, is that right?"

Cl: "I don't know. I'm not sure."

Co: "At any rate, people who give in to the force are pretty vulgar."

Cl: "Yes, if they take it outside of its proper place."

Co: "You feel that between two married people it's all right, but otherwise it's very cheap and sinful."

Cl: "It's cheap and it's dirty."

Co: "And you're somewhat afraid of it."

Cl: "Very much afraid of it. I don't like things I can't understand, and I most certainly don't understand that. I understand the functions of the body. I understand everything except the emotional factors involved. One reason why I don't like it is because of understanding the process."

Co: "You want to carry that farther?"

Cl: "A great deal of heat is involved. Heat produces sweat. I don't like sweat. That's one of the big reasons."

Co: "You find sex disgusting. And is it possible that you felt certain tensions yourself and therefore you're afraid of it?"

Cl: "Yes, you're afraid of it. There isn't anything you can do about it. You know it's there and you have got to accept it."

Co: "So you're forced into a position where you can't live as idealistic a life as you'd like to."

Cl: "I don't know. I'm afraid of it, that's all. Just plain afraid of it."

Co: "M-hm. You feel something of disgust because it's sweaty."

Cl: "Sweaty and so darn intimate. It's the closest two people can get without chopping them up and making hash of them. It's so animal-like."

Co: "And you feel people should be superior to animals?"

Cl: "They're supposed to be."

Co: "Sex isn't very modest either, is it?"

Cl: "No, there are no secrets. There's not a bit of modesty in it. It's not the place for a shy person like me."

Co: "You feel it's somewhat revealing of the personality."

Cl: "M-hm. You feel a person who gives in to sex urge has to feel very inferior or unclean about it."

Cl: "Yes, it brings a king down to the equal level of the lowest pig on earth. The meanest animal you can find is just as good as a king in that sense. And Einstein is just as good as one of the feeble-minded patients out at the hospital."

Co: "How do you mean?"

Cl: "A Phi Beta Kappa man isn't any better sexually than a feeble-minded gink."

Co: "In other words, it doesn't take much brains."

Cl: "It doesn't take *any* brains. It's purely an animal instinct. Purely a motor impulse. It's automatic."

Co: "But unfortunately you feel it's still a pretty dynamic force."

26

Cl: "I don't know whether that's exactly right or not. I can't put my finger on it. Sometimes I feel lonely and sometimes I feel another way. Do you have cases this bad?"

Co: "You really wonder whether anybody else could be — "

Cl: "I think I'm worse than anybody that I know. That's just it. I feel as though I am terribly, terribly low. It just does not seem worth — bothering with it, it doesn't seem worth while, that I can't get up there to first base."

Co: "You think about making the struggle, but it doesn't seem possible."

Cl: "That's right. I just wonder what other people do when they find problems and stuff. I just wonder whether they see it through or try to find out something else."

Co: "You feel that you'd like to know how somebody else would handle it."

27

Cl: "Well, I guess that is so. I don't see what it is that has changed me so much. Yes, I do. These talks have helped a lot, and then the books that I've read. Well, I've just noticed such a difference. I find that when I feel things, even when I feel hate, I don't care. I don't mind. I feel more free somehow. I don't feel guilty about things."

Co: "You feel as though these talks and the thinking you've been doing have just changed you so you feel more comfortable with yourself."

Cl: "Yes." (*Pause*)

Co: "You find that you can even feel hatred toward somebody and not be bothered about it."

28

Cl: "So you see I've come a long way. I've faced some of these things. I've realized I'm not so bright, but I begin to think I can get along anyway."

Co: "Yes, you have come a long way and you really have faced some of these things pretty deeply."

29

Cl: "Yes, but how can her husband accept her? Can a man accept a woman who is a lot lower than he is in ability? What do you think?"

Co: "I expect we all see examples of that."

30

Cl: "That's right. (*Pause*) On the other hand, I suppose you can balance it off. The other person might be very intelligent but might have a serious fault that would make it hard for him to get along with people. That would sort of balance it off perhaps."

Co: "You feel that the husband might have real flaws in his personality which would sort of make up for a slight lack of ability on your part."

Cl: "You say it is a slight lack; it seems very great to me. I don't think I'll ever get over what I wanted to be. Of course, though, I suppose everybody wants better things, but I don't know whether I'll really get over not being able to reach the standards that I've always thought about."

Co: "Your deficiency seems pretty great to you and you wonder if you really ever will give up the heights you used to want."

31

Cl: "I think you could say that. When we got to Lexington, I went on to graduate school and got along O.K. But we were living in Marie's mother's home, and after we were married things began happening. My role of dominance found me in the role of critic. I became very critical of Marie. It evolved around the fact that she did little in the line of domestic responsibilities. The girls in her family never did cook at home, or clean house, or do all the things necessary to keep a home going. And I felt that our being in their house was an imposition on Mother to begin with, so I pitched in and took over many of the household responsibilities myself. I'd cook, clean, wash dishes and so on, and then resent the fact that she didn't help very much."

Co: "You felt rather resentful at Marie for not taking hold of the household tasks which you felt needed to be done."

32

Cl: "That's the only kind of experience that has worked in the past, although I'm not saying that nothing else can work. I just now thought of one thing. While we were talking it just occurred to me; that is, I wonder if it would have helped at the outset for you to tell me to call an armistice to my affairs. You see you may not know what I've been doing lately. I haven't altered abruptly *any* of these experiences; I haven't made any attempt to forego these extra-marital experiences. If you had told me to halt these affairs temporarily, the same impulses and urges would have been there, but I think I would have played ball with you. At least it would have had some value in terms of having gotten over a certain difficult period — like a period without a drink. Now it may not have any value, I don't know."

Co: "I appreciate your comments in this regard and they are well taken. However, I'm not interested in the least in either asking, suggesting, or telling you to do something that you really fundamentally may not want to do. I believe you mentioned a few minutes ago that that sort of influence has had little value for you. In fact, I'm not concerned at all in any behavior you desire to engage in. I am interested, however, in talking and thinking these things through with you so that *you* feel what you are doing is really what you want to do. Your coming here in the first place was indicative of the fact that things were not going exactly as you wanted them to go. I am here specifically to help you work out this business, if possible, so that what you do, you really *want* to do in terms of your total life-span."

33

Cl: "All that I'm sure of is that there is a general relaxation of domestic duties. For example, I came home the other evening around five-thirty. Mother [client's mother-in-law] was there, but there was no bread and no food for me. That makes me resentful. I'd just like to have it go for a week with her [client's wife] making meals on time. It's only one meal a day that I eat at home. I don't ask her [the wife] in the morning to get up and get my breakfast; I do it myself, and I eat my noon meal downtown. But that one meal I eat at home, I feel ought to be done — and on time for me to eat when I get home. If for no other reason than to win the battle for me. And yet, I've said little about it. I've kept it pretty much to myself."

Co: "It burns you up, but you haven't said much about it."

34

Cl: "That's about it. Things just seem to be going more smoothly at home, although the work situation is relatively the same. That hasn't materially improved, since there are still the usual work difficulties. But those things seem less important now. The real changes seem to be showing up, and it seems to go back to the decisions on my part to change."

Co: "As I understand it, you feel that things are going more smoothly at least in part due to the fact that you have put your back upon these extramarital affairs. You also said [a moment ago] you felt no qualms about your recent visit to this girl's house. I didn't understand what you meant there. Would you care to explain that a little further?"

35

Cl: "The relationship, I know now, could stand in spite of anything else that might occur. I could coldly anticipate something else, but I know I would do so only because I wanted to continue these sessions which have meant so much to me. But I have the feeling that, since I've come to these conclusions, your responsibilities as far as I'm concerned ought to be permitted to cease."

Co: "You feel, then, that perhaps it might be a good plan to think of terminating our sessions together."

Cl: "I can see the value of keeping me reporting every week. But the point is that I'm sensitive enough not to impose upon you any more than necessary."

Co: "Well, it's certainly not an imposition, and if you feel that you'd like to continue, we could arrange it, I'm sure."

36

Cl: "No." (*Pause.*)

Co: "It seems pretty elusive. These things are hard to express. I can see how they might be. Just go ahead as you like. Through talking these things over together, we may be able to find some new ways of dealing with these things. Just feel perfectly free to talk about anything you like."

37

Cl: "I'd like to keep on trying. I was sure that it was the right thing to do, when I was trying to get myself to act naturally about my hand. But somehow I think that it prevents me from trying another thing which might yield something. I remember in phobias they say if you remember the original situation it helps to do away with the fear. I don't remember the original situation, but in this case I seem to be able to remember more recent things. I was talking to my mother over the week end at home. She said that until I was three I never hid it from anybody. It was after that that it started."

Co: "This has been going on for a long time."

Cl: "My parents remember when I was about ten. They said that they always tried to stop me from hiding my hand. When I was about four I was in a doctor's office and I was hiding my hand, then I remember. There was a girl in there who was very badly burned and was forcing herself on other people. I remember my mother's saying that she was glad that I wasn't like that. Maybe that had something to do with my not wanting to force it on people. But that was when I was already starting to hide it."

Co: "M-hm."

Cl: "I don't know the cause — I can't remember."

Co: "You feel that if you find the cause that it might help."

38

Cl: "Often I feel that way. I have always felt that way. No matter how realistic I try to be. I remember one time my freshman year, one of the girls was getting a date for my roommate. My roommate said, 'Edith and I were going to go out together,' and she asked if this girl could get me a date. She said, 'I don't know. You see, Edith has a bad hand.' I was terribly hurt. I think the fact that it was so important to her made it much more important to me."

Co: "I can see how it would. That must have hurt badly." (*Pause.*)

39

Cl: "Well, here I am. This is perfectly silly, but the doctor *insisted* that I come in and see you. I promised the doctor that I would come for *one hour* and here I am."

Co: "You're here because of the doctor's insistence and not because you feel any need for it."

40

Cl: "I cried myself to sleep many a night. Then one of my profs talked to me and he said, among other things, that a person who lost an eye wore a glass eye, and a person who lost an arm or a leg wore an artificial limb and it was considered a godsend. 'You're no more of a fraud than they are,' he said. 'No more of a fraud than all the girls who wear rouge and lipstick and who permanent their hair. You had the advantage of correcting a flaw of nature. There isn't any reason for you to feel like you do about it.' And so — (*Begins to cry again.*) And so I got over it."

Co: "After he talked it over with you, you were able to accept it and you got over your feelings."

This completes the post-test. In Appendix B are given a set of "answers" against which the reader may wish to compare his responses to the test items.

Appendix A

SCORING THE PRE-TEST

Parts I through III are designed to measure the same fundamental characteristics of the counselor, the attitudes which he implements when confronted by different client attitudes in different situations. In the alternatives following items 1 through 45 each alternative exemplifies a basically different counselor attitude. These five attitudes are:

E — *Evaluative.* A response which indicates the counselor has made a judgment of relative goodness, appropriateness, effectiveness, rightness. He has in some way implied what the client *might or ought to do*: grossly or subtly.

I — *Interpretive.* A response which indicates the counselor's intent is to teach, to impart meaning to the client, to show him. He has in some way implied what the client *might or ought to think*: grossly or subtly.

S — *Supportive.* A response which indicates the counselor's intent is to reassure, to reduce the client's intensity of feeling, to pacify. He has in some way implied that client *need not feel as he does.*

P — *Probing.* A response which indicates the counselor's intent is to seek further information, provoke further discussion along a certain line, to query. He has in some way implied that the client *ought or might profitably develop or discuss a point further.*

U — *Understanding.* A response which indicates the counselor's intent is to so respond as in effect to ask the client whether the counselor understands correctly what the client is "saying," how the client "feels" about it, how it "strikes" the client, how the client "sees" it.

In Part IV all of the alternatives following the test item are so phrased as to appear to be attempts to effect an *Understanding* attitude as described above. In each question, however, the alternatives differ in the following ways.

C — *Content.* A response in which the attempt at understanding is implemented in large part by a simple repetition of the same words used by the client.

S — *Shallow or Partial.* A response in which the attempt at understanding is implemented in a limited way by involving only a portion of what the client expressed or by "undercutting" or "watering-down" the feeling tone expressed.

R — *Reflection.* A response in which the attempt at understanding is implemented by a rephrasing in fresh words the gist of the client's expression without changing either the meaning or feeling tone.

I — *Interpretive.* A response in which the attempt to understand actually goes beyond the meaning of the client and adds meaning not expressed by the client.

Instructions for Scoring Parts I, II and III

In the scoring table below the number of each item appears in the extreme left column. To the right are the numbers of the alternatives for each item. These numbers are placed in the column at the top of which appears the first letter of the name of the attitude the alternative represents: E — evaluative; I — interpretive; S — supportive; P — probing, and U — understanding. Score parts I, II, and III by circling the number of the alternative you chose in each test item. Adding up the number of circles in each column (for each part and for the three parts) gives a distribution of the attitudes which you favored. You may wish to make a profile of these results.

Instructions for Scoring Part IV

In the scoring of the table below, the number of each item appears in the left column. To the right are the numbers of the alternatives for each item. These numbers are placed in the col-

Part I

Item No.	E	I	S	P	U
1	2	4	3	1	5
2	3	1	2	5	4
3	1	3	5	4	2
4	4	5	1	2	3
5	5	2	4	3	1
6	4	2	3	5	1
7	3	5	4	1	2
8	5	4	1	2	3
9	2	1	5	4	3
10	1	4	2	3	5
11	4	3	5	1	2
12	1	2	4	3	5
13	3	1	2	5	4
14	2	5	1	4	3
15	3	5	4	2	1
16	1	4	2	5	3
17	3	5	4	1	2
18	2	1	3	5	4
19	5	3	1	2	4
20	4	5	2	3	1
21	1	2	5	4	3
22	4	5	3	2	1
23	4	3	1	2	5
24	2	1	4	5	3
25	3	4	5	1	2
Totals					

Part II

Item No.	E	I	S	P	U
26	5	4	2	3	1
27	1	3	4	2	5
28	4	2	1	5	3
29	2	5	3	1	4
30	5	1	2	4	3
31	3	4	5	2	1
32	1	3	4	5	2
33	3	2	1	4	5
34	2	1	5	3	4
35	4	5	3	1	2
Totals					

Part III

Item No.	E	I	S	P	U
36	5	4	2	3	1
37	2	5	3	1	4
38	1	3	5	4	2
39	4	2	1	5	3
40	3	1	4	2	5
41	1	2	4	3	5
42	4	1	3	5	2
43	5	3	1	2	4
44	1	4	5	2	3
45	3	5	2	4	1
Totals					
Grand Totals					

umn at the top of which appears the first letter of the name of the factor which most characterizes the alternative: C — content repetition; S — shallowness; R — reflection; and I — interpretive. Score Part IV by circling the number of the alternative you chose in each test item. Adding up the number of circles in each column will give the distribution of responses. Since the items in the R column are considered most accurate, the totals of other items suggest the frequencies and types of errors made.

Item No.	C	S	R	I
46	1	3	4	2
47	2	1	3	4
48	3	2	4	1
49	4	3	1	2
50	1	4	2	3
51	4	2	1	3
52	3	4	2	1
53	2	3	1	4
54	1	2	4	3
55	4	1	3	2
Totals				

Instructions for Scoring Part V

No numerical score is directly obtainable for this part of the test. Below there appear responses which are designed to be illustrative of what would be appropriate from a non-directive or client-centered point of view. The reader may wish to compare his responses to those given and to analyze for any differences in the attitudes or purposes behind the responses.

56. You're coming at his instigation, then, rather than because of something that you wanted to see me about?
57. That's the way he looks at it — but I gather you don't agree with him?
58. You're not sure in your own mind that it is, is that it?
59. I can give you until —— .

60. Wondering just how far you can go? Wondering if it isn't too late?
61. On that point you feel pretty certain.
62. Fairly certain of what you'd like to do but not at all certain of whether it's attainable, is that it?
63. You feel he's pretty strongly opposed to your interests.
64. For you it's the *most* important thing, is that it?
65. You feel that that's what may be behind your ambition.
66. Feel that you're pressed into doing something now, is that it?
67. You want a sense of satisfaction and achievement as well as a living.
68. I gather that this is something that is of real concern to you.
69. This is something that is really puzzling to you.
70. The idea that it might be your parents has been brought up but you aren't satisfied that that's the whole story.
71. You feel that you're not getting what you want here.
72. Feel that you can cope with this yourself.
73. It's been helpful even though you feel reluctant to bring out some things.
74. That's been one of the things that's made your situation serious, is that it?
75. Feel that you're imposing on me, in that sense?

Appendix B

SCORING THE POST-TEST

Part I of the post-test represents a situation comparable in feelings expressed with Part V of the pre-test. The reader may wish to compare his performance on these two sections in light of the material discussed in the intervening chapters. No numerical score is suggested. There are reproduced on the following pages responses which currently might be deemed appropriate from a nondirective or client-centered point of view.

Part II is scored qualitatively, not numerically. In the pages which follow the writer presents his analyses of the passages presented. These may be used as bases for comparisons by the reader.

Suggested "Answers" to Part I

1. I see. You're coming to see me because *he* thinks you should, is that it?
2. That's the way he sees the situation but I gather you aren't so certain he's right.
3. If you could feel reasonably sure it would help, you'd like to go into it.
4. Right now I can give you until ——.
5. In other words, you don't feel you're entirely to blame.
6. That's the part that sticks in your craw.
7. In other words, you feel he's threatening you.
8. You're under pressure; you just can't afford to lose out.
9. For you it's something *really* desirable.
10. There's some connection there.

11. Regardless of what might be behind it, the pressing thing is to do something about it, is that it?
12. You not only have to make good but you really want to, too.
13. You feel it's silly, in a sense, but nevertheless, that is how he does affect you.
14. I gather that it's really puzzling to you.
15. The notion of your brother has been brought up but I gather you're not entirely satisfied with the idea.
16. You feel that this is not doing the job you wanted.
17. Feel that you can handle it yourself, is that it?
18. In other words, maybe you're in the clear without going into a lot of more intimate details.
19. I gather that that is hanging over your head and forcing the issue for you.
20. Feeling grateful, in part, yet feeling that you may have imposed on me, is that it?

Suggested "Answers" to Part II

21. (a) Basically a reassuring attitude with some teaching or structuring.
    (b) External frame of reference. The counselor has presumed a number of things about the client.
    (c) The implication is that the client is untutored and can't make this judgment himself.
22. (a) Essentially interpretive with an element of support.
    (b) External frame of reference. The counselor is not following the client but is pointing out some of his behavior to him.
    (c) The implication here would seem to be that even though the client is acting in a rather infantile way the counselor still likes him in a big-brotherly way.
23. (a) An evaluative attitude and an understanding attitude.
    (b) External frame of reference. The counselor is throwing his weight behind the goodness of a decision as well as understanding the satisfaction the client feels. This latter part is in an internal frame of reference.
    (c) The implication here is immediately that the client has done a good thing and is thereby praiseworthy. The attitude behind it is that the client can't be trusted to really judge the value of the experience himself.

24. (*a*) Evaluative and/or supportive attitude.
    (*b*) External frame of reference. The client clearly is not referring to what he traced the time before.
    (*c*) This is not too clear. If the attitude is evaluative, (You achieved insight into that last time, why are you acting like this now?) it implies that the client is either somewhat inferior or somewhat culpable. If the attitude is supportive, (You don't need to feel that way any longer: remember the insight you achieved last time?) the implication is also one of an inferior person who needs a crutch.

25. (*a*) Essentially interpretive with strong moralistic or evaluative elements.
    (*b*) Almost wholly in the external frame of reference. The counselor is pushing the client most forcefully, leading him into the feelings which the counselor feels the client should explore.
    (*c*) The implication here is that the client has an inferior set of notions about sex. There is clearly the implication, too, that the client has to be pushed, that he can't or won't take the responsibility for himself.

26. (*a*) Understanding or reflecting attitude.
    (*b*) Internal frame of reference. The counselor continues to "match the perceptions" of the client even though a strong invitation exists to depart into reassurance or interpretation.
    (*c*) The implication to the client here is one of worth and integrity. (This may be understood by recognizing what the counselor does not do which would ordinarily be expected by the client.)

27. (*a*) Counselor's first response indicates attitude of understanding. The second response seems to indicate either a probing attitude or a pushing, interpretive attitude.
    (*b*) Counselor's first response: internal frame of reference. Counselor's second response: external frame of reference. It appears that the counselor is seeking to bring the client to further expression on this topic.
    (*c*) Counselor's first response sets same climate as in 26. Counselor's second response implies the client's need to not bypass this important point — an implication of her weakness or incompetence.

28. (*a*) Reassuring attitude.
    (*b*) External frame of reference. Counselor has made a judgment about the client's progress and depth of experience.
    (*c*) The implication here seems to be more one of the client's being

praiseworthy. This carries the implication that any other judgment is incorrect and not praiseworthy.

29. (a) Essentially reassuring attitude.

(b) External frame of reference. Counselor responds to his own conception of reality, not to the client's.

(c) The implication here seems to be that of incompetence. The response implies that the client's doubting attitude is immature or unrealistic, something not worth worrying over.

30. (a) First response is either reassuring in reference to a "slight lack" to balance a "serious fault" or is a mistake in an otherwise understanding attitude. Second response is similarly reassuring in reference to "the heights you used to want" or is a mistake in an understanding attitude.

(b) In both cases the response seems to be largely from an internal frame of reference but with two elements in an external frame. The counselor apparently judged the client to be overestimating the lack of ability and introduced this judgment into his response. The counselor apparently judged the client's reference to "the standards that I've always thought about" as implying that her wishes were in the past.

(c) The climate the counselor provides here seems quite sound as far as the attitudes are concerned (presuming that they are essentially understanding) but the mistaken judgments made by the counselor may be quite threatening to the client in the lack of close understanding they may convey. If the attitudes are reassuring, the implication of weakness is apparent.

31. (a) The attitude here seems clearly an understanding attitude.

(b) External frame of reference. The counselor here misses the feeling being expressed and responds to a feeling the client reports having had in the past. It is more likely the client is expressing the feeling "My dominance led me to act in a way I feel was wrong, even though justified."

(c) The climate here seems positive except for the threat the client may feel from not being closely understood.

32. (a) The attitude here seems largely reassuring.

(b) The reference frame is external. The counselor does not come to grips directly with the client's attitude toward the counselor or toward himself but seems to provide a course of instruction for the client designed to reassure the client that the counselor does not wish to intervene in the client's life. (The counselor may be reassuring himself after the client's comments earlier in the interview. See response S29, page 222 in *Casebook of*

Non-Directive Counseling, William U. Snyder, Houghton Mifflin: Boston. 1947.)

(c) It is difficult to decide just what climate is set for the client here. The fact that the counselor feels a need to explain to the client that the client is really his own master implies weakness in the client. On the other hand, the message of independence conveyed by the content of the counselor's response implies strength and integrity in the client.

33. (a) Clearly the attitude is one of understanding.

(b) The frame of reference is clearly that of the client's; an internal reference frame.

(c) The climate here is positive in every sense that it is possible to make it. The implication of integrity in the client is complete.

34. (a) The attitude here is either a probing attitude in the sense of satisfying curiosity or in the sense of digging for something the counselor thinks is important.

(b) The frame of reference is external: this is thinking about or thinking for the client.

(c) To the extent that this represents the satisfaction of curiosity, the climate sets up the implication that the client's thinking is less important than the counselor's curiosity. If the counselor's intent is to probe for something of significance it implies that the client is inadequate to judge what is of importance and is incapable of understanding it.

35. (a) In the counselor's first response the attitude is one of understanding: in the second response the attitude is openly reassuring.

(b) The frame of reference is internal in the first response even though the counselor has not perceived accurately that the client is expressing the notion of an obligation to terminate rather than expressing the conclusion that it would be a good plan to terminate. In the second response the counselor adopts the external frame of reference, denies the client's feeling of imposing (which may well be a dependent invitation for reassurance), and openly reassures the client.

(c) The climate set by the understanding attitude has been previously discussed. It might be noted that the inaccuracy of the counselor's apprehension of the client's meaning puts the client in the position of having to justify himself. The climate set by the reassuring attitude seems to imply a weakness in the client, in this case a weakness in ability to decide for himself whether or not he wants further interviews.

36. (a) Possibly understanding but in greatest part the attitude is reassuring and moralistic; moralistic in the sense that it establishes values for the client to accept.

   (b) In part this may be based on an internal frame of reference, that is, the client may see the situation as involving elusiveness and difficulty of expression. Largely, however, the response is from an external frame of reference and seeks to reassure the client and to teach the client how to act.

   (c) Essentially this response sets the warm, friendly atmosphere of the paternal counselor who sees the client as somewhat infantile, inadequate and weak.

37. (a) The counselor's attitude here is essentially understanding, that is, he is trying to see the situation as the client sees it.

   (b) The frame of reference is internal. One might notice, however, that the responses are not as accurate as they might be, they seem to be more general and somewhat more shallow than the client's feelings.

   (c) It is not clear just what climate is set when a client is dealing initially with material which leads to insights of central significance and the counselor does not follow closely. It may be perceived by the client as an area of exploration which is forbidden or fruitless.

38. (a) The attitude here seems to be essentially a supportive attitude, especially in its agreement with the reasonableness of her feelings.

   (b) The frame of reference here is a mixture of the external and internal. The counselor is responding to what the client is feeling but only in part. The more characteristic element of the response is the introduction of the counselor's standards of what was a reasonable feeling for the client to have.

   (c) The climate here seems to carry the implication that the client is right in viewing herself as a pitiable object. The implication of weakness would appear to be reinforced.

39. (a) Clearly an attitude of understanding.

   (b) Internal frame of reference.

   (c) This is a clear illustration of a climate which implies the client is capable of caring for her own integrity.

40. (a) Clearly an understanding attitude.

   (b) Wholly in the internal frame of reference.

   (c) The climate here clearly implies strength and capacity within the client to maintain her own integrity.

Appendix C

READING SOURCES

I. Periodic publications which frequently carry research reports and articles relative to the issues involved in therapeutic counseling.

1. American Journal of Orthopsychiatry.
2. American Journal of Psychiatry.
3. American Journal of Psychotherapy.
4. American Psychologist.
5. Applied Psychology Monographs.
6. Bulletin of the Menninger Clinic.
7. Educational and Psychological Measurement.
8. Etc. (A General Semantics publication.)
9. Human Relations.
10. Journal of Abnormal and Social Psychology.
11. Journal of Clinical Psychology.
12. Journal of Consulting Psychology.
13. Journal of General Psychology.
14. Journal of Personality.
15. Journal of Psychology.
16. Journal of Social Issues.
17. Marriage and Family Living.
18. Mental Hygiene.
19. Occupations.
20. Psychiatric Quarterly.
21. Psychiatry.
22. Psychological Abstracts. (Contains abstracts of articles published in journals. Excellent source for rapidly locating articles of interest.)
23. Psychological Bulletin.
24. Psychological Review.

25. Psychosomatic Medicine.
26. Reports of the Group For The Advancement of Psychiatry, 3617 West Sixth Street, Topeka, Kansas. (Of special interest is Report No. 10, "The Relation of Clinical Psychology to Psychiatry.")
27. Sociatry.

II. Sources relating to personality formation and personality theory.

28. Adler, Alfred. *Practice and Theory of Individual Psychology.* New York: Harcourt Brace, 1924.
29. Angyal, A. *Foundations For A Science of Personality.* New York: The Commonwealth Fund, 1941.
30. Barker, R. G., Kounin, J. S., and Wright, H. F. *Child Behavior And Development.* New York: McGraw-Hill, 1943.
31. Cameron, N. *The Psychology of Behavior Disorders.* Boston: Houghton Mifflin, 1947.
32. Curran, C. A. *Personality Factors In Counseling.* New York: Grune and Stratton, 1945.
33. Dreikurs, R. *An Introduction to Individual Psychology.* London: Kegan Paul, Trench, Trubner, 1935.
34. Fenichel, O. *The Psychoanalytic Theory of Neurosis.* New York: Norton, 1945.
35. Freud, S. *An Outline of Psychoanalysis.* New York: W. W. Norton, 1949.
36. Goldstein, K. *The Organism.* New York: American Book Company, 1939.
37. Hunt, J. McV. (Ed.) *Personality And The Behavior Disorders.* New York: Ronald Press, 1945.
38. Lecky, P. *Self-Consistency — A Theory of Personality.* New York: Island Press, 1945.
39. Leeper, R. *Psychology of Personality.* Ann Arbor: Edwards Brothers, 1941.
40. Lewin, K. *A Dynamic Theory of Personality.* New York: McGraw-Hill, 1935.
41. Miller, J. G. *Unconsciousness.* New York: Wiley, 1942.
42. Raimy, V. C. *The Self-Concept As A Factor In Counseling and Personality.* Doctoral dissertation, Ohio State University Library, 1943. (The student who seriously wishes to read in this area will do well to read the original study.) A condensation of a portion of the thesis appears as "Self-reference in counseling interviews," *Journal of Consulting Psychology,* 1948, *12,* 153–163.
43. Rogers, C. R. *Client-Centered Therapy.* (In preparation.)

44. Snygg, D., and Combs, A. W. *Individual Behavior*. New York: Harper, 1949.

45. White, R. W. *The Abnormal Personality*. New York: Ronald Press, 1948.

III. Sources relating to psychotherapeutic procedures and theories.

46. Adler, Alexandra. *Guiding Human Misfits. A Practical Application of Individual Psychology*. New York: Macmillan, 1939.

47. Adler, Alfred. *Practice And Theory Of Individual Psychology*. New York: Harcourt Brace, 1924.

48. Alexander, F., French, T. M., (et al.) *Psychoanalytic Therapy*. New York: Ronald, 1946.

49. Axline, V. M. *Play Therapy*. Boston: Houghton Mifflin, 1947.

50. Barker, L. F. *Psychotherapy*. New York: D. Appleton-Century, 1940.

51. Fenichel, O. *The Psychoanalytic Theory Of Neurosis*. New York: Norton, 1945.

52. Garrett, A. *Interviewing*. New York: Family Welfare Association of America, 1942.

53. Garrett, A. *Counseling Methods For Personnel Workers*. New York: Family Welfare Association of America, 1945.

54. Kubie, L. S. *Practical Aspects of Psychoanalysis*. New York: Norton, 1936.

55. Law, S. G. *Therapy Through Interview*. New York: McGraw-Hill, 1948.

56. Lecky, P. *Self-Consistency — A Theory Of Personality*. New York: Island Press, 1945.

57. Raimy, V. C. *The Self-Concept As A Factor In Counseling and Personality*. Doctoral dissertation, Ohio State University Library, 1943. (The student who seriously wishes to read in this area will do well to read the original study.) A condensation of a portion of the thesis appears as "Self-reference in counseling interviews," *Journal of Consulting Psychology*, 1948, *12*, 153–163.

58. Rank, O. *Will Therapy*. New York: Knopf, 1936.

59. Raskin, N. J. "The development of non-directive therapy," *Journal of Consulting Psychology*, 1948, *12*, 92–110.

60. Rogers, C. R. *Client-Centered Therapy*. (In preparation.)

61. Rogers, C. R. *Counseling and Psychotherapy*. Boston: Houghton Mifflin, 1942.

62. Snyder, W. U. "The present status of psychotherapeutic counseling," *Psychological Bulletin*, 1947, *44*, 297–386.

63. Snyder, W. U., Rogers, C. R., Muench, G. A., Combs, A. W., and Axline, V. M. *Casebook of Non-Directive Counseling.* Boston: Houghton Mifflin, 1947.
64. Sullivan, H. S. *Conceptions of Modern Psychiatry.* Washington, D.C.: William Alanson White Psychiatric Foundation, 1945.
65. Taft, J. J. *The Dynamics Of Therapy In A Controlled Relationship.* New York: Macmillan, 1933.
66. Williamson, E. G. *How To Counsel Students.* New York: McGraw-Hill, 1939.

IV. Sources relating to learning theories and theories of perception and concept formation.

67. Cantor, N. *The Dynamics of Learning.* Buffalo: Foster and Stewart, 1946.
68. Köhler, W. *Gestalt Psychology.* New York: Liveright, 1929.
69. Lecky, P. *Self-Consistency — A Theory of Personality.* New York: Island Press, 1945.
70. Leeper, R. "Dr. Hull's *Principles of Behavior,*" *Journal of Genetic Psychology,* 1944, *65,* 3–52.
71. Mowrer, O. H. "Learning theory and the neurotic paradox," *American Journal of Orthopsychiatry,* 1948, *18,* 571–610.
72. Mowrer, O. H. (Ed.) *Psychotherapy As Social Learning.* (Approximate title. May appear in 1950.)
73. Raimy, V. C. *The Self-Concept As A Factor In Counseling and Personality.* Doctoral dissertation, Ohio State University Library, 1943. (The student who seriously wishes to read in this area will do well to read the original study.) A condensation of a portion of the thesis appears as "Self reference in counseling interviews," *Journal of Consulting Psychology,* 1948, *12,* 153–163.
74. Shaw, F. J. "A stimulus-response analysis of repression and insight in psychotherapy," *Psychological Review,* 1946, *53,* 36–42.
75. Snygg, D., and Combs, A. W. *Individual Behavior.* New York: Harper, 1949.
76. Tolman, E. C. *Purposive Behavior In Animals and Men.* New York: Century, 1932. Reprinted by University of California Press, 1949.
77. Tolman, E. C. "Cognitive maps in rats and men," *Psychological Review,* 1948, 55, 189–208.

V. Sources relating to different areas of relevance or application of therapeutic principles and procedures.

78. Allen, F. *Psychotherapy With Children.* New York: Norton, 1942.
79. Axline, V. M. "Nondirective therapy for poor readers," *Journal of Consulting Psychology,* 1947, *11,* 61–69.
80. Axline, V. M. *Play Therapy.* Boston: Houghton Mifflin, 1947.
81. Baruch, D. W. "Mental hygiene counseling as a part of teacher education," *Journal of Psychology,* 1942, *13,* 69–108.
82. Baruch, D. W. "Therapeutic procedures as a part of the educative process," *Journal of Consulting Psychology,* 1940, *4,* 165–172.
83. Cantor, N. *Employee Counseling.* New York: McGraw-Hill, 1945.
84. Cantor, N. *The Dynamics of Learning.* Buffalo: Foster and Stewart, 1946.
85. Corey, S. M., and Herrick, V. "Adjustment counseling with teachers," *Educational Administration and Supervision,* 1944, *30,* 87–96.
86. Corsini, R. J. "Nondirective vocational counseling of prison inmates," *Journal of Clinical Psychology,* 1947, *3,* 96–100.
87. Cruickshank, W. M., and Emory, L. C. "Group therapy with physically handicapped children. I. Report of study," *Journal of Educational Psychology,* 1948, *39,* 193–215.
88. Curran, C. A. "Nondirective counseling in allergic complaints," *Journal of Abnormal and Social Psychology,* 1948, *43,* 442–451.
89. Dicks, R. L. *Pastoral Work and Personal Counseling.* New York: Macmillan, 1944.
90. Dickson, W. J. "The Hawthorne plan of personnel counseling," *American Journal of Orthopsychiatry,* 1945, *15,* 343–347.
91. Fiedler, F. E. "An experimental approach to preventive psychotherapy," *The Journal of Abnormal and Social Psychology,* 1949, *44,* 8 pp.
92. Froehlich, C. P. *Evaluating Guidance Procedures: A Review Of The Literature.* Washington, D.C.: Federal Security Agency, Office of Education, Misc. No. 3310, January, 1949.
93. Garrett, A. *Counseling Methods For Personnel Workers.*

New York: Family Welfare Association of America, 1945.

94. Green, A. W. "Social values and psychotherapy," *Journal of Personality*, 1946, *14*, 199–228.

95. Johnson, P. E. "Methods of pastoral counseling," *Journal of Pastoral Care*, 1947, *1*, (6 p.)

96. Jones, E. *Psycho-Analysis*. New York: Jonathan Cape and Harrison Smith, 1929.

97. Law, S. G. *Therapy Through Interview*. New York: McGraw-Hill, 1948.

98. Lewin, K., and Grabbe, P. "Conduct, knowledge and the acceptance of new values," *Journal of Social Issues*, 1945, August, 53–64.

99. Lewis, V. W. "Changing the behavior of adolescent girls," *Archives of Psychology*, 1943, No. 279, pp. 87.

100. Miller, J. G. "Mental hygiene for the counselor," *Journal of the National Association of Deans of Women*, 1949, January, 51–58.

101. Mitchell, J. H., Curran, C. A., and Myers, R. "Some psychosomatic aspects of allergic diseases," *Psychosomatic Medicine*, 1947, *9*, 184–191.

102. Mayer, N. A. "Non-directive employment interviewing," *Personnel*, 1948, *24*, 377–396.

103. Pearse, I. H. and Crocker, L. H. *Peckham Experiment*. London: George Allen and Unwin, 1943.

104. Rogers, C. R. "The non-directive method as a technique for social research," *American Journal of Sociology*, 1945, *50*, 279–283.

105. Rogers, C. R. "Some implications of client-centered counseling for college personnel work," *Educational and Psychological Measurement*, 1948, *8*, 540–549.

106. Rogers, C. R. *Dealing With Social Tensions*. New York: Hinds, Hayden and Eldredge, 1948.

107. Schultz, D. A. "A study of nondirective counseling as applied to adult stutters," *Journal of Speech Disorders*. 1947, *12*, 421–427.

108. Seeman, J. "Interview methods in vocational counseling," *Journal of Consulting Psychology*, 1948, *12*, 321–330.

109. Smith, A. J., and McGrath, F. "Parent education and group therapy: An episode," *Journal of Clinical Psychology*, 1948, *4*, 214–216.

110. Taft, J. J. (Ed.) *Counseling And Protective Service As Family Case Work: A Functional Approach*. Philadelphia: Pennsylvania School of Social Work, 1946, pp. 162.

111. Williamson, E. G. *How To Counsel Students*. New York: McGraw-Hill, 1939.

VI. Sources from which an historical perspective may be obtained. (These are listed in chronological order of their publication.)

112. Freud, S. *An Outline of Psychoanalysis.* New York: Norton, 1949. (Papers dating from 1893.)
113. Dubois, P. *The Psychic Treatment of Nervous Disorders.* New York: Funk and Wagnalls, 1909.
114. Münsterberg, H. *Psychotherapy.* New York: Moffat, Yard and Company, 1909.
115. Jacoby, G. W. *Suggestion and Psychotherapy.* New York: Scribner's, 1912.
116. Adler, Alfred. *The Neurotic Constitution.* New York: Moffat, Yard and Company, 1917.
117. Adler, Alfred. *Practice and Theory of Individual Psychology.* New York: Harcourt Brace, 1924.
118. Janet, P. *Principles of Psychotherapy.* New York: Macmillan, 1924.
119. Janet, P. *Psychological Healing.* New York: Macmillan, 1925.
120. Jones, E. *Psycho-Analysis.* New York: Jonathan Cape and Harrison Smith, 1929.
121. Alexander, F. M. *The Use of The Self.* New York: E. P. Dutton, 1932.
122. Rank, O. *Will Therapy.* New York: Knopf, 1936.
123. Raskin, N. J. "The development of nondirective therapy," *Journal of Consulting Psychology,* 1948, *12,* 92–110.

INDEX

Accuracy of perception of client attitudes, test of, 37–40
Acknowledgment of help, example of, 43, 191–192
Admiration, example of, and different methods of handling, 23
Advice, example of request for, and different methods of handling, 16–17
Ambitiousness, example of, and different methods of handling, 13–14
Ambivalence, example of, and different counseling aims, 33–34, 34–35
Analysis of interviews, 171–188; checklist for, 187–188; objective approaches to, 177–179, 180–182, 183, 183–184, 184–185, 185, 186; subjective approaches to, 174–175, 175–177, 182
Anger, example of, and different counseling aims, 32–33; and different methods of handling, 25
Answers, issues in handling demand for, 118–119
Answers to exercises; *see* Responses, suggested formulations of
Answers to tests; *see* Scoring
Anxiety, example of, and different methods of handling, 15
Apparent feeling, issues in handling recitation of facts without, 91–92
Aptness of response to client, in different counselor roles, test of, 25–31; in same counselor role, test of, 11–25
Attitude, issues in handling desire to retain unsatisfactory, 145–147
Attitudinal learning, 45–46, 49; exercises for analysis of, 50–52, 52–53, 54–56, 57–58, 58–59, 60; illustrative example of, 46; limiting factors in, 49–50
Axline, Virginia M., 10

Beginning an interview, problems in, 88–96
Blocking, example of, and different methods of handling, 22
Blocksma, Douglas D., 40, 190

Cause, example of evaluation of, 43, 191; example of inquiry into, 43, 191
Client attitudes, accuracy of perception of, test of, 37–40; and counselor techniques, 4; free response to, test of, 40–44, 190–192; research methods on, 182–186; and therapeutic outcomes, 9; and therapy goals, 4
Closing a beginning interview, problems in, 107–120
Closing phases of interviewing, problems in, 123–160
Competence, example of assertion of, 43, 191
Competitiveness, example of, and different methods of handling, 21–22
Concern with symptoms, example of, 42–43, 191; example of, with differences in accuracy of handling, 39–40; example of, and different counseling aims, 33
Condemnation, example of, with differences in accuracy of handling, 37–38
Confirmation of judgment, example of request for, and different counseling aims, 34
Conflict, example of, and different methods of handling, 14–15
Continuation of counseling, issues in handling attempt to force decision for onto counselor, 109; issues in handling expression of no further need for, 112–113; issues in handling panic with idea of, 119–120
Counseling, special problems in, 161–170; typical problems in, 87–160
Counseling procedures, issues in handling demand for justification of, 114–116
Counselor aims, test of, 31–36
Counselor attitude, frame of reference and psychological climate, test of, 192–200
Counselor attitudes, control of, 2; importance of, 1; projection of, 1; self-knowledge of, 2, 4; and techniques, 2,

Initial statements of difficulty, problems in, 96–107

Inquiries about clients, from friends or relatives, 166; from referring authority or agency, 166–167

Insight, example of, 42, 191; issues in handling expression of, 143–145, 157–158

Instructions, issues in handling request for, 90–91

Interpretation, and moralization, example of use of, 194–195; and support, example of use of, 192–193

Interruption of counseling by client, 168–169

Interruptions during counseling hour, 170

Internal frame of reference, 61; and client's perceptions, 64; diagrammatic sketch of, 63; identification of, exercise in, 64–67; implications of for techniques, 62; importance of, 61–62; and perception, 61; responding to; see Responding to the internal frame of reference.

Internal motivation and resistance, 7–8, 62

Interviewing, problems in beginning, 88–96; problems in closing, 107–120, 123; problems in handling initial statements of difficulty in, 96–107; problems in middle and closing phases of, 123–160

Isolation, example of, and different methods of handling, 15–16

Jake and the Analyst, 58–59
Jim Gets a Lickin', 54–56
Johnny and His Mother, 46; analysis of, 46–49

Justification by counselor, example of demand for, 41, 190

Lead taking, issues in handling of pressure on counselor to engage in, 147–151

Learning, and therapy, 123–124, 175–177; *see also* Attitudinal learning

Linda and Dr. A., 57–58

Marriage counselor role, 27–28

Medical problem, issues in handling when raised by client, 100–101

Middle phases of interviewing, problems in, 123–160

Misunderstanding of counseling, issues in handling when expressed by client, 93–94

Motivation; *see* External motivation, *also* Internal motivation

Mr. W and the Jumping-Board, 50–52; students' reactions to, 52–53

Non-directive hypothesis, 173

Pauses, issues in handling prolonged, 155–157

Perception, and defensiveness, 62; and internal frame of reference, 61; and techniques, 62

Personality, and capacity for expression of, 5–6; relation of to techniques, 5–6; and self-evaluative attitudes, 45

Personality disorder, issues in handling expressed fear of, 129–131

Planning activity, example of, and different methods of handling, 17, 18–19, 20–21; issues in handling when related to next appointment, 131–132

Porter, E. H., Jr., 40, 177, 190

Presenting problem, issues in handling when stated as need for advice, 89; issues in handling when blocked in stating, 97; issues in handling when study habits stated as, 105–106

Pressure, example of felt presence of, 42, 191

Probing, example of use of, 198

Problem, example of initial statement of, 41, 190; issues in handling when client faces seriousness of, 151–152

Proving experience, 50

Psychological climate, 46, 49, exercises for analysis of, 50–60; illustrative example of, 46–49; and learning of attitudes, 46–50; and therapeutic process, 176

Raimy, Victor C., 183

Reason for entering counseling, issues in handling when stated as curiosity, 92–93

Reassurance, example of use of, 196, 199; and evaluation, example of use of, 196; and moralization, example of use of,